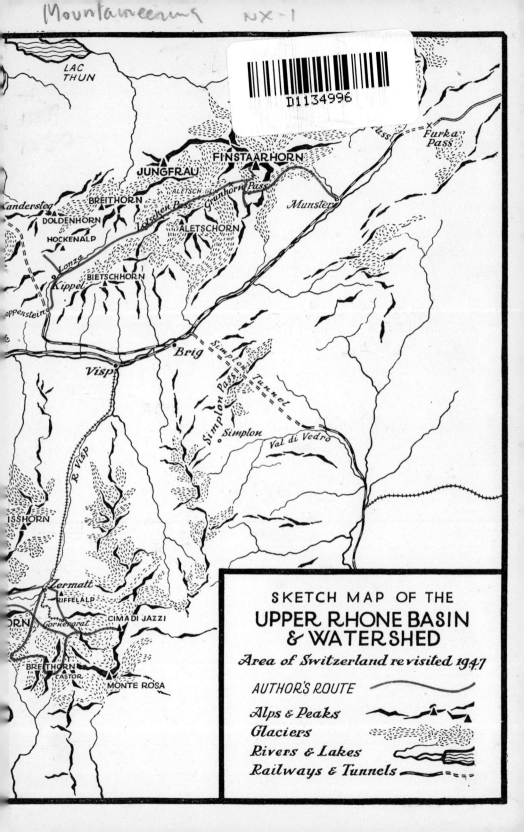

LAC THUN

FINSTAARHORN

JUNGFRAU

Furka Pass

BREITHORN

ALETSCH

Grunhorn Pass

Munster

DOLDENHORN

Lotschen Pass

HOCKENALP

ALETSCHORN

Kandersteg

Lonza

Kippel

BIETSCHHORN

oppenstein

Brig

Visp

Simplon Pass

Simplon Tunnel

R. Visp

Simplon

Val di Vedro

ISHORN

Zermatt

RIFFELALP

CIMA DI JAZZI

ORN

Gornergrat

BREITHORN

CASTOR

MONTE ROSA

SKETCH MAP OF THE
UPPER RHONE BASIN & WATERSHED

Area of Switzerland revisited 1947

AUTHOR'S ROUTE ——————

Alps & Peaks

Glaciers

Rivers & Lakes

Railways & Tunnels

AGAIN
SWITZERLAND

BOOKS BY
FRANK S. SMYTHE

CLIMBS IN THE CANADIAN ROCKIES
THE SPIRIT OF THE HILLS
CAMP SIX
OVER TYROLESE HILLS
MOUNTAINEERING HOLIDAY
THE MOUNTAIN VISION
THE VALLEY OF FLOWERS
KAMET CONQUERED
THE KANGCHENJUNGA ADVENTURE
ALPINE JOURNEY
EDWARD WHYMPER
THE MOUNTAIN TOP
and his novel
SECRET MISSION

Old Zermatt

AGAIN
SWITZERLAND

By
FRANK S. SMYTHE

Photographs by the Author

HODDER AND STOUGHTON
LIMITED · PUBLISHERS · LONDON

FIRST PUBLISHED . . DECEMBER 1947
SECOND IMPRESSION . . . 1952

MADE AND PRINTED IN GREAT BRITAIN FOR
HODDER AND STOUGHTON LTD., LONDON, BY
HAZELL, WATSON AND VINEY, LTD., AYLESBURY AND LONDON

TO

MY SWISS FRIENDS

CONTENTS

vi

ILLUSTRATIONS

By the Author

CHAPTER I

AGAIN SWITZERLAND

ON the day I left England for Switzerland, February 5th, 1946, grey clouds sagged low over Croydon Airport, and the long runways disappeared into a blue mixture of mist and rain. It had rained for days past, coldly, steadily, persistently, and before that there had been gales. This was an English winter, this was something from which before the war lucky mortals, sometimes myself among them, had managed to escape to the sunshine and snow of the Alps. And now, after seven years, seven years better forgotten, I was returning to Switzerland.

The Customs, the Exchange Control Office, the passport examination were behind, weeks of form filling were already forgotten. A door was opened, and the penned travellers streamed out on to the airfield towards the aluminium-sheathed monster that shone like some knight in armour with its promise of errant adventure.

" Swissair," the name is subtly magical. Perhaps not to some of my fellow-passengers, sedate, dark-suited fellows with sallow complexions and well-filled waistcoats, business men perhaps, or jaded remnants of some forlorn political mission. For them air travel merely linked noisy cities, stuffy hotels and droning conference tables, but for me it conjured up something altogether different, something in the nature of the " vision and the faculty Divine." Once again I was returning to the mountains.

A stewardess with blonde untidy hair bid us fasten our safety-belts, and a few minutes later the fields, copses and orchards of Kent were slipping past beneath. Then we climbed into the clouds.

In delightful theory, the traveller should leave England on just such a winter's day as I have described, and a few hours later emerge into the sunshine of Switzerland: this, at any rate, is what the tourist agencies would have their customers believe.   But brutal practice has a knack of defeating the most eloquent theories, and of knocking on the head the most cherished ideals of Messrs. Cook, Frame and Lunn.

For nearly three hours we pulsed through a mist-filled void, and I watched the ice crystals building up along the leading edges of the aircraft until the de-icer slid comfortingly forward to dislodge them.   Then down we came, and down.   Objects faintly appeared, the loom of a hill, the framework of a small town, and chequered dull-green fields, then, suddenly, as we changed course, the convolutions of a mighty river, the Rhine.

A few minutes later Switzerland lay at our feet, a dim Switzerland, of trim little farmsteads and villages over which drove leaden sheets of snow, only to melt into rain before reaching the ground.   Then down we came again, finally this time, and two minutes before we were due, and this despite a blind flight of some 400 miles, the wheels touched on the rain-soaked turf of Zürich airfield.

My first impressions as always were of cleanliness and tidiness.   On this occasion, however, there was something else—an atmosphere, cheerful, carefree, even gay, an atmosphere unpermeated with the horrors of war and the privations of peace, very different from the one I had so recently left.

The young Customs official, nattily attired in a checked sports suit with voluminous plus fours, who casually and smilingly chalked my kit, was representative of this post-war Switzerland.   The passport officer was friendliness itself.   How long was I staying?   Two months—a very good two months, he hoped, with plenty of ski-ing.

A blue, brightly polished motor-coach, with tall windows extending past the angle of the roof so that passengers could view the hill-tops, rolled luxuriously into Zürich between shop windows that glittered enticingly with goods.

We arrived at the main railway station. As we stopped there was a sudden rush forward of blue-coated men. For a moment it seemed that a revolution, a riot or some other form of civil commotion had broken out, and we were to be victims of a blood-thirsty crowd; then, out of the mêlée, a broad-shouldered, round-faced elderly man clad in a loose-fitting smock appeared before me. " Excuse me, sir," said he in perfect English, " but may I have the privilege of conveying your luggage to your hotel? " I suppose I must have gaped a trifle blankly, for he went on, still in the same academic English: " Yes, sir, I see you are surprised; but the fact is I was educated at a private school in Herne Bay."

A few minutes later my luggage was whisked away by my friend on his bicycle, and I set off to walk to my hotel. I had proceeded some way when it suddenly occurred to me that I had entrusted all my possessions to a railway porter of very plausible address whose number I had omitted to take. But almost simultaneous with this chilling thought there arrived another and a warmer thought. I was no longer in thief-ridden England, where a citizen cannot leave his car unattended with safety, or turn his back on his baggage in a railway station, but in Switzerland. And with this I proceeded on my way to find my luggage awaiting me and my elderly friend beaming at me from beneath his rain-soaked hat.

My hotel, which was close to the great clock tower of the church, had been recommended to me by a Swiss friend. Needless to say it was a good one, designed, not to accommodate tourists, but the wealthier class of Swiss business men. It was, of course, scrupulously clean; in fact, everything shone and gleamed from the efforts of the staff. As to the quality, variety and quantity of the fare, it seems scarcely decent to particularise after the British ration. The cooking also displayed an artistry commensurate with the fare, and there was a bar stocked with a prodigious number of bottles, more than I had seen for many a long day, and with prices so moderate that it appeared I had dropped into some Bacchic Eden.

I was wondering what to order from this *embarras des richesse* when a lean, dark, leathery-faced man seated himself next to me.

" You are an Englishman, aren't you? " he inquired in excellent English, but with a trace of French accent. " And just arrived in Zürich? "

I admitted that was the case. There is presumably not only something immediately distinguishable about the breed, but also even something by which the discerning foreigner can tell that he has come directly from England. I was about to ask him by what means he had discovered this when he went on:

" I am myself a Belgian—you must have a drink. It would be a privilege to stand an Englishman a drink." Then, noticing my hesitation, he continued, smiling: " It is necessary, is it not, to wash out the fog, the ' what-do-you-call-it ' in London? "

The " London Particular," I told him.

" That is it, ' the Particular.' "

" It's not so bad nowadays," I said defensively.

" I'm not so sure." He smiled. " I was there not long ago. *Parbleu!* they were lighting fires in the streets. You should be proud of it; there is nothing like it in the whole world."

" I daresay we are," I said. " It's a part of our tradition and our life."

" And death too, I should think, breathing that. But

I like your London. I go there often on business; I am from Belgium."

Over the drink I asked him what conditions were like in Belgium. He replied:

" There is much market gardening and small farming. Most of us live off the Black Market. It is bad, I know, but what would you? You have food and I have money. I am hungry, and I buy your food, regulations or no regulations."

" But what about those who cannot afford to buy food? " I asked him.

He shrugged.

" It is sad, I know, very sad. But it is the law of the jungle; that is what war teaches man, the law of the jungle."

" Do you think that law will survive? "

" It is always there behind civilisation, behind a man's mind; it is a part of his instinct. You can only drug it by food, by safe and easy living; as you would say in England, by ' Safety First.' "

" We don't now," I told him. " We are beginning to realise that we too live in the jungle."

" It is as well," he replied, " for on England much depends. In America there are some who have seen the jungle and what it means, but not many, and you are never in such danger in the jungle as when you think yourself to be safe. And do you know where the jungle is thickest and the animals most dangerous? "

" I think I do," I replied; " it is in the East."

" Yes," he said, " it is in the East."

Our talk turned to Switzerland.

" It is a wonderful little country," he said. " It has put the law of the jungle farther away than any of us on the Continent. Think of it! Peoples of four languages living peacefully together under one constitution. They are almost too good, too law-abiding to be true in this wicked world. Perhaps they should have a little bit of war, not too much, just a shaking up, then they would find their heroes again, William Tell and Arnold von Winkelried, yes, I am sure they would. As it is, they live on the level, good people, steady, honest, reliable, industrious, but on a level, none high, none low, perfect socialists. But where do you get the spirit, the art, the genius, the heroes and the saints? No, no, not from a level, not from a perfect socialism. But we must admire them. They too have had their struggles, and they deserve their peace and tranquillity. We go through our struggles now. Perhaps they will end in peace, but only in the end. And what then? Can you picture, *mon ami*, a world at peace, and the perfect socialism, that dead level? What then? Where does man go? What is life without some struggle, some risk, some achievement? "

" Is war the only answer to this need? " I asked him. " What about the sports and pastimes, the open air, exploring, sailing, ski-ing, mountaineering, even walking? Do they not promote that virility of mind and spirit, that sense of achievement and adventure? "

" Yes," he replied, " they do; but only for a few, not for the masses who live in cities and work in factories and offices—those are the people who make wars, or at least are led into wars. They live so dully, so mechanically that they must have excitement, and the only excitement they know is something that disrupts that dull uneventful life, war or revolution. War is bred in the masses by the masses and it needs only a leader to fertilise it. You heard Hitler speaking? He appealed to the masses, but to the single sensible man who listened it was the voice of a maniac."

" But the Swiss don't want war," I pointed out.

" That is true," he agreed. " They are a peace-loving people, but there are reasons. They are too small in numbers to fight anyone around them, and then there is their country—the mountains. There is adventure for them there. It is so easy for them to escape from their cities into the open air, to climb and ski."

" Are you a mountaineer? " I asked him.

" No, I am not," he replied; " at least, only a little piece of one; but I like ski-ing, ah, how I like ski-ing! "

His dark eyes lit up, and he swung round on his stool with a lithe movement.

" Tell me," he cried ecstatically, " is there anything better than to stand at the top of a long, steep snow-slope, and to look down at the snow all sparkling in the sun, and without a track on it, pure snow, falling and falling in big curves, like waves, down and down into the valley, and then to say to yourself: ' Is that too steep for me, dare I take it straight down? ' And when you think of that you get a little feeling in your stomach. There is no one there who cares where you go or whether you take it straight; it is so easy to descend from side to side, so easy and so safe. There is no one there but yourself, and something within you says: ' Come on, you—you imbecile, down you go—straight.' And then something else says: ' Don't be a fool, of course you can't, mutton-head. You might hurt yourself.' And so you stand and argue with yourself until at last you get impatient and you say: ' What the big hell or what the heck '; then with a sudden jump you point your ski straight down the slope and off you go. Ah, that is the moment! Your heart has come for a second—zut—into your mouth, and you clench your teeth in case it might come out, but next moment you are thinking, so clearly and so calmly, and everything is moving, rushing at you, then slipping away under you. And the air, so cold, is against you. Whoo! it goes in the ears, and whish! go the ski in the snow. Then over a wave of snow you go. You bend your knees, then come up again as you go over the edge. And for a moment you fly—yes, fly in the air and

Near Adelboden

CHAPTER II

ADELBODEN

FROM Zürich I travelled via Berne to Adelboden. Torrential rain was still falling as the electric train purred across the lowlands to Berne, but this could not dim the brightness of a gracious landscape. Few Englishmen visiting Switzerland make a tour of the lowlands beyond visiting the principal towns such as Berne, Basle and Zürich, yet such a tour is not only worth while for its own sake, it is an excellent substitute for a bad-weather holiday spent kicking the heels in mountain huts and hotels.

This lowland country has the charm of spaciousness and fertility. Had Switzerland possessed a Constable it would have been his country. The compositions in breadth, depth and scope are those he loved to depict, a rolling network of fields and copses melting into dim distances, and above, in the wide heavens, great strolling clouds. But there the resemblance to the Eastern Counties ends. In every southward view from the higher ground the scene is dominated by the Alps. They are always there, surprising the blue distances where the earth should end.

Many a time when I lived at Baden I climbed a hill to watch the evening light flow and ebb along them. The eye passed swiftly over the fertile meads, the orchards, the forest-clad ridges to find repose in their snows. And even when mist concealed them they were still there, a presence, until once again they shone out in kingly procession across the plains.

To-day the distances were hidden behind curtains of steel-grey cloud white-shot with snow in their heaviest folds. Indeed, it was evident as we approached Berne that the temperature was falling, and first sleet, then snow slowly replaced the teeming rain.

Perhaps the most impressive feature of the Swiss agricultural landscape after the cows (primary motivators of Swiss life, Swiss philosophy and Swiss finance) is the fruit. Nowhere are healthier apple and cherry orchards to be found than in the lowlands, and the trees are invariably well shaped and meticulously pruned. Few growers bother to protect their fruit from marauders, and many trees line roads or stand in public places. It must be positively dull to be a small boy in Switzerland; a surfeit is no incentive to appetite or to crime!

At Berne a stern-visaged, elderly porter with glacier-blue eyes took charge of my luggage, inquiring at the same time in precise Oxford English as to my destination. From his accent he would have been taken for a cultivated Englishman anywhere; his vocabulary, however, was strictly limited, an unusual combination.

From the restaurant-car of the train to Brig, and in between sips of an acidulous white wine which the anxious-to-please attendant had euphemistically described as having " the most kick of all," I watched the snow-veiled landscape quietly change from low hills to high with a dusting of freshly fallen snow on their flanks.

Thun, Spiez, Frutigen, Kandersteg—these are names to conjure up memories and visions. Perhaps they seem most romantic in the spring, when the cherries and apples blossom in a froth of white and pink along the banks of Thun, and the snows of the Oberland are mirrored with scarcely a quiver in the cobalt-blue waters.

Between Spiez and Frutigen we passed the snow-line, that enchanted region where the rain-drop is transmuted to the snowflake. Something of childhood's romance is still to be woven into the snow-line and the adventures to be found beyond it.

The snow-line was quite a sudden affair. At one level

no snow lay on the brown, rain-sodden ground, then a few feet higher a sprinkling maintained a precarious foothold just sufficient to whiten the earth, while higher it had collected on every blade and twig, a quantity that deepened rapidly with every upward yard: and all this within a hundred feet or so of altitude.

From Frutigen a postal motor service conveys the traveller to Adelboden. It was Saturday, and the train disgorged a horde of Swiss week-enders, who crowded into five buses waiting to take them to the latter winter-sports resort.

Snow was falling heavily as we climbed up the road. There was nothing visible of the scenery, as the windows of the bus were rendered opaque from the exhalations of the heated mass within. How fortunate the Swiss are in their excellent communications between the mountains and the cities. It is possible to leave Berne or Zürich on a Saturday midday, spend Sunday ski-ing or climbing, and be home the same evening.

At Adelboden the buses disgorged their loads of winter-sportsmen. The new snow already lay over a foot deep, and more was falling, the air was thick with dry, feathery flakes. I had no room booked at any hotel, but a stout concierge with " Hotel Adler " on his cap quickly took charge of me.

Of English hotels it has been said that there is no hotel so good as a good one and no hotel so bad as a bad one. In Switzerland the limits are not so far apart. I know of no Swiss hotel to be preferred to the best in this country and certainly none, not even the simplest and cheapest inns, to be compared with the chill, unfriendly barracks of so many British provincial towns. The difference between the best of both countries lies in such details as the cosiness of the bar and the open fire, in those deep leather upholstered settees and armchairs beloved by the Anglo-Saxon, for which the foreigner has no use whatsoever; in tradition and antiquity, often exploited as a sop to discomfort, and above all, in cheerful and willing service.

The Swiss hotel proprietor attaches little importance to tradition; he is concerned with the immediate and material welfare of his guests, and of the application of the acid test—will they come back? There is nothing more indicative of the character and taste of its owner than his own hotel, the quality of its comfort, and the manner in which it is run. Men and women who have been brought up in discomfort, who have been inadequately educated and led narrow, circumscribed lives, will own uncomfortable little hotels in which the food and cooking will be a reflection of their prejudice and ignorance, the decorations and furniture will be tawdry and in poor taste, and all those amenities great and small, which make for comfort, will be conspicuous by their absence. This is the ilk that regards comfort as anti-Christian, and with sadistic relish enforces a journey from bed over bare boards or icy linoleum to turn off a light-switch at the far end of an unheated bedroom.

The reverse applies with equal force. The ideal hotel proprietor is a man of culture, sound taste and good education. Above all, he must have travelled and studied the methods of others. In these days, when the word " culture " has come to have a sinister meaning, and a " gentleman " is synonymous with " capitalist," such qualifications are rare among British hotel keepers, primarily, I suppose, because the business does not attract them, which is not to be wondered at, as of all businesses there cannot be one necessitating a greater financial tenacity, a more blooming optimism and a finer tact.

My hotel was a good one. The food was excellent— fresh produce, admirably cooked. Beware of those hotels—and there are not a few—which provide, not the products of the country, but those of Mr. Armour and other kings of tins. At one hotel where I stayed shortly before the outbreak of war there was evidently a surfeit of tinned mushrooms, for these in different guises, and beneath different sauces and relishes, appeared at almost every meal. As Mr. E. E. Shipton remarked on Mount Everest with force and feeling. " These tinned mucks all taste the same after a month."

There is one item the traveller to Switzerland must always allow for—the extras. Hotels advertise two prices, one the weekly total at pension rates, and the other the weekly total including most extras, such as heating, kurtaxe, etc. The latter gives a rough idea of the actual living costs, but extras like Gremlins will always creep in. The extra which sticks in the gizzard of the English-man is a bath, for which two francs are normally charged. Yet the Swiss support of this imposition is both logical and convincing. In smoky England, they argue, baths are a necessary part of personal hygiene, but in the clean mountain air of Switzerland they are not, and become therefore a luxury. Coal, also, is difficult or impossible to obtain, and central heating has to be maintained by wood fuel, which is rationed, since not even Alpine timber is inexhaustible. At Adelboden, and other winter-sports centres, baths are to be had for the order-ing; but in the remoter parts of Switzerland, where the English tourist seldom penetrates, they are still anomalous, and he who demands one is regarded as a Dives in Sparta.

After dinner I chatted with the proprietor, and it was no surprise to discover that he was a connoisseur both of food and wine. In these rushing, hurly-burly days, in which the palate and digestion of the human species is being ruined at snack counters and caféterias, and " meat and two veg." represent the highest flight in the gastronomical fancy of the average citizen, it is a privilege to talk with one to whom food and drink are something more than solid and liquid fuels to be disposed of thoughtlessly and with the maximum dispatch.

For French and Swiss wines, he told me, the years 1939, '41, '43 and '45 were all good. Beware, he warned me, of wines that are chemically treated in order artificially to mature them, for they are acidulous and hard on the stomach. I thought of what I had already imbibed on the railway journey and agreed. Dôle, he declared to be the best Swiss red wine, but there were several good white wines from the Rhone Valley, the soil of which could produce excellent still wines, but not sparkling wines, and certainly not champagne. Furthermore, Swiss wine had not the keeping qualities of French wines. It matured quickly, and was at its best within ten or twelve years.

I told him how in the spring of 1940 I had been shown over the cellars of Pommery and Greno at Rheims by the manager of that firm. There were two or three million bottles of champagne there and we sampled one or two. Finally we drank to the damnation of " Le sale Bosche " who, declaimed the manager, would " never again defile Rheims." Unhappily, within a few weeks he had once again overrun that fair and prosperous city.

To be born an Englishman in this present age is to be denied or restricted in some of the best things of life, and wine is one of them. In Switzerland half a bottle of a very fair Fendant wine can be purchased for the equivalent of one and sixpence or two shillings, and French wines are little if anything more expensive. The prohibitive duties placed on imported wines have turned us into a spirit-drinking race. Nowadays, the ignorance of the spirit-tippling Englishman on the subject of wine would be farcical were it not tragic. In 1940 I was entertained by a certain Major at a French hotel world-famous for its cellar of Château Yquem. My host demanded the wine list and scanned it—on it were enumerated the various vintages of this great wine. Finally, he threw it down and turned to me. "They don't seem to have much of a variety here," he remarked peevishly. "Nothing but this stuff—this Château Yquem. We'd better have a whisky."

Sleeping in a Swiss hotel is something of a problem to an Englishman. First there is the duvet, that mountainous monstrosity stuffed with feathers which is the equal in warmth of some half a dozen heavy blankets. At first sight there seems no alternative with a duvet; either you have it and sweat or you go without it and shiver. Thus, the duvet alternates between the floor and the bed during the night, under the inexpert management of the unskilled traveller. Experience, however, teaches the correct management of the beast. It must be brutally hammered into shape. If too thick at the head end it must be vigorously attacked with the fists and its feathers driven down to the far end. Or vice versa; the permutations and combinations possible with a duvet are well-nigh infinite. Second, there is the central heating. The problem here is that with the window open the room becomes too cold and vice versa. Furthermore, the arrangement of the duvet is directly dependent on the temperature of the room. It will be seen, therefore, that there are many variables, and it needs experience and skill to manage them efficiently and enjoy an unbroken night's rest at a Swiss hotel in winter.

I was awakened next morning by a considerable commotion. Outside on the snow-laden pine tops a concourse of several hundreds of Alpine choughs had gathered. These birds are well known to the mountaineer, and they will appear miraculously out of the blue at the remotest and highest huts in search of scraps. They follow the climber up Mount Everest, and I have seen them soaring, apparently without effort, at heights of over 25,000 feet. However, it is evident that, like the sensible and catholic-minded mountaineer, they can appreciate the amenities of civilisation as much as the sublimities of the wild, for here they were in their hundreds at fashionable Adelboden, obviously engaged in a winter-sports meeting of their own.

Snow was still falling at breakfast-time, but later the sky lightened. Shortly before midday the miracle occurred. There was a glimpse of blue, faint at first, then deepening and strengthening. Of a sudden the sun broke through, hotly, gloriously, and the mists rolled back on a splendid world.

A few minutes before, the village had been imprisoned in sluggish mists, now there was space, wide, deep, shining space, and in it the peaks rose, brilliantly silver, celestially blue.

The snow had fallen without wind. It was light and feathery, and it clung to everything; it had spilled deeply on the trees, every twig was laden, and it sparkled and winked with small, many-coloured lights, blue, yellow, green and orange. It had transformed the world in form, substance and colour. Where harsh lines and sharp angles had been there were flowing contours, curves, dips and undulations. A soothing hand had rested on the forehead of the earth and smoothed away the wrinkles.

The atmosphere partook of this same beauty of freshly fallen snow. It was not merely limpid and brilliant, but charged with some subtle power, so that I found myself drawing it, cold and pure, deeply into my lungs, as though to replace the feeble vitiated airs of the lowlands. It was possible in a sense to see this atmosphere, for in it were suspended millions of minute ice crystals that sparkled and scintillated in the sun like star-dust. The mountain air—is it really different from the air of sea-level? Doubtless it is composed of the same gases in the same proportions. There is not a ha'p'orth of physical difference between the two. And yet what is there about this Alpine air that refreshes and restores our jaded bodies, that stimulates and revivifies our tired minds? What is this magic, this panacea of ills, we find in Switzerland?

There were many Americans on leave from occupied Germany. All were enjoying themselves hugely. Everyone had a camera. and these cameras were soon clicking determinedly at the snowy scene. The light was brilliant, and my exposure meter indicated an exposure of one seventy-fifth of a second at stop F 16. As a matter of interest, I approached a sergeant and asked him what exposure he was giving. " I don't rightly know," was the reply. " I guess I just point the blamed thing and hope for the best." The " blamed thing " in question, an expensive and complicated camera of German make, had been adjusted to its largest aperture F 2, and the shutter speed had been set to one twenty-fifth of a second. I pointed out that all his pictures would be hopelessly over-exposed, but not with much effect. The sergeant's photographic knowledge seemed to be on a par with that of the old lady who, on being told by the chemist that her films were all fogged, replied indignantly, " Nonsense, I opened the camera in bright sunlight."

The break in the weather was only temporary, and by evening snow was again falling. My ski had not arrived from Zermatt, so I hired a pair. Hired ski are no more satisfactory than a hired gun or cricket bat. It is true that they are made merely of wood and metal, and are subject to the same physical laws whoever employs them, but there are qualities not so easily definable. And more than these, there is something about a tried and trusted article which cannot be analysed in material terms; it is not merely that you become used to it, but that it becomes used to you. In Tibet, if you would harm your enemy, you send him some small object into which you have concentrated all your ill-will, so that when he touches the object he will receive and suffer from that ill-will.

My pair of hired ski acted on much the same principle, for they seemed to have been worn by a succession of highly incompetent persons, whose perverseness and inefficiency they at once proceeded to demonstrate in no uncertain fashion. When I wanted to go one way they automatically went the other, and even when I thought I had them safely stationary they would suddenly leap forwards and deposit me on my seat. It was, I admit, a long time since I had last ski-ed, but even this could not entirely explain the unaccountable performance of that pair of hired ski, which exhibited every diversity of natural and unnatural motion.

In an attempt to establish some kind of an ascendancy over them I spent the morning climbing the Hahnenmoos. Normally, motor-buses convey the ski-er to this alp from Adelboden, but the road was now blocked by the freshly fallen snow, and would take a day or two to clear. The ski-ers, therefore, very sensibly remained at Adelboden eating and drinking until such time as the road should be reopened to traffic, since at Adelboden and other winter-sports places, to walk uphill by one's own unaided efforts has come to be regarded almost as a social solecism. The modern ski-er must above all things remain elegant and immaculate in appearance and attire, and to sweat, literally to sweat, uphill is something most definitely not done in the best circles.

Yet, despite any guilty feelings I may have possessed in this respect, and the untractable behaviour of my ski, I thoroughly enjoyed the trudge up to Hahnenmoos. I had been there once before, in the spring of 1935 during a solitary ski traverse of Switzerland, when the slopes were gay with crocuses; now winter's hand lay on alp, forest and stream, and snowflakes in a vast and stealthy multitude were slowly falling.

There was silence. The air was motionless, without the slightest stirring or movement, and all around the snow-burdened pines stood immobile as though carved out of ebony and alabaster. Between them, along their aisles, the eye searched for something that moved and lived, but nothing moved, nothing lived, and there was no sound except for the faintest of whisperings, the falling snowflakes.

I halted, and instantly the silence encompassed me. As I stood there I realised for the first time that I was back among the mountains where I properly belong. The snow was falling more densely now, yet with the same unhurried calm. It was interesting to fix the attention on a single flake and follow it as it floated down, sometimes without movement, and sometimes twisting slowly on its axis, to add its infinitesimal quota to the vast accumulation of its predecessors.

Up I went along the twisting path through the forest, my ski clumsy and heavy on my feet. My legs ached slightly, my heart was beating hurriedly, there was a constricted, slightly muzzy feeling about my head, and I was sweating. So much for civilisation. When a man is young he shakes it off easily, but as he grows older it clings more tightly and the effort required to escape increases. Yet, I doubt whether there is any sport to compare with mountaineering in restoring physical fitness to the city dweller. Many persons imagine that mountain climbing demands a high degree of athleticism. This is a misconception: athleticism is not only unnecessary, it may even lead to the over-development of the wrong muscles. Given only a reasonably fit body, the rest follows, for mountain climbing is much more a matter of mind than of muscle.

On the alp above the forest I overtook three young

Swiss from Bâle, and together we ascended the open slopes to the chalet-restaurant which stands on the ridge separating Adelboden from Lenk. It was their last day of a week's holiday, and they referred ruefully to the horrors of civilisation as represented by Bâle. At lunch they insisted on my sharing their soup while they plied me with questions, for I was the first Englishman they had seen for several years. The first question, and this applied to almost every Swiss I met, was what about Russia? The intentions of the Soviet Union form a big question-mark in the Swiss mind. They had served in the Swiss army during the war, and had been stationed in the St. Gotthard district. In the event of a Nazi invasion it had been the intention to abandon the lowlands, and to withdraw into the mountains, where supplies had been assembled sufficient for several months. " We would have fought to the last," they declared; " for to us freedom means as much as it does to you." There is no doubt that had Hitler invaded Switzerland the stand of the small but splendidly trained and equipped Swiss army in the mountains would have provided an epic in the tradition of Morgarten and Arnold von Winkelried.

Snow was falling heavily when we set off to Adelboden. I had looked forward to a slow and solitary descent on this my first day, during which I would practise my turns at my leisure; but my Swiss companions appeared to think that I was not safe enough to be left to my own devices, and despite my protestations, insisted on accompanying me and, what was worse, waiting for me. The snow was good, too good, for it seemed uncommonly fast, and the conscientious hirer-out of my ski had seen to it that the latter were efficiently waxed. The descent began over the open alp, where light and visibility were poor. Up this alp to the chalet-restaurant are disposed sundry wires, apparently something to do with a cable railway, and now, owing to the deep new snow, these wires were at a height calculated neatly to decapitate an unwary ski-er. Mr. Alfred Jingle, drawing perhaps even more than usual upon his fertile imagination, would have neatly summed up such a contingency.

" Ski-er ski-ing fast, very fast—thinking only of cocktail bar—never saw wire—next moment head off—but going so fast went on ski-ing—head rolling down behind, still with thoughts on cocktail—strange sight—arrived bar—cocktail waiting, but no head to put it in—great tragedy—everyone sympathetic—one moment, though—head rolled in door—picked it up—put it on—drank cocktail—all's well that ends well. Glad my own head is still on—what's that? A Scotch? Certainly, sir, Scotch all round. My respects, sir—your very good health—keep your head, sir—that's the ticket—keep your head. Ha! Ha! "

Below the open alp a steep and narrow track descended through the forest. Track ski-ing, as opposed to ski-ing on open slopes, is a technique of its own, a form indeed of racing ski-ing. For a great many ski-ers, ski-ing consists in ascending by a funicular or ski-lift, and running down a track over and over again throughout the day, perhaps to the extent of 20,000 to 30,000 feet of downhill running between breakfast and dinner. Such ski-ing bears little relation to mountain ski-ing; it involves no knowledge of snow-craft or route finding. It does, however, develop a high degree of skill on hard snow, the capacity to go fast, and the strength of nerve and will associated with high speeds on ski. To some extent at least the mountain ski-er must learn to ski at speed over hard-tracked snow, since the routes leading down into Alpine valleys more often than not include such tracks through the forests and fields. Ski-ing is a sport in which speed is a prime motivator. Any ski-er worthy of the name measures his skill, nerve and determination against the

yardstick of speed.   Where speed involves a risk of accident on a mountain or in any situation far from help, it
is not justifiable; but on standard runs, where stretcher
parties are always at hand, it is perfectly justifiable and a
substantial source of income to the Swiss medical pro-
fession.   The point I wish to make is that there is a
world of difference between mountain ski-ing over untracked snow and ski-ing down a prepared track; it is
the difference between track motor-racing and cross-
country touring; it is, however, out of the track-raced car
that the touring model has been evolved, and similarly
with ski—much that has been learned in the hard school
of racing is of value to the mountain ski-er and cross-
country runner.

   All ski-ing text-books enlarge on the virtues of falling
forward.   To fall forward, they claim, is a sign of
courage and determination, while to fall backwards and
sitzmark is the hallmark of the craven.   To fall forward
when one is young and lissom is nothing, but nowadays,
with the signpost pointing the way towards the fifties, I
must confess to a dislike of a fast forward fall, and on
occasions when I find myself out of control, or unable
to turn adequately or quickly enough, I seat myself in
the snow with the utmost deliberation, caring nothing
for appearances or text-books.   So it was on the track
through the forest.   It was fast and it was narrow; there
was no possibility of stemming; one had to go flat-out
all the time.   Here it switchbacked and there dived
alarmingly.   It was perfectly simple, but it was my first
day, my legs ached; and when the ski dived they seemed,
like a New York elevator, to leave something vital
behind.   The ranks of pines flew past; there was no time
to see anything, or to concentrate on anything, except the
narrow icy track, and when the speed became too break-
neck I had no option but to relapse into the undignified
position to which I have already adverted.   I have

already said it was perfectly simple, an easy run, but I
say again it was my first day, and my ski were hired and
possessed of the devil.

Yet I enjoyed it. For all my aching legs, my fear of
hitting something hard at speed, and the devilish nature
of my hired ski, I enjoyed it. Many a time I have remarked to myself—I have even ventured it to friends—
that for me ski are only a means of getting up mountains
and across country, and that beyond this the wooden
boards have no meaning, but I have known, even in the
sorest moments (I once *sitzmarked* heavily on to a sharp
splinter of rock), that this is not true, and for me, in-
efficient as I am, there will always be a thrill and a delight
in ski-ing.

Ski-ing enjoyment begins the moment that ski are put
on for the first time, but there is nothing remarkable in
this; the same applies to many sports and games. The
indifferent cricketer who miraculously hits up twenty or
thirty runs on the village green gets as much out of the
game as a Bradman. So it is with ski-ing; indeed, it is
questionable whether the expert, concerned only with
knocking a second or so off his previous time on a run,
gets as much out of it as the novice struggling with
his first stem turn. Perfection and boredom are too
often synonymous, yet, such is human nature, it must
needs struggle towards perfection.

And so to Adelboden, tea and pâtisserie, to watch the
ski-ers (who had been eating and drinking all day)
clumping round a dance floor to the strains of a Swiss
string orchestra playing jazz in that sober classical style
peculiar to Swiss orchestras.

The weather continued bad with intermittent snow-
storms during the next two days, but the morning of
February 14th promised better things; the sky was misty,
but here and there were gleams and suggestions of sun
and sky. The motor road to Hahnenmoos had been

cleared by rotary snow-ploughs, so I took the first bus after breakfast in the company of a cheerful crowd of Swiss ski-ers.

In Britain a few inches of snow are sufficient to paralyse transport, while there are many contemporary as well as legendary stories of trains being lost and passengers starved. In Switzerland, however, snow is not only part and parcel of the scheme of things, but an important source of national revenue. It is necessary, therefore, that it should be efficiently controlled. There are occasions, as I shall relate subsequently, when even the best-controlled Swiss snow becomes revolutionary-minded and, breaking loose from all restraints, indulges in an orgy of obstruction and destruction. In the main, however, the Swiss, through long and at times bitter experience, have learned how to deal with natural phenomena, and to them the idiosyncrasies of the weather and snow are not so much acts of God as matters to be dealt with energetically and turned to good advantage. Hence the rotary snow-plough, which of recent years has been developed by the great engineering firms of the country into a most efficient instrument for clearing roads and railways. One of these machines is worth a hundred of the antiquated snow-ploughs employed by the town councils of Britain. In all such matters the Swiss are realists. They do not try to delude themselves that their climate is temperate, and they believe in comfort. Instead, therefore, of shivering in front of an open fire of which ninety per cent. of the heat goes up the chimney, with their backs exposed to cutting draughts from a single ill-fitting window, they have highly efficient systems of heating. Were we to renounce the foolish idea that we live in a temperate climate instead of one of the coldest, because the dampest, in the whole world, and adopt similar methods in place of our present mediæval contrivances, it is certain that we could

An alp above Adelboden

Hahnenmoos and the Wildstrubel

subsist, and with far greater comfort, on half our present fuel consumption.

Above Adelboden new snow had fallen to a depth of over three feet, and drifts several times deeper had formed on the road; but the rotary snow-ploughs had made short work of these, and the bus mounted steadily between walls of snow which in places were as high as the roof. At one point we had to wait while a plough ahead completed its work, and it was amazing to watch it eating through a depth of fully nine feet of wind-compacted snow. A few minutes later we alighted at the terminus, which is situated about 1,000 feet beneath the chalet-restaurant I had already visited.

The promise of finer weather was being rapidly fulfilled. The mists were thinning, shredding out and dissolving. Areas of blue sky were expanding every instant, spilling across an unsubstantial land of silvery mist, and brilliant sunlight flooded down on the snowy mountain-sides. It was one of those scenes of which a photographer dreams, but so seldom meets with—half an hour of witchery and magic. I hastened off with my camera along the alp. There were pines there, solitary, or in small groups above the fringe of the parent forest, bowed down and hoary with gleaming accumulations of crystalline snow, and brown-timbered hay huts with the snow piled on their roofs in gleaming volutes. Then there were the shadows, blue shadows transparent with reflected light, shadows that revealed the delicate mouldings of snow, that picked out every subtlety, the texture, the ripples, the ridges, the undulations; and lastly the wind, which with infinite dexterity and delicacy had moulded and shaped this dazzling scene. Beyond was mist, thin wisps of mist that curled languidly upwards like dissolving steam, and denser masses that clung to the shadowed hollows; mists opaque and mists transparent. And in between these mists, the mountains rose; ridges

A.S.—3

gleaming, slopes pendant, shining in the blue vacancies
of heaven.

What can a poor photographer do but point and peer
and hope for the best?   How can he arrange such visions
within his view-finder and concentrate such scenes into a
space an inch or so square?   How can he hope to capture
the evanescent mists, transmute to a chemical black-and-
white the tender gradations of the tones, the ethereal
qualities of the lights and shadows?   As I fiddled with
my filters the gods laughed out of that silver-and-blue
morning.

For an hour or more I nosed about the alp, while the
mists presently vanished, leaving the sun in undisputed
possession of the snow-fields.   A peasant and his two
sons were engaged in bringing down sleigh-loads of hay
from one of the huts on the alp, and for a time I watched
and photographed the operation, the trio, beyond the
customary " Grüss Gott," taking not the slightest notice
of me, but continuing methodically with their work, the
father smoking his pipe the while.

It is interesting to watch a Swiss peasant at work.   His
every action is slow and deliberate, planned and calculated to perform the work with the least possible expendi-
ture of energy; energy, as he has learned, is a precious
commodity on mountains, something to be conserved, not
frittered away.   It is out of the peasant that the guide is
evolved with his rhythmical uphill pace, and his reserve
of strength and energy against an emergency.   And so,
as I watched the trio slowly loading the sledge with hay,
it came to me how perfectly they fitted into the scene.
But did they extract the same from it as I?   Were they
conscious of its beauty?   What did the mountains mean
to them except as a means of livelihood, an inconvenient
means involving a lifetime of toil for but little material
reward?   Unnecessary questions perhaps, for I was outside the scene, a visitor who came to see, analyse and

describe. For me the mountains were the supreme contrast to the city and the lowlands. These peasants, on the other hand, were part of the scene, they had learned to accept it, not analyse it, love it or hate it. Would they gladly exchange a fat farm in the lowlands for what they already had?

There is a story of a Swiss guide who was brought by his employer to London. As the train passed through the depressing suburbs of that city, the employer remarked what a miserable prospect it was compared with the mountains where they had climbed together. " Miserable? " replied the guide. " Ah, sir, it is much finer." Yet, I daresay that were such a man to settle in such a spot he would " in his dreams behold . . . "—the mountains of his native land. To us the Swiss peasant, like many others of his ilk, may appear dull, slow-witted and lacking an æsthetic appreciation of his splendid environment, but the love is there, perhaps all the stronger because inarticulate. Many men have music in their souls, but cannot utter it.

Towards midday I made my way up to the chalet-restaurant. The sun had assumed command of an unclouded sky, and the terrace and *gastzimmer* were crowded with ski-ers all endeavouring to acquire the deepest possible sun tan in the least possible time. Writing as a fair-haired person who reddens like a lobster, peels like a leper, and cracks like a mud-pan, I should like to inquire as to the benefit of sun bathing? With most persons the object appears to be to simulate a negro.

A temporary pigmentation of the skin has the curious psychological effect on many persons of a temporary superiority complex, so that meek and mild-mannered men and women with normally wishy-washy complexions, when under the subtle influence of sun tan, lose their sense of proportion, and strut about, and swank and boast, as though they had acquired some new and subtle merit unpossessed by their fellows. They would even, given the opportunity and a relaxation of public morals, expose a far greater area of their bodies than they would dream of doing in normal circumstances.

In the German Alps such sun bathers are positively unblushing in regard to the area they are prepared to expose. I speak not as a prude, but as an æsthete, for the human body is seldom beautiful, and to arrive at a club hut and find scores of stout Teutons and their fraus sprawled meatily outside is suggestive, not of Botticelli's blithesome cupids, but of the mordacious inventions of Picasso.

It is a remarkable fact that the majority of Alpine guides take good care never to expose their bodies to the sun, and I well remember my surprise on seeing one of the greatest stripped to the waist. His face and neck had been burned by countless suns to the colour of seasoned mahogany, but the remainder of his body was a milky white, a whiter skin I have never seen on any man.

There are even misguided people who, failing to acquire a genuine sun tan, employ artificial colouring matter, and I saw a number of women from French Switzerland who had resorted to this singular substitute.

The sun has an undoubted value in the treatment of certain diseases, but it does not follow that it has any effect whatsoever on healthy persons beyond transforming them to a negro or a lobster according to whether they are dark or fair, and if any reader can adduce scientific proof of its value to the body, it would be interesting to hear it. On the contrary, the sun can render high Alpine ski-ing thoroughly miserable, while an overdose of it can be positively dangerous and lead to a high fever. The best protection against it is one or other of the brick-red glacier creams, which have the property of filtering out the harmful ultra-violet rays. Ordinary face creams are useless. They may even aggravate sunburn, and I well remember crossing a Himalayan snow-pass on one occasion with nothing better to hand than a white cold cream. My face not only fried: I could hear it frizzling.

The sufferer from sunburn is provided with a fine test of will power. For when skin begins to peel, a well-nigh irresistible urge will come over him to assist that peeling. He will pick, and he will pull; little by little, and more and more. He pulls too far; there is a sore place left; it oozes a sticky gum-like substance; the sore place cracks—cracks horribly and painfully. His face feels like dried leather, and like dried leather it goes on cracking. It is painful to eat, and hot or acidulous liquids are a torture to the lips. To blow the nose is not to be thought of—better to sniff and go on sniffing. It is tactful to remain sympathetic and sombre, not to joke in his presence, for smiles are taboo and laughter an agony. It is best not to talk to him; he will merely glare and growl, for he has slept little if at all. And still, with an awful, an irresistible and horrid fascination, he goes on pulling at the wreck that was once his face.

I lunched at one of the crowded tables in the company of a party of Swiss, one of whom was a Canadian by birth. She it was who insisted on presenting me with her chocolate coupons for the month and would take no refusal. This was but one of many acts of generosity and kindness that I met with in Switzerland. Such acts both warm the heart and restore faith in international values. If every country could budget a large sum to send its citizens travelling to other countries, this would be the best possible form of insurance against war and international misunderstanding. In the welter of politics it is easy to lose sight of fundamentals, and individual contacts are the basis of international co-operation, not only between politicians and diplomats, but between the common peoples. Speedy and cheap travel in the future is going to have a far greater influence than ever before on the common weal.

Once again the Russian question cropped up. If there is anything the Swiss detest it is social or political opportunism and extremism. To no country does Abraham Lincoln's receipt of government apply with greater force, and the " Middle Way " of Confucius and Lao Tsu finds its perfect expression in the welding together into a single entity of four peoples of different speech and racial tradition. " We believe," said one of my Swiss friends, " in the nationalisation of national services, such as transport and power, since a single network centrally administered is more efficient; but outside such services we believe in the right of every man to trade freely with every other man."

An example of the jealous regard of the Swiss for his political system, and his ingrained dislike of revolutionary measures and abrupt reforms, was the rejection by the electorate of a proposal for a capital levy. Although this levy would have affected only a well-to-do minority, and not the vast majority of voters, it was rejected by the country as a whole. This was a proof, not only of a sturdy independence in political thought, but of an absence of class consciousness.

There are, of course, social strata in Switzerland, and the Swiss themselves would be the first to admit the difference between culture and the reverse; but Swiss society does not suffer those uneasy attributes of pride, cupidity and covetousness which make for violent revolutionary doctrines, and arouse internal bitterness and hostility within a nation. Each stratum fits snugly into its place, an essential part of the whole structure. The general effect is to produce a degree of peaceful uniformity in social life which to visitors from countries where class consciousness still persists may seem a trifle dull and

parochial. I prefer the word " stolid," and this I think
rightly describes the Swiss temperament. In the stolidity
of the Swiss, and especially the German-Swiss, lies his
political and social strength. He likes to chew the cud
of political and social change; he will not be bounced
and flounced into unconsidered decisions; he is poor
material for any dictator, but there is within him so great
a devotion to his country, so jealous a regard for tradition,
so supreme a love of freedom, that he would rally without thought of self to any cause that sought to resist an
onslaught on his inheritance.

After lunch I set off to climb the Albristhorn, 9,075
feet, an ascent of 2,665 feet from Hahnenmoos. From
the restaurant a broad snow-ridge led up for a considerable distance. The snow was a trifle soft, but safe
enough so long as I followed the ridge. A hot sun, the
first I had seen, burned down with an Alpine fury as I
tacked upwards. Perhaps 1,000 feet higher the ridge
narrowed and steepened into a rocky edge. It was possible to ascend on ski the unbroken snow-slopes to the
left, but the afternoon sun shone full on them, and the
risk of treading loose an avalanche was all too obvious.
I removed my ski, therefore, and proceeded on foot.

Most ski-ers naturally and rightly object to foot-slogging, but I am neither a natural nor a right-minded
ski-er. When the difficulties of the ground are such that
it is necessary to remove ski, I experience a distinct thrill.
I say to myself: " So far I have done no more than
any Tom, Dick or Harry on ski could have done, but
now, now I am mountaineering."

The change from two promiscuously sliding planks of
hickory to the grit of clinkers on rock is for me eminently
satisfactory. Let me hasten to add that I am not one of
those old fogies, if there are any left, who compare mountaineering and ski-ing to the detriment of the latter, and
from their foot-won heights mouth criticism and con-

tempt at another sport, for the only apparent reason that it is also associated with hills and mountains; he would be a rash cricketer who would criticise polo because it is also played on grass. The fact is that mountaineering and ski-ing can exist happily apart. They also make an idealic married pair, even though, like any husband and wife, they retain their separate and distinct personalities.

I had no ice axe, but on an easy mountain a ski stick is a substitute. It was late in the afternoon as I made my way along the ridge. I had hoped to find the crest reasonably firm and wind-blown, but the new snow had fallen with little wind and had not yet compacted. At every step I sank in knee-deep, and between rocks sometimes floundered in to the waist. Nevertheless, I was enjoying every moment. Up on that sun-smitten ridge the cares and anxieties of past years vanished. Again I was young, again I knew the brave magic of the mountains; it was in every curve of the ridge, in every upward step, in every hand-clasp of the rough warm rock.

There was a point ahead, the summit? No, merely the end of a rocky ridge leading to a small peak. The summit lay beyond. To reach it, it was necessary to descend from the ridge on to a small snow-field, and to trudge across the latter to the final peak.

It was a pleasant scramble. There was no difficulty, but with so much powdery snow on it the rocky crest enjoined caution. It was one of those little indeterminate climbs about which the climber remembers little; just an up-and-down crest, with here and there a steeper step, which was best avoided to one side or the other. I do not even remember the details of the summit, but I remember the sun and a calm in which a chill little wind came and went like some mischievous elf. I remember also something of the view. The intellect of a Sherlock Holmes could not have coped with its manifold details, its wealth of ridges, its slopes and crests, its thousand peaks, but I do remember some old friends. It is natural with a mountaineer that on arriving at a summit he should first seek to identify and greet his old friends. The Wildstrubel was opposite beyond the Hahnenmoos, but my gaze passed unheeding over its level ramparts and, with scarcely a pause on the sturdy massif of the Gross Lohner, alighted on that well-loved and remembered skyline of the Jungfrau, the Mönch and the Eiger. What memories were locked up there! It was twenty-three years ago that I first climbed them, and long before that their magic had struck deep into the heart of a small boy.

Next to the Matterhorn, the Jungfrau is the most publicised mountain in Switzerland, yet in its presence men forget that they have seen it before on picture postcard, tourist poster, trinket and chocolate box. For the Oberland wall is unique; there is nothing like it in the world. There is the mighty lift of the Himalayas from the Indian plains, the icy savagery and remoteness of the mountains of Yukon and Alaska, the southern fall of Mont Blanc. It is possible to think of greater heights and grandeurs, yet in the memories and affections of all who know it, and have climbed on it, there is nothing quite like the Oberland.

From my viewpoint it appeared almost end on, and I could see how the inmost keep of glacier was contained and upheld by the wall buttressed in its turn by the Jungfrau, Mönch, Eiger and Wetterhorn. Small wonder that the natives of bygone generations invested these peaks with a romantic awe. For them they became the Maiden, the Monk, the Ogre and the Peak of Storms. No names were ever better bestowed, the flowing snow robes of the Jungfrau suggest the feminine and the dark top of the Mönch a monk's cowl, while the fearsome stone-swept precipices of the Eiger are certainly reminiscent of an ogre's lair. But it is in the contrast between these stern watch towers with the gentle meadows and foothills beneath that constitutes the charm of the Oberland.

Such a wall, so abrupt and severe, has no business to be there without some intermediate peaks of moderate elevation to transport the eye in an easier and more conventional passage.   Thus, however many times you have seen the Oberland before, it comes always as a great surprise.   The angle its crest makes when viewed from Thun can only be a degree or two, yet, it is not where you expect to see it, but always higher, so that you forget that you have ever trodden it, and long again to identify yourself with its shining snows and translucent airs.

Yet, if the Oberland is new in one sense, it is old and friendly in another.   On it untold generations of men have gazed and wondered—wondered what lay behind, what mysteries it concealed.   Its ramparts are the same to-day; only we know them better.   Men have delved into them to wrest their secrets, fared forth up the grim wall of the Eiger, burrowed with drill and pick through the living rock to the very crest.   But essentially it remains the same; it is only we at its feet who change.

There are other and higher mountains, peaks unknown and untrodden in far ranges, but always the mountaineer will return to the Alpine Mother who nourished him to seek her love and counsel.   Always will he return to refresh himself anew amidst the well-remembered scenes, to renew old friendships and to dream new dreams.

Long I sat on my summit.   I had no thought of continuing to the highest point; it would have been a hard slog—too much for a first day's mountaineering; and it had little more to offer in the way of view.   That is the charm of solitary climbing, to stop when and where and as long as you like.   Had I had a companion with me, one or both of us would have felt obliged to suggest that the summit must be reached, and thenceforward we should have moiled and toiled through the soft snow, knowing that almost as soon as we got there we should have to retire.   The solitary climber can snap his fingers at such moral obligations and physical castigations.   He is not bound to do anything, and his conscience is pleasantly amenable to the mood and inclination of the moment.

So I sat where I was.   The sun was fast declining and the small cold wind had fallen to a complete calm.   And as I looked at the Oberland snows, remote now in the yellowing afternoon sun, it seemed that all I had seen and done was concentrated in a single sentimental journey lasting a single moment of time, just as a succession of events lasting hours and days will run in a matter of a second or so through the mind of a falling man.   I was a small boy on the Wengernalp listening to the avalanches from the Jungfrau.   The snow was shining through the trees, and the sound of cowbells, remote and sweet, stole like a benediction across the warm, pine-scented air.   It was all new and wonderful, and yet, and yet I had seen and experienced it somewhere before. And climbing, a panorama of friendship and adventure, of storm and shine, of failure and success, the sum of all I had seen and done, running through memory like a film geared to some speeding time machine.   And then . . .

It was after four o'clock.   An hour had vanished in the single wave of a magician's wand.   The margin between the sun and the horizon was narrowing every instant, and darkness would fall within two hours more. Down I went, plunging through the soft snow.

I rejoined my ski and slid through the sticky snow, keeping close to the ridge crest, to the point from which it is possible to descend into the Allenbach Thal.   Others coming up the ridge behind me had already made this

descent, the best ski route from Hahnenmoos to Adelboden, and I watched a party of Swiss girls skimming
down the slopes towards the rolling alps far beneath.
They all ski-ed gracefully and well; indeed, the standard
of skill among Swiss women ski-ers is something to marvel at.   It has been said that women have a finer sense of
balance than men, though whether this is a physiological
fact I do not know.   They have certainly a sense of
rhythm and a natural neatness and aptitude both as ski-
ers and rock climbers, and it is only in strength and
stamina that they are inferior to men.   Yet, even in these
last two qualities there have been some notable excep-
tions, and the late Brigadier-General C. G. Bruce told me
of a strange encounter with a certain eminent lady
mountaineer on the Baltoro glacier in the Karakoram.
She climbed and travelled with her husband, and an
oddly assorted pair they made, since she was powerful
and brawny and her husband a somewhat puny fellow.
The unfortunate little man had collapsed from fatigue,
and lay on the ice unable to proceed another step.   His
partner, however, thought otherwise, and was standing
over him administering sundry telling kicks with her
climbing boots, while she angrily exclaimed: " Get up,
you pig dog.   I did not bring you here for this! "
    The sun was now very near the horizon.   For a few
minutes I sat in its warm rays, not the shrivelling rays of
midday reflected from the snow in blistering waves, but
gentle and beneficent.   The ski-ers had all gone.   I
could just discern them, mere specks on the broad-
bosomed alp twisting and turning like scurrying ants.
The glowing mountains, the deepening sky, the snows
were mine.   The valleys were blue and dim, and in slow
march the shadows paced the hill-sides.   Already in the
east beyond the Oberland the night was casting its dusky
veil.
    One hour to Adelboden?   Perhaps.   I clipped on my

ski. An instant later I was in cold shadow bumping along in the deeply worn track of my predecessors.

The slope from the ridge was steep at first, but the sun had long passed from it and the snow was safely frozen. Then came gentler and broader slopes easing down in great undulations. And here for the first time I found " pulver schnee." And what snow! The perfect powder of the ski-runner's dreams. You who live in England do not see such snow, at least not more than once or twice in a lifetime, and then it is sadly deficient in depth. Such snow is a product, not only of frost, low temperatures and a modicum of sun, but of blue skies and mountain air. There is about it an indescribable vitality. It does not clog or obstruct; there is nothing harsh about it; it is silky and smooth; the ski glide over it with a dry whispering swish, the sound of a ballerina's skirts on a polished floor. Lift a handful, and its dry crystalline powder pours like sugar from the grip. Such snow is beautiful; it has never the dead wrinkled appearance of old snow long exposed to the sun; there is about it a quality and a texture which rejoice the eye; in its purity and serenity it resembles a starry essence deposited on earth for the greater glorification of the hills.

Such was the snow down which I floated towards Adelboden. The underlying snow had compacted during the past few days, but the uppermost layer consisted of this powder-snow.

Down to the broad-backed ridge beneath and the first of the alp huts, the last few hundred feet in a glorious " schuss." Off the alp, plunging over the slopes to the north, the parted snow hissing like steam, the still air burdening coldly against the face. Down into a deep well of shadow. Down a great convex slope ribboned faintly with ski tracks, and across an elliptical sweep, then swinging out below into another " schuss." Down to the pine forest, slipping past the outpost sentinels, then into crowding ranks of silent snow-burdened trees, levelling out at last to a standstill.

Motionless, and a few instants before the world had been drifting by. Its details were already forgotten; only the broad pattern of the descent remained, that and the thrill of a perfect run. Life was no longer cinematic, no longer a succession of fleeting impressions.

The evening was supremely calm, the atmosphere motionless, the pines standing without a quiver as though encased in crystal. Between their snowy tops the day flared out on the crags of the Gross Lohner, and behind the ruddy serrated edge of the mountain a deepening purple spread up the eastern sky, pierced by a solitary star.

Through the forest, and the dimming eventide, I slid, to emerge on to open slopes. There was a scattered hamlet at the foot of them, and there I found myself on the broad road to Hahnenmoos, a mile or so from Adelboden. The welcoming lights of the village shone steadily before me as I rasped and skidded through the frosty twilight.

CHAPTER III
THE LÖTSCHENTHAL

FROM Adelboden I travelled to Kippel, in the Lötschen-thal. I had visited the Lötschenthal twenty years pre-viously, when I had walked with a friend from Goppenstein to the hut on the Bietschhorn. It was a summer afternoon, hot and lazy, and we had tramped along a dusty path with cool meadows on either hand and banks gay with flowers. We halted for a drink before climbing up through the forest to the hut, and I remember an old-world village of weather-browned chalets congregated about a tall church. But most of all I remember tranquillity. Cut off from a bustling world, the valley dreamed the years away.

There are many beautiful valleys and villages in Swit-zerland, yet, when I came to remember the Lötschenthal, I was more tempted to return there than to any valley I had yet visited. Not only is it remote and unspoiled, but its villages are among the oldest and most beautiful in Switzerland.

The day following upon the ascent of the Albristhorn was as fine as its predecessor, and the post bus splashed down to Frutigen through fast-thawing snow. At Fruti-gen I had but a few minutes' wait for the train which, as Swiss trains usually are, was punctual to the minute.

Both from scenic and engineering points of view the journey from Frutigen to Brig via the Lötschberg railway is the most interesting in the Alps.

Main routes across the Alps, such as the St. Gotthard, the Simplon and the Mont Cenis, although they involved immense difficulties in their construction, are at least reasonably straightforward in their main conception. They run as far as possible up one valley, then tunnel beneath the Alps to another valley. Such routes are internationally significant, and are mutually advantageous to the countries they link. The Lötschberg railway was, however, solely a Swiss conception. The initial difficulties were greater than those confronting the engineers of the other routes, though the Simplon tunnel, $12\frac{1}{4}$ miles, and St. Gotthard tunnel, $9\frac{1}{2}$ miles, take pride of place as the two longest tunnels in the world. To construct a line $9\frac{1}{4}$ miles long up the steep and rocky Kanderthal was in itself a formidable undertaking, whilst the route from the other end of the tunnel to Brig, across many miles of steep mountainsides broken into buttresses, ridges and ravines, was among the most daring and skilful engineering ventures of all time. And more than this, the line is double-tracked throughout, thanks to the far-sightedness of the Swiss Government, which granted a subsidy of six million francs to the Grand Council of the Canton of Berne, who were primarily responsible for financing the scheme.

Owing to a climb of 1,385 feet in a distance of only 8 miles between Frutigen and Kandersteg, it was found necessary to construct a double loop and a spiral tunnel over a mile long. There are no such loops and tunnels between Goppenstein and Brig, but there are twenty-one ordinary tunnels and ten viaducts, as well as numerous avalanche sheds to protect the line from snow slides.

Work on the tunnel was begun from both ends in October 1906. All went well until July 24th, 1908, when a disaster occurred. The tunnel had been planned to pass beneath the floor of the Gastern Thal, and it had been estimated by geologists that the detritus in the valley would be well above the line of the boring, which would be through solid rock. The detritus, however, extended much deeper than had been supposed, and a dynamite charge opened up the roof of the tunnel to a mass of sand, gravel and water. This poured into the

The Oberland from the Albristhorn

Avalanche in the Lötschenthal

latter, filling it for nearly a mile and killing twenty-five Italian workmen. As a result, a new heading had to be started about three-quarters of a mile from the mouth, increasing the length by half a mile, and forming a curve in the tunnel. Eventually, the two headings from north and south met on March 31st, 1911. Thus, after four and a half years, was completed a great feat of railroad engineering, one of which the Swiss are justly proud.

I can never surround the electric locomotive and train with quite the same degree of romance as the steam train. My generation was nourished on the true-blue romance of railways, and no electric locomotive, however efficient and powerful, can ever supplant the puffing, smelly, noisy, dirty steam locomotive of boyhood's dreams. Yet there is something surprising and romantic in being borne through the Alps with effortless ease. It is scarcely possible, when seated in an electrically heated compartment, with the snowy mountains fleeting past, to put ourselves in the places of those who, in the pre-railway days, had to cross the Alpine passes on foot, mule-back or in draughty stage-coaches. Furthermore, the inns were crude, dirty, flea-ridden and uncomfortable. To such, the mountains were equally crude and uncomfortable, horrid and hideous excrescences to be abhorred by all honest travellers and God-fearing men. It cannot be doubted that efficient travel, and cleanly hotel accommodation, have had much to do with man's appreciation of Swiss scenery.

While I maintain that scenery is best enjoyed on Shanks's mare, I am not so bigoted as to deny that I thoroughly enjoy travelling by train, and if the journey lies through mountainous country so much the better. The ascent to Kandersteg discloses much noble and savage scenery, the limestone country being typical of its kind, with steep cliffs blackened and rusted with water, alternating with dark forest and bright-green alps.

Waterfalls hang thread-like from the beetling crags, and torrents imprisoned in narrow gorges dash furiously into the valley, impatient for their freedom.

All too soon came Kandersteg, an admirable mountaineering centre, but to my taste too crowded about with steep cliffs and high mountains. A minute later we were humming through the Lötschberg tunnel.

I alighted at Goppenstein, the only passenger to do so. As there is no vehicular traffic up the Lötschenthal, at least in winter, I sought information from the stationmaster as to whether my luggage could be conveyed on the postal sleigh. The former, neat and sleek in his blue uniform and gold-braided cap, did not at first seem very helpful.

"There is no post to-day," he said. "Look, the avalanches."

I looked, following his outstretched arm. Two huge avalanches had fallen across the valley close to the station.

"They are big avalanches," he continued complacently, "very big."

I thought I could detect a suspicion of pride in his voice.

"Six men were caught, but they escaped with their lives. Two were buried for three hours, but we dug them out."

It was evident that an event of the first magnitude had occurred at Goppenstein.

He turned and left me, and I made my way towards the refreshment-room for a cup of coffee; but a few moments later he returned, accompanied by a peasant clad in a rough greenish homespun, with baggy, bell-mouthed trousers.

"This man has a sleigh; he will take your luggage to Kippel."

I thanked the stationmaster, who was now content at

having solved the difficulties of "der Engländer," and
after a cup of coffee at the station restaurant I followed
the peasant, who was a man of few words, to his sleigh.
To reach it we had first to clamber over the debris of the
two avalanches. They were both monsters; I have seen
none larger in the Alps. Fully 50 feet deep, they formed
a mass of sodden snow, earth, rock and the remains of
pine trees, some 300 yards in breadth. A gang of men
was busily engaged in tunnelling, though it was evident
that some days must elapse before the road could be
opened to any form of vehicle.

A recent Föhn (the warm wind from the south), accompanied by rain, had been the cause of these wet-snow
avalanches, which had slid off the steep slopes of the
Meiggengrat. This locality is indeed notorious for
avalanches, and on February 29th, 1908, during the construction of the Lötschberg tunnel, there occurred a
major disaster.

In ignorance of the dangerous nature of the area, the
French engineers working on the tunnel had a hostel
built for their men. During the days before the disaster
new snow fell to a great depth, and a large powder-snow
avalanche descended into the Lötschenthal from the
Meiggengrat.

It should be explained that powder-snow avalanches
are in a different category from the wet-snow avalanches
already mentioned, which are released only after a heavy
thaw. The former falls at a temperature at or below
freezing-point, and consists of light dry snow, the
particles of which, being unable to adhere together, pour
off from the steeper slopes like salt and sugar. It might
be thought that such light snow would be comparatively
harmless, but this is far from being the case. Freshly
fallen snow contains an appreciable amount of air, and
when large quantities slide, not only is this air released,
but the displacement of the atmosphere by the enormous

masses of snow is such that a wind blast of great volume and velocity accompanies the avalanche. This air blast, which sometimes extends far in front of the avalanche, is capable of snapping stout pine trees like matches, and of blowing houses to fragments. I had ocular evidence of its power when in 1931 I visited Wengen, and saw the remains of strong steel pylons torn from their concrete bases, and hurled many yards through the air, by the wind of an avalanche that descended between Wengen and Wengern Alp.

Some fifty persons were dining in the hostel when the avalanche fell. It was accompanied by masses of suffocating powdery snow, which overwhelmed and smothered the unfortunate diners with such suddenness that, when the rescue parties managed to extricate them, it was found that of the twelve dead and fifteen injured all had been seated at table facing the oncoming avalanche. Happily, as is often the case in avalanche accidents in which rescue work is promptly and efficiently organised, the remaining victims were dug out alive.

In powder-snow avalanches of this nature the large percentage of air contained in the loose crystalline snow often enables an imprisoned man to breathe for hours. Prompt action by means of sounding-rods will often extricate persons alive from beneath several feet of snow, though in some instances artificial respiration may be necessary.

The sleigh, a rude, primitive affair, drawn by a single jaded horse, was waiting on the far side of the avalanches. My suitcase and rucksack were placed on it, together with sundry other sacks and parcels, and we set off up the valley track.

It was a remarkable little procession. First came the peasant, who had carried my luggage, leading the horse by the bridle, while behind the sleigh trudged a youth and a girl. Seated on a pile of potato sacks at the front of the sleigh was an old lady. She was dressed in the conventional peasant costume. A white silk scarf was wound round her head, and another and larger black silk scarf edged with beautifully worked lace was wrapped about her shoulders over a high-corseted, flowing black silk dress.

Yet it was not her attire, tasteful and simple though it was, that drew the attention, but her carriage, and above all her face. She sat bolt upright, as straight and stiff as our Victorian grandmothers were wont to sit, her hands clasped in her lap. Her hair beneath the silk scarf was a pure white, so pure that, in the deep-shadowed valley, it seemed to catch and hold the reflection from the sun-lit snows so that her face was framed in an aureole of silvery light. And what a face! It was old, very old, white and transparent with age, yet it was the face of a Madonna, a perfect oval out of which two large dark eyes gazed steadfastly ahead. If it were wrinkled, then I do not remember the wrinkles; I remember only something to which it was impossible to apply a span of years, something serene and remote. There she sat, upright, without movement, without speaking, while the sleigh slid gently along the valley, her white silk scarf, her hair and her face seeming to glow ethereally out of the deepening shadow.

I could only surmise as to where she had been, perhaps to a wedding or a funeral, perhaps to bury one of her children or grandchildren. I felt it would be impolite to inquire, and I doubted whether my German was the equal to their *patois*.

A mile from Goppenstein the track had been cut through the debris of a third enormous avalanche. Although not so deep as the others, the snow had fanned out to a breadth of nearly a quarter of a mile. The fall had originated not only on open or shrub-covered slopes, but on a well-timbered mountainside, and such had been the weight and momentum of the sliding masses, that hundreds of pines large and small had been shorn away and now lay broken and splintered among the heaped-up masses of snow.

In normal circumstances a pine forest is a barrier, not only from an avalanche falling from above it, but from one originating on the slopes where it grows. It is only in exceptional circumstances, such as a sudden Föhn after an unusually heavy snowfall, that it does not provide an adequate protection to the lower slopes of a valley; but it is a mistaken idea that avalanches cannot originate on tree-clad slopes; not indeed where the forest is really dense, but in areas where the trees are thin or scattered. More than one fatal accident has occurred to ski-ing parties in thin timber, a notable one being that which brought disaster to some British runners in the Aletschwald.

In the apparent path of the avalanche stood the workings of one of Switzerland's few coal-mines, a small but precious pit which produces some two truck-loads of anthracite daily. Luckily, the workings were situated on a ridge which caused the thousands of tons of sliding snow to divide. Some slight damage was caused, but the majority of the pit-head buildings and equipment escaped, although masses of snow 20 feet deep were piled about them. A dozen or so men are employed at this mine, and the coal is transported down the mountainside to the hamlet of Goltschried by an overhead conveyor. I have never before heard of a coal-mine in which the danger of outside avalanches is added to the danger of inside roof falls. To work a shift at a coal-face, and then have to dodge avalanches at the pit-head, and on the way home from work, appears a somewhat *outré* method of earning a livelihood. The Swiss, however, are philosophers, and accept patiently the worst that Nature can do, an enviable and necessary trait in a mountain people.

Close to Goltschried we met with some of the miners, evidently just off a shift, since they were as black as sweeps. A cheerful-looking crowd, they wished us " Grüss Gott " with broad grins, then swung down the path, their lamps swinging from their grimy hands, an incongruous spectacle against the snow.

At the village of Ferden the valley bends almost at right angles, and opens out into broad meadows, whence rise wooded mountainsides and spacious alp-lands. Afar off lies the long, gently inclined Lötschen glacier and the snowy parabola of the Lötschenlücke, as beautiful and as obvious a pass as any in the Alps.

The declining sun was still pouring its rays into the valley, and the scene was in striking contrast to the dark sunless rift through which we passed from Goppenstein; it reminded me of the Bhyundar Valley in the Garhwal Himalayas, where the traveller emerges with dramatic suddenness from the jaws of a boulder-strewn gorge to find himself amidst smiling meadows bright with flowers. In these contrasts between the savage and the gentle, the fertile and the infertile, the pastoral and the sublime, lies the charm of Switzerland.

A mile or so ahead on a grassy shelf above the valley stream was Kippel, the tall thin spire of its church soaring above a huddle of snow-mantled huts and houses. From it the eye lifts over a sweep of pine forest to the open alps, and thence scales crag and glacier to the rocky pile of the Bietschhorn, King of the Lötschenthal. This mountain, 12,970 feet high, dominates the western wing of the Oberland. It is best viewed from the south, and its solitary pyramid is seen at its sharpest and shapeliest from the Visp Thal looking across the Rhone. From the Lötschenthal it appears foreshortened, and to appreciate its scale the traveller must mount the slopes to the north of the valley, whence the beauty of its sweeping ridges is evident.

The Bietschhorn was first climbed in 1859 by Sir Leslie Stephen with four Lötschenthal natives, among them being a parson. According to their " Herr " in his amusing account of the expedition they—

". . . appeared in full dress-coats and ' chimney-pot ' hats, or such imitations of those civilised articles of torture as pass current in the Lötschenthal. A certain air of shabby respectability was thus communicated to the party, in singular contrast to the wild scenery around; and with our clerical guide in shorts and a shovel-hat, we had the appearance of being on our way to some outlandish Young Men's Christian Association, rather than the ascent of a new mountain."

A cat completed the party, but on encountering a glacier torrent retreated with pitiful mews. The parson did not long survive either. He was slow and was left far behind. Finally, when some loose stones were dislodged and bounded down towards him, he turned and fled.

The spirit of the past was for me very much alive that evening as our own singular little party jogged along the road towards Kippel. The prospect had changed but little during the past century. An ugly barrack-like hotel with plastered walls of a dirty-grey colour had been erected for summer visitors on the outskirts of the village in disagreeable contrast to the age-browned chalets, and there were other and less offensive buildings. That was all. I should hardly have been surprised had anyone come forth to question me as to the progress of the Crimean War or the first ministry of Mr. Gladstone, while " chimney-pot " hats and tail coats were obvious concomitants of the scene.

So I mused as we approached the village. The sunlight was fast retreating before the tide of shadow, but the glowing mountainsides were reflected into the valley, and the deepening dusk was suffused with a faint opalescence. Wind there was none, and a profound silence reigned, broken only by the crackle of the fast-freezing snow as the valley filled with a frosty cold.

We stopped opposite to a trim chalet with a tree-shaded terrace now deep in snow, and a balcony above, on which was painted " Pension Bietschhorn." The peasant carried my luggage and dumped it down on the threshold. " How much is the cost? " I asked him. He muttered something, then said awkwardly, " Two francs." It was little enough. I bade him " Grüss Gott —auf wiedersehen " and he, the youth and the girl returned the salutation. The old lady spoke no word; she continued to sit immobile, a queen lost to the world and its small affairs. Then the sleigh moved off quietly into the evening.

The proprietress met me at the door.

" Can I have a room? " I inquired. " I wish to stay some days."

Her face wrinkled with consternation.

" A room, yes, but food—there is no food. There are no tourists here, not one in the valley."

" Is there any other hotel open now in the Lötschen-thal? "

" There is none."

It was time to play my trump card. At Andermatt the Swiss proprietor of the sports shop from whom I had hired my ski had recommended the Pension Bietschhorn, and told me to mention his name.

" A gentleman I met at Adelboden told me to come here. He wishes to be remembered to you—Frau Belwald, is it not? And to Herr Belwald. He said that you would look after me, and that I should be very comfortable."

Frau Belwald smiled.

" He said that, did he? But we have only plain food, not food for tourists; however, perhaps . . ."

Half an hour later I sat down to a dinner consisting of

vegetable soup, delicious sun-dried meat cut into thin slices with green salad and potatoes, and a jam omelet, together with the excellent dark rye bread of the valley, the whole accompanied by a half-bottle of an excellent Dôle. What, I wondered, over my coffee, does the tourist get if this is not considered good enough for him? The sun-dried meat was somewhat similar to that I have eaten in Tibet. It is raw meat dried in the pure air and hot sun of the mountains. It is cut thin, and is so easily digested that it is an ideal food for the mountaineer and walker.

Later, Herr Belwald, the proprietor, joined me. A burly, ruddy-cheeked man with wide blue eyes, he had for many years been a guide; now he had settled down in this quiet retreat, in the village where he had been born and bred, as owner of an inn. It was seven years since an English mountaineer had stopped at the Pension Bietschhorn, and he was delighted to see me.

Mine host, I soon discovered, was a well-read man, keenly interested in national and international affairs. Like many educated Swiss, he could discard Swiss-German in favour of high German. Thus, we were able to get along famously—at least to the limit of my vocabulary, not to mention my vile grammar, over which he preserved a demeanour of unwearying courtesy. The talk ranged widely, including, as it was bound to do, the spread of Communism in Europe. I think that he spoke, not only for himself and his countrymen, but for all free peoples when he said: " Even though I live in this one place amidst the high mountains, I can if I wish go elsewhere. I can also say what I like and trade with whom I like. If I were not free to do these things, then I should not want to live, nor would there any longer be a Switzerland."

That night I slept in a clean little pine-walled bedroom with simple furniture to match, and woke next morning to see the sun shining on the high snows.

As I was anxious to spend a day with my camera, I decided to ascend to the Hockenalp, one of a range of alps above forest level to the north of the Lötschenthal, to which the inhabitants of the valley ascend in summer for cattle grazing and cheese-making.

From Kippel a steep foot-track led up through the lower pastures into the forest. The snow had frozen board-hard in the overnight frost, and I had to carry my ski over an icy track in nailless ski boots.

As I climbed the sun crept down the slopes, and I paused to photograph the Bietschhorn between the pines. Such photographs are conventional, everyone takes them, and the results are usually disappointing, since the jump between foreground and background is so abrupt that depth lacks in the composition, but I must confess that in this matter I have never profited by experience; I still point the camera hopefully, even enthusiastically, and I am still disappointed at the results.

Hope, enthusiasm, anticipation, these are the attributes of the keen photographer, be he expert or inexpert, amateur or professional. Photography has one thing, at least, in common with the arts: the true photographer is never wholly satisfied with what he has done; he must go " always a little farther." He may indeed rejoice at a beautiful negative, but in the midst of rejoicing he will wonder whether he could not have done better—" So vast is art, so narrow human wit."

Presently I was able to put on ski, and a little later emerged from the forest on to the alp above. Several caravans of ski-ers now appeared from below, and a man passed in a hurry carrying a bundle of flags. There was evidently to be a ski race among the locals, and I decided to watch it.

A chilly wind was spurting viciously across the alp, and clouds of driven snow were streaming from the ridges.

Making my way upwards over open slopes, I came presently to some huts, and halting on the leeside of one made myself comfortable in the sun. This hut formed a turning-point in the race-course, and flags had already been planted to signify this.

It was pleasantly warm, and a good hour elapsed before the wind found me out. Wind has a knack of invading the most sheltered place, and its malignancy and perverseness are sometimes beyond belief. After a prolonged local reconnaissance you find what appears to be a perfectly sheltered place. There you make yourself comfortable, open your rucksack and unpack your lunch. Everything is beautifully arranged, the bread is cut and the butter spread; the sun is genial; and then, suddenly and unexpectedly, comes the wind. In a matter of a minute or so your fingers are numbed, and you are chilled to the marrow.

You gobble down lunch hurriedly and joylessly, and fumblingly repack your rucksack harried relentlessly the while by the enemy. At length you are ready to go on again, numbed, miserable and cursing the wind. But the moment you begin to plod off, chilly and disgruntled, your precious halt ruined, the wind, taking its cue, falls to a complete calm.

The worthy Frau Belwald had provided me with an excellent lunch. There is nothing second-rate about Swiss food, and the plainest fare of the simplest peasant is to be preferred to the doubtful viands disguised by sauces and relishes of many city restaurants.

During my two months in Switzerland it was difficult to believe in a world food shortage, and to envisage peoples outside the narrow frontiers who were living on the verge of starvation. The Swiss had their lean times during the war, but by 1946 these had passed away, and their standard of living was but little removed from the pre-war years, even in respect of many imports which the

British people had been told were unobtainable. I remember eating a sweet and juicy orange (excellent oranges were in plentiful supply in the most remote parts of Switzerland) with a feeling almost of guilt, not unmixed with anger at the thought of my austerity-ridden friends and countrymen still denied the good things of life after many years of sacrifice. Then there was an apple, a couple of eggs, a packet of biscuits, and a large slice of the tasty local cheese—what a change from the eternal " mousetrap "!—not to mention a generous helping of ham and cooked meat.

There can be no doubt that any view, however majestic and beautiful, is best appreciated when the soul of man is comfortably housed in a warm, well-nourished body. So it was on this occasion. The wind had not yet found me out, and I scarcely noticed an occasional whiff of loose snow blown off the roof. An eager sun poured down its warmth from the blue cupola of heaven.

From my position above the bend of the Lötschenthal I could see down the valley towards Goppenstein. Beyond that hamlet a band of haze marked the line of the Rhone, and farther still, framed between the nearer valley sides, rose the Weisshorn.

Even in this present age of desultory fashions and ephemeral opinions there are still fixed values, absolutes in beauty, and none, I think, would deny that the Weisshorn is a beautiful mountain. It expresses better than any mountain I know Nature's preference for elliptical curves. It is built up of these ellipses in one of the simplest, and in some respects the most elemental, of mountain forms; yet one of the rarest, since the original formation, out of which time and weather have sculptured what we now see, must have been accidental in the first place.

I am no geologist, and cannot enter here into a dissertation on the complex forces that manufacture mountains, such as volcanic and glacial action, sun, ice, snow, rain, frost, lightning; I can only write that mountains, like men, possess their individuality. No two mountains are precisely alike. Nature may standardise her species, but never her forms.

Presently a tall young fellow, one of the umpires, appeared, and a little later a number of other umpires ran at speed down the flagged course. Then the race began, and the first of the runners shot down the slopes above, " christied " round the bend, and re-gathering speed fled down the alp into the forest. There is no doubt that to the participants ski racing is a thrilling sport, but as a spectacle it leaves something to be desired. If the spectator is personally acquainted with the racers, or is himself an authority on racing style and technique, then he can of course muster interest and enthusiasm. There is also something artistically satisfying in seeing a man slide expertly down a steep slope on a pair of planks. For the rest, however, there is a certain monotony. The racers are set loose at intervals, and it is only afterwards when the times are announced that the winner is known. Thus, a ski race is much less exciting to watch than a race on foot, in which the competitors set out all together.

At certain points every ski-er must turn and at other points run straight; thus the manœuvres of all are substantially the same, and the interest lies solely in watching how well they are executed. Furthermore, even though each member ski-es as a member of a team, the team spirit and team manœuvres are lacking. Each man is out to do his best for his team, but to all intents and purposes he is doing it solely for himself. This, of course, applies to many sports and games, but in ski racing the immediate competitive element is lacking. It is not like watching a tennis singles between two experts with all its subtlety and jockeying for length and position, nor can it compare as a team spectacle with football or cricket. Undoubtedly, the charm of ski racing is for the ski-er himself; it is too fine an art, and not thrilling enough as a spectacle, to attract the ordinary spectator, and, except on national or international grounds, it will never in its present form enjoy the wide popularity of many other sports.

The ski-er will justly and doubtless angrily inquire, " Who cares about spectators, anyway? " The answer is that spectators, apart from providing " gate " money, do improve any competitive form of sport. What Test cricketer fighting to save his side has not been influenced by the crowd of anxious fellow-countrymen about him, or what footballer has not been urged into putting forth that extra bit which has made all the difference? I maintain, therefore, that ski racing could be improved as a spectacle.

How is this to be done? Is there any reason why race tracks should not be doubled or quadrupled, so that members of opposing teams could run in heats? The trouble with modern ski racing is that it has become a scientific matter of " times " in which the split-second bulks larger in the mind of the competitor than anything else. He becomes like a cricketer who thinks of nothing but his average. The only way of eliminating this is to make ski racing directly competitive. Let me confess that I have only taken part in one ski race, and that was a very mixed and jolly affair, in which all the competitors, male and female, started off at the same time. This is obviously not practicable in a big race, but a compromise is surely possible? The essence of a race and a game is that it should be directly competitive, a duel in skill and stamina between opposing personalities. The Greeks would have extracted little enjoyment from the stop-watched ski racing of to-day.

One by one the racers passed. Some of them fell, and one took a spectacular forward toss on the straight above.

By now the wind had found me out and was assaulting me shrewdly, so I leisurely followed them towards the valley.

There was no wind in the forest, and I stopped once again in a glade to enjoy the afternoon sun. It was an hour of peace. The ski race was over, and the competitors had long since descended into the valley. The tall pines, hoary with moss, stood unmoving, and in the valley a faint blue dimness was deepening beneath the levelling rays of the sun. Only on the Bietschhorn was there evidence of ruder things, and its ridges were blurry with wind-blown snow. The mountain seemed to shrink, and withdraw into a cold heaven under the attack of the blast. Nothing in all Nature is more terrible than a great mountain smoking in the wind.

The snow was hardening in the evening frost as I emerged from the forest and ran down the lower meadows to Kippel.

While in the Lötschenthal I took the opportunity of visiting the Reverend J. Siegel, the Prior of Kippel, and he very kindly presented me with an autographed copy of his illustrated tourist guide to the valley. Prior Siegel is a remarkable man. It is only necessary to spend a day in the valley to learn with what affection and esteem he is held by his parishioners. Quiet, gentle and kindly, he dwells in an unpretentious chalet near the church. There in his spare time he devotes himself to reading, and is a keen collector of old books.

But a minister so devoted to his work has little time for leisure, and he described with enthusiasm the valley, its villages, alps and people. The Lötschenthal, he declared, was one of the healthiest valleys in Switzerland, and an American dietetic expert who had visited it had spoken enthusiastically about it. Tuberculosis among its 2,000 inhabitants is practically unknown, and teeth are exceptionally sound. This was due, averred the Prior, to simple and happy living:

A peasant of the Lötschenthal

Ski racing above Kippel

" We live here on what we grow. We eat rye bread, meat, eggs, vegetables, butter, cheese and fruit. Tinned foods are unknown, but where they are eaten in some of the more sophisticated valleys the health is not so good, and the teeth in the young decay quickly. My people are contented also. Crime, there is none among them."

" Is there anything else you think contributes to this happy state of affairs? " I asked him.

" Perhaps there is," he replied. " I endeavour to teach not only the word of God but His bountiful power and His glory. In the springtime, when the herds ascend to the pastures, I go with them and bless them. I tell them that the butter and cheese which they eat are products of the good soil, the air and the sun, all of which God made, and that they must think when they eat that this is going into and strengthening them, that and the power of God. No one hurries here. There is time to eat, and to think, and to pray. That I think is the secret of true happiness, because it brings contentment. I teach also that covetousness brings only discontentment and unhappiness. It is the greatest of all sins in man."

" Did you not hold Mass on the summit of the Bietschhorn? " I asked.

" Yes," he replied. " Some people thought it was merely something to do and to advertise, but this it was not to me. To me all mountains are examples of the power of God, and I try to make my people appreciate their beauty. When I said Mass on the Bietschhorn I was very conscious of this power; it was all around us."

Thus spoke a simple and earnest prelate, a man whose first care and charge was the spiritual and physical well-being of his people, who lived simply and preached simply, a man of a serene faith. Small wonder that the Prior of Kippel is beloved by his people; his fame has gone far outside the Lötschenthal.

Other days I spent wandering about the valley and

photographing the villages. The Lötschenthal is well known in Switzerland for the antiquity of its dwellings. It is mentioned in Stumpf's *Chronique of 1548*, and as late as 1810 Ebel, in his *Manuel du Voyageur en Suisse*, remarks that it was among the four or five remotest valleys in the Alps and that strangers were never seen there.

Like most Alpine villages, those in the Lötschenthal have suffered from fire from time to time. To this they are still highly susceptible, since to avoid avalanche-swept ground the houses are clustered closely together in safe spots. Thus the oldest houses now existent go back to the sixteenth century. Many of them, as with other districts in Switzerland, have inscriptions carved on them, sometimes inside and sometimes outside. The late Mr. Walter Larden, a member of the Alpine Club, made a collection of these which he published under the title, *Inscriptions from Swiss Chalets*.

The following are typical examples. The first relates to the Bellwald family:

" In 1703 did Joseph Bellwald and Maria Hasler have this room constructed. . . . Two things shouldst thou set store on, that no man can bring again: Time and Virginity."

One of the older inscriptions on a house at the village of Ferden, dated 1591, is in a jumbled mixture of Latin and German. It has been the cause of considerable controversy between Swiss " savants " at Basle, Berne and Oxford. It reads:

" When God wills it, then is our end."

On an adjoining beam, dated 1670, is another inscription:

" It is certain that thou wilt die; but thou knowest not

where, when, or how; for everywhere Death is awaiting me. Therefore do thou also, if thou art wise, expect Death everywhere."

This gloomy and warning note is common to many inscriptions, and implies a resignation to the ultimate in life characteristic of a mountain people. Some, however, express thanks for Divine gifts and mercies:

"In the year when one counted 1730 then has God stood by us. For then is the avalanche from the Bach-gorge gone past the house to this side and to that."

Houses in the Lötschenthal are built of pine, a damp wood lacking resin, judging from the amount of cracking. They are often large and several stories high, each story being occupied by one family.

Some of the houses have a solidly built internal stone staircase connecting every story. They were formerly badly lit, but electricity has come as one modern advantage to the valley.

Winter is, of course, the slack season, but a good deal of wood cutting is needed, since little coal from the neighbouring mine appears to be burned, and the women spend much of their time at the open-air washing-troughs cleansing the family garments. But apart from these activities there is little to do except feed the goats and cattle, and fetch down on sleighs the hay stored on the alps above.

In all, life proceeds regularly and placidly in this as in many other Alpine valleys. The days pass, the sun comes and goes, the bells toll for Mass. There are births and marriages and deaths. Men and women congregate and talk at the corners of the narrow streets as they always have. Life pursues a gentle even tenor beneath the towering mountains. And who would have it otherwise?

CHAPTER IV
THE LÖTSCHENLÜCKE

FOR all the beauty and interest of the Lötschenthal, no mountaineer should leave the valley without visiting the Lötschenlücke. This pass was first crossed in 1811 by the Meyer brothers during the course of their remarkable expedition. It has been often stated that Mr. Justice Wills's ascent of the Wetterhorn in 1854 was the first purely sporting mountain climb, but the Meyers' expedition in design and execution, and the results achieved, was not only far ahead of its time, but was thoroughly sporting, in that it was made primarily for the love of exploration and adventure.

The brothers set out from their home in Aarau with several of their servants, and having engaged a porter, crossed the Grimsel pass into the Rhone Valley. They then ascended to the Ober Aletsch glacier, and crossing the Beich pass, 10,290 feet, descended into the upper Lötschenthal. They next traversed the Lötschenlücke, and on August 3rd, 1811, made the first ascent of the Jungrau, 13,669 feet, afterwards retracing their steps to the Rhone Valley and returning to Aarau over the Grimsel.

Many persons disbelieved the exploit, so another expedition was undertaken during 1812. This resulted in the ascent of the Finsteraarhorn, 14,026 feet, the highest peak of the Bernese Alps,[1] the first crossings of three new passes—the Oberaarjoch, 10,607 feet, the Grünhornlücke,

---

[1] This ascent was long a matter of controversy. It is now generally accepted that the party did not reach the highest point, but a minor summit on the south-east ridge. Meyer himself got no higher than another and lower point on the ridge. From there, two of his guides advanced to the minor summit. The first ascent of the highest point on the evidence available must be attributed to J. Sulger, of Basel, and his chief guide, Hans Jaun, of Meiringen, in 1842.

10,844 feet, and the Strahlegg pass, 10,995 feet—and a second and triumphal ascent of the Jungfrau. The modern mountaineer, with mountain railways, hotels, club huts, accurate maps, warm clothing, efficiently nailed boots and proper mountaineering equipment, might well think twice before undertaking such journeys were he deprived of these amenities, and when we consider the nature of the country, the complicated system of peaks, ridges and glaciers, the continual risk of mist and bad weather, and join these to the subtle fear of the unknown that still existed in many minds at that time, it is only possible to marvel at the skill and hardihood of these early explorers.

I had toyed with the idea of making a solitary traverse of the Lötschenlücke, the Grunhornlücke and the Oberaarjoch to the Grimsel pass, but the weather was manifestly unsuited to such a venture. Snowstorm had succeeded snowstorm, and the barometer remained uncompromisingly low. There is no technical mountaineering difficulty whatsoever in the traverse of the Oberland glaciers, and the expedition is carried out entirely on ski. The risk to a solitary man lies in the possibility of accident, such as a sprain or broken limb when descending from one or other of the passes, or of falling through a snow-bridge into a concealed crevasse. Both can be greatly minimised by care allied to skill and experience. The final word on risk in the mountains must always rest with the weather, and this risk is increased considerably in the case of a solitary climber or ski-er, especially with the latter, since it is fatally easy in bad visibility to blunder into a crevasse, or on to an unsafe snow-bridge, which could be seen and avoided in bright light. To sum up this question of risk: if I were engaged in weighing odds, I should say that to ski alone in good weather under spring conditions across the Oberland is, for an experienced mountaineer, less risky than

the ascent with companions of many a standard mountaineering route. At the same time, it is only fair to
state that it is less risky to traverse the Oberland with
companions than to go alone. There is no point in
labouring the argument, since many " unknowns " enter
into even the simplest mountaineering or ski-ing expedition. To climb or ski alone demands, not only the
requisite confidence, skill and experience, but a special
psychic capacity, and I use " psychic " in its exact sense
as " belonging to the soul, spirit or mind." To travel
safely across mountains alone a man must be *en rapport*
with Nature and his surroundings. In a word, he must
love the experience. It is only through genuine mountain love that there develops in the mountaineer a sixth
sense, a fineness and quickness of perception, a genius
for route finding, an instinct for weather change, an
animal anticipation, even premonition, of danger. Not
until he has acquired these qualities is he justified in
venturing over the mountains alone. Then will the
mountains offer him their choicest gifts of peace, solitude
and beauty.

I decided, therefore, to employ a guide. This decision
was in part inspired by the fact that during twenty-five
years' mountaineering I had not once employed a guide,
except during a search party, in which three had taken
part. It would be a new and interesting experience to
climb with a guide for the first time.

Inquiries of my worthy host elicited the facts that he
would like to come himself, but had for some time past
suffered from a stiff arm; it was undeniable also that he
was not as young as he used to be. The only possible
substitute for himself, he told me, was one Willy Lehner.
Accordingly Lehner was sent for. He proved a fine
young fellow, aged about twenty-five, with a brick-red,
wide and happy countenance, in which was set a pair of
fearless blue eyes. Of medium height, he was unusually

broad shouldered and deep chested.   He was obviously
a man of great physical strength and endurance;
indeed, a young Burgener [1] in the making.   And, what
was more important still, was his evident keenness.   He
had, he told me, been granted his guide's certificate three
years previously.   Since then, owing to the war, there
had been few " Herrs " in the Lötschenthal—I was
among his earliest employers, and the first Englishman
he had ever guided.

It is refreshing to meet a genuine enthusiasm in a
professional sportsman.   The task of conducting inex-
perienced tourists over peaks, passes and glaciers is liable
to have a debilitating, even souring, effect on the Alpine
guide.   And small wonder.   It is said that the tariff for
the Matterhorn is disproportionate to that of neighbouring peaks, having regard to the fact that the ascent by the
Zermatt route is comparatively easy; but the guides who
throughout the season drag tourists of all shapes, sizes
and descriptions up that mountain earn every centime
of their pay; indeed, the fatigue, both mental and
physical, that they undergo is worth far more than a
modest 200 francs.   Anyone interested to learn how
much, should spend twelve hours of a single day lifting
and raising a hundredweight sack of coal up and down
a step-ladder.

I planned to start the day after the morrow, as this
would give some time for the weather to show its hand.
My guide, I noticed, would neither drink nor smoke.   It
presently transpired that he was participating in the local
slalom race that was being held on the morrow, and was
therefore in strict training.

The barometer had climbed slightly, but the weather
seemed to have lost all power of rising from the doldrums

---

[1] Alexander Burgener was reputed the strongest guide of his time.
It is said that he could lift a twelve-stone man with a single arm
stretched out to its full length.

into which it had been plunged since my arrival at Zürich, and the following day dawned with an overcast sky, a gusty wind and a drizzle of fine snow. It was Sunday, February 17th, and in the afternoon a crowd of several hundreds, a substantial proportion of the total populace of the Lötschenthal, gathered on the slopes just outside the village. Despite the bitter wind and driving snow, all were clad in their Sunday-best, the women for the most part in black, high-waisted dresses with embroidered shawls over their heads and shoulders, and the men in black coats, black, broad-brimmed Homburg hats, waist-coats ornamented with substantial gold watch-chains, and the inevitable drain-pipe trousers so beloved by the Swiss.

The course had been marked out, and at length, after much shouting and signalling between the judges at either end, the competitors came twisting and turning down through the complicated labyrinth of flags. It was evident that Willy Lehner was among the most fancied and popular runners and a great roar greeted his appear-ance. It was also evident that he was a fine ski-er, and it was no surprise when I learned that he had won the race.

The afternoon ended in revelry. I have often noticed on these occasions that it is not the champions, but those who champion them who imbibe most freely. I saw no sign of Willy Lehner until late in the evening, when he arrived to discuss plans, but his friends and fellow-vil-lagers had by then hit all the high spots there were to hit and fallen heavily to earth again. The climax was reached at about six o'clock, when from the ground-floor of the inn there arose such a screaming, shouting and banging that bloodshed at least seemed imminent. In England a free fight and the intervention of the police would most certainly have occurred, but there was no free fight and as to police, I saw none in the Lötschenthal. At the moment, when the hubbub reached its climax, the participants, embracing one another lovingly, and for

mutual support, were gently assisted by the worthy land-
lord down the passage and out of the door into the snow-
swept night where, I should imagine, they were cooled
down in next to no time.

In view of the bad weather the start was again postponed, but as is so often the case on these occasions, the
snow-storm blew itself out during the night, and the sun
rose next morning in a cloudless sky. That evening I
was initiated into the mysteries of Herr Belwald's store-
room, and very intriguing, not to say titivating, mysteries
they proved; I had not seen so goodly a number of well-
stocked shelves for many a long day.

Preparing the provisions for a mountaineering expedition always requires a certain amount of moral resolution, especially when such preparations are made after an
excellent dinner. The amount always seems altogether
disproportionate to the length of the expedition. In the
present instance I had decided upon a five days' trip, but
it seemed that we were taking enough food to last a week
or longer; and if the delicacies so freely produced were
tasty enough, the thought of having to carry them up to
the Lötschenlücke was another matter. In the end, the
load Lehner and I would have to divide had risen to such
mountainous proportions that when he tentatively suggested hiring a porter I gladly agreed.

There are those who appear to revel in back-packing on
a mountain. Their attitude as they pass on a path bound
for a hut, weighed down beneath enormous rucksacks wreathed in ropes and jangling with crampons,
pitons and all the paraphernalia of their craft, is at times
positively offensive. It exudes a superior he-mannish-
ness that seems to shout aloud: " Look at me, see how
strong and tough I am. Look at my nailed boots, my
rope and my ice axe. See how sunburnt I am. Note
my torn, patched clothing. I am going to do hard,
dangerous things. And now look at you, you miserable

tourist, slipping about in your town shoes and girlish tweed suit, with that petty little rucksack on your back purchased at the bazaar, your absurd walking-stick, and your miserable milk-and-water complexion. You poor miserable little—Bah! " And so they go on their way, striking contemptuous sparks from the rocks with the he-mannish impact of their nailed boots and ice axes.

Let me hasten to explain that I hope and trust I am not one of these fanatics. I do not like, have never liked, or tried to emulate the he-man. I like all the comfort I can get when such comfort is available. Good food, choice wines, and a well-sprung bed are for me essentials in an Alpine holiday. I am not of that discomfort-revelling ilk. I dislike a heavy load on my back, and always have done, and as for Alpine huts, I still remember with a shudder a night spent in the Italian Cabane on the Matterhorn, a sleepless night in a cold, evil-smelling fug with an oily, straw-filled pallet for my head, wedged between two unwashed Italians, who gurked garlic into my face. Is it not strange that civilised man should endure such things for the sake of climbing a mountain? I have never ceased to wonder.

It is impossible also to regard as anything but profoundly uncomfortable and depressing the necessity to rise from bed in the small hours in order to climb a mountain. This is supposed to be an exciting, even romantic experience, and Alpine literature is full of elevating accounts of tramping along beneath the stars behind a candle lantern. What these descriptions usually omit is the actual getting up, and the vulgar business of clothing oneself and eating breakfast at an hour when the life force is indubitably at its lowest ebb. To be awakened suddenly from a deep sleep by a sudden knocking at the door, or what is worse an alarm clock, to have to wash and dress, then creep like a thief along the hostile corridors into a repellent salle à manger, there to force a surprised and rebellious stomach into action, are matters which the romanticists of mountaineering conveniently omit to mention, or else attempt to gloss over with some tepid and futile joke. And this is wrong of them, for how can we appreciate the strength of man unless we know his frailty?

The porter was waiting downstairs, a tall young man attired in voluminous plus-fours, widely and vividly checked. Frau Belwald had insisted on rising, and the excellent breakfast she prepared, which included a brew of coffee, went far towards minimising the horrors of an early start.

> "Coffee which makes the sleepy climber wise,
> And see through all things with his half-shut eyes."

If I may so misuse Pope.

I gave the barometer a parting thump—it reacted not at all—and at four o'clock we sallied forth into the night. The sky had been clear at sunset, but it was now overcast once more. However, the clouds were thin and low, and here and there a gleam of moonlight was visible on the mountainsides. Low mists overhanging a valley often herald a fine day, but this is conditional on there being no higher layers of cloud.

Through sleeping Kippel we marched, carrying our ski, since it was easier to walk than ski on the hard-trodden track up the valley, then through Wiler and Ried. We were not the only early birds. On a hill near Blatten there was a sudden " Achtung! " and a couple of ski-ers swept by going full tilt in the dark.

Once the mountaineer is fairly on his way, and has overcome the disagreeable preliminaries of the early start already alluded to, there is a certain charm about trudging along at night—not, I should hasten to add, over one of those loose and shin-barking moraines which are so often a feature of an early start from an Alpine hut, but along a nicely surfaced and well-conducted footpath, where it is possible to pursue a steady rhythm and meditate on things other than the heaviness of the rucksack, the possibility of twisting an ankle, or the uneasy condition of the stomach.

In the above manner we presently passed Blatten and halted to attach our ski. The first of the daylight was now quenching the patches of wan moonlight on the hillsides; and as we made our way along the undulating valley floor, a snowy world filled slowly with the dawn. Sunrise is supposed to be a dramatic moment in the life of the mountaineer. In this instance it was a failure, since we did not see it owing to the low clouds which, instead of dissolving as they are supposed to do in the morning sun, remained obstinately overhead.

We passed various alps, and in one place crossed the debris of a large avalanche which had fallen across the stream and piled up on the opposite side of the valley for fully 100 feet. The pines became smaller as we progressed, until the forest ran out in a level sprinkled with small trees three-quarters buried beneath the snow, which cannot have been less than 15 feet deep. Beyond were the moraines and the terminal ice of the Lötschen glacier. The latter had arched up at its snout to form a cave, and here we congregated for second breakfast, a ceremony long overdue, as I had been reminded by the autocrat within.

In Alpine theory the function known as second breakfast is a delightful interlude partaken of in the warm, newly risen sun, and an altogether jolly preliminary to a day's climbing. In the present instance there was no sun, and we huddled on what spare clothing we could, endeavouring at the same time to crouch in a corner of the cave out of a cutting wind that had risen during the past half-hour. The cave itself was a singularly unprepossessing and shelterless arch. Doubtless, were there sufficient tourists to the Lötschenthal in summer, the shrewd and industrious Swiss would hew it out a yard or two deeper, place a kiosk with a display of postcards, ash trays and carved bears at the entrance, and charge one franc for admission. In our case we were soon ready to pay a larger sum to get out of it, and when, after a few minutes spent in a hasty and unappreciative mastication of the good things provided by Frau Belwald, we again set off, I know that my hands were already numb and lifeless from a damp and bitter cold.

Up to then we had progressed with extreme slowness. Since both guide and porter had heavier loads than I, I had said nothing, but when presently Lehner turned to me and asked whether he was going too *fast*, my reply was so emphatic that the party was suddenly galvanised into activity, and from then on we proceeded at a reasonable and warming speed up the glacier.

The Lötschen glacier is a smooth, gently sloping tongue some 5 miles long, and in late winter, when the snow is well consolidated over such crevasses as exist, a rope is unnecessary. We were now above the low mist, and could look over its dull grey surface down the Lötschen-thal towards the distant Rhone Valley; but we were still out of the sun, which skulked dismally behind the rocky wall of the Distelhorn, and in no way alleviated the chill-ing wind which poured like douches of cold water down the glacier into our faces. Meanwhile, the snowy curve of the Lötschenlücke remained as far off as ever, and our objective, the Hollandia hut, which was clearly visible, refused to grow in size despite our labours.

Although this was my first serious expedition for some years, I was agreeably surprised to find that I was going much better than I had expected. Beneath a heavy ruck-sack I was, however, exuding steadily those fats and by-products which are so quickly and easily amassed in civilised life, and at the same time gaining a compensatory thirst of which a stoker on the Red Sea run might well be proud.

At last, very slowly, the sun, which had been smiling for some hours on the slopes of the Ebnefluh, at length condescended to unbend in our direction, but it was too late and too weak to counter the icy wind which lashed the loose snow about in sportive gusts. I was relieved, however, to find that the Lötschenlücke, so far from being an illusory product of Looking-glass Land, had suddenly approached considerably nearer, so near indeed that it was possible to distinguish the shuttered windows of the hut. This discovery was so exhilarating to us all that the porter conjurously produced a fair-sized aluminium bottle which he opened and handed to me. Thinking this to contain tea, coffee or some such innocuous liquid, I took a long deep pull, only to pause gasping, my mouth and gullet suddenly aflame from what appeared to be liquid fire. The donor grinned and remarked that it was good cognac. I daresay it was; it was certainly stimulating, to such an extent indeed that, after the bottle had circulated to all concerned, we shot up the final slopes to the Lötschenlücke at a speed which would have out-distanced the village fire engine had this been capable of making the ascent.

The Hollandia hut, which is situated some 300 yards to the north of the Lötschenlücke, was built a few years ago in replacement of the old Egon von Steiger hut, and is stoutly constructed of stone and timber. We found it three-quarters buried beneath snow-drifts. The Swiss, however, are adepts in allowing for such contingencies, and the end containing the door was wind-swept and clear. Like the majority of huts accessible to ski-ers in winter and spring, the accommodation includes a special winter room, an apartment considerably smaller than the *gastzimmer* provided for summer visitors, which it would be impossible to heat adequately in low temperatures.

One end of this room was taken up by a kitchen, whilst two tiers of bunks occupied the remainder. Even so, it was decidedly chilly, and during our stay there we were unable to raise the temperature above minus 5 degrees Centigrade, an indication of the low temperature outside, especially having regard to the fact that the hut was mostly snow buried and should have been reasonably warm.

Firewood is always a problem at these high huts, since it must be carried up by hand over miles of difficult ground, and it is not surprising, therefore, that its cost is considerable; if I remember aright, it cost $2\frac{1}{2}$ francs a bundle, weighing about a kilo, at the Hollandia hut, and $3\frac{1}{2}$ francs at the remoter Finsteraarhorn hut. Such prices impose economy; it is also a point of honour not to burn more than is strictly necessary.

The first and natural action on arrival at a hut is to get a fire going and brew a hot drink, the second is to change damp clothing, and the third to substitute " hausschuhe " for ski-ing boots. These last are wooden, felt-lined clogs, which are to be found in varying stages of decay and repair according to the age of the hut. A thing I have noticed is that " haus-schuhe " are either immensely large or absurdly small. Thus, a visitor arriving at an Alpine hut from another planet would conclude that mountaineers consist of two clans of giants and pigmies living amicably together. He might also, did he come from a land of open fires, deduce that the Swiss is an ingenious and thrifty person. In England, we and generations of our ancestors have laboured to heat the open air outside our houses while retaining ten per cent. of such heat for the interior. The net result of these labours is that the open air remains at approximately the same temperature, while the inside air is but little affected except in the immediate vicinity of the fire, owing to the convection currents generated by the passage of so much hot air up the chimney, and the consequent inrush of new cold air through the cracks in windows and around doors, which are a permanent feature of the English home. This method of heating is said to be healthy and homely. Whether or not a circulation of air and a distribution of heat, which puts a human being in a position analogous to that of an unbasted beef steak hung one side to the flame and the other to a refrigerator, is healthy I will leave it to my medical friends to decide. As for the homeliness associated with this method of heating, there is an undeniable pleasure in looking into an open fire, one which cats and dogs as well as humans appreciate, and this pleasure, which dates back to the beginnings of time, and is associated with the turnspit and the roast, is unquestionably a part of our rugged tradition.

The Swiss, however, is more realistic as well as more thrifty. He is certainly a respecter of tradition where it concerns the evolution of his political system and heroic ancestors, but not where it retards or impinges upon his efficiency and comfort. Furthermore, coal is in short supply in Switzerland, and timber must be carefully and scientifically deforested. He has set to work, therefore, to evolve wood-burning stoves in which the position already mentioned is reversed, the open air receiving but ten per cent. of the heat, the remaining ninety per cent. being employed for the interior. This is quite simply done by passing the smoke and heat through a kind of radiator, thus distributing the heat over a wide area. Any remaining heat is trapped by a long flue, which passes halfway round a room before emerging into the open air. The fire itself is controlled by a damper and by regulating the flow of air to the burning wood. Rings above the stove allow for various sizes of receptacles, while an oven on one side and an oblong division on the other, in which snow can be

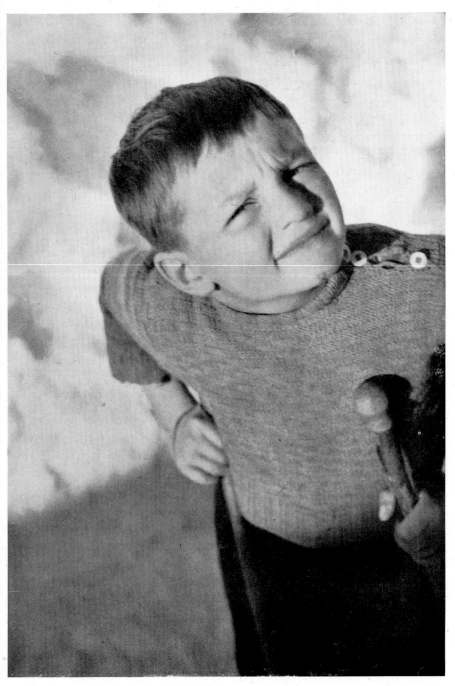

The young idea. A boy of the Lötschenthal

Wiler, Lötschenthal

melted, complete the assembly. On one of these stoves, if it is skilfully handled, a pound or so of wood will suffice to cook a two-course meal for several persons as well as heat the room.

Perhaps some impressions of my first climb with a guide may now be of interest. During the ascent to the hut I had been a trifle bored. To climb behind a guide in his own country is a process so certain and so mechanical as to remove any doubts and uncertainties, and are not doubts and uncertainties more than half the fun of guideless mountaineering? One analogy is gardening. While we can rejoice with our particular "Angus MacFungus" on the successful raising of some choice plant, or the production of a fine crop of peaches, how infinitely greater is the satisfaction of doing it oneself! Decisions made for you are poor, sapless things compared with the decisions you make yourself. These factors, important perhaps to some climbers and less important to others, have opposed to them other factors which find favour with many. The guided climber does not have to think for himself in anything like the degree he must when climbing without guides. Apart from the concentration required in having to place his hands and feet in the same position in which the guide places his, he can, on all but really difficult ground, relapse into a reverie, which is materially assisted by the fact that the guide and porter are carrying the bulk of the load. Thus to hire a couple of sturdy peasants to carry up your belongings is undeniably delightful, though I must confess to a faint but noticeable feeling that mountaineering in such circumstances has not the sparkling thrill and later satisfaction that it has when the climber does all the work himself.

In a hut, however, guided climbing is infinitely superior to guideless climbing. For here it is possible to renounce without a single qualm all those duties so onerous to the guideless climber. In a matter of minutes the wood is cut up, the fire lit and the weary " Herr " tucked up in bed if need be. The meal is cooked and the snow brought in from outside ready for melting. To attempt to assist in these operations is merely to be a nuisance, as is evident from the guide's tolerant smile. It is better to desist, even to allow the guide to unlace your boots, since this is obviously pleasurable to him, giving him as it does that sense of fatherly superiority which is the characteristic of all good guides.

Finally, when the washing-up has been done, the guide *may* allow the " Herr " to dry one or two utensils, if the latter can do so without breaking them. After this the guide arranges the bedding and blows out the candle. Only one act that would complete this pleasant panorama of paternal duty is omitted—he does not as a rule kiss his " Herr " good-night.

After tea, the porter set off for Kippel. It was now late in the afternoon, but he was an expert ski-er and would, so Lehner assured me, take a mere two hours to descend, as against our eight hours of ascent. Off he went at a spanking pace, his plus-fours wide in the breeze like the hairy legs of an eagle. In a matter of minutes he was a mere speck on the broad glacier, and was curveting from side to side in beautiful rhythmic stems. Once, and once only, he fell, apparently on a piece of crusted snow, and Willy Lehner caught his breath in a sudden hiss of disapprobation, as one who watches a Bradman make a false stroke. I wondered how many times he would catch his breath when he saw me ski-ing downhill—enough to incur a grave risk of choking.

Soon the porter had vanished into the gathering shadows, and we turned into the hut out of the bitter wind.

The weather conditions were by no means propitious. The hut barometer, already at " Regen," responded to the usual suasion with a vicious jerk backwards towards " Stürm," and outside an hour later this promise of impending evil was in certain process of fulfilment.

From the hut the view westwards extended to Mont Blanc. I had already greeted the Mountain King with affectionate respect. Although 70 miles distant, he was still visible, but all around him the storm was congregating its forces, and he stood out inkily blue, his mighty shoulders humped hard and gaunt against a sky of pale sour green, banded with long strips of cloud, between which the sinking sun glared fiercely crimson as though through furnace bars. Far into heaven these clouds extended, and in the north-west united like the spokes of a gigantic wheel in a bulbous hub of murky grey, beneath which the far-distant mountains vanished as though into some impalpable tide. And if anything else was wanting to amplify the threat, the clouds still brooding over the Lötschenthal were beginning to extend their dominion and push their sluggish vapours towards the pass on which we stood. It was a magnificent, a beautiful, a terrible sky. I have seen such skies before, but never one more spectacular—once before a devastating thunderstorm on the Schreckhorn and on Mont Blanc two or three times. Substantially, they had exhibited the same violent contrasts and colours with layers of cloud above and below the mountain tops. The question was unnecessary, but as a matter of conversation I asked Lehner what he thought of the weather. He pursed his lips and slowly shook his head, but made no other reply.

I photographed the scene, then we went inside to escape the wind, which was now blowing in sudden violent gusts with short intervals of calm in between. Half an hour later I emerged for another glimpse and some more photographs. The sun was about to set, and the dark bars of cloud had expanded and were crowding in closer and closer. The sky near the sun was red, not the calm peaceful red of a fine-weather sunset, but a furious fiery crimson, as though the sun had set afire the very tenements of heaven. And above, the pale green had deepened into an opaque colour, a colour without light and life, cold, expressionless and cruel like a feline eye. Of orange there was strangely little. Red and green merged into one another almost without pause, and the former was branded on the latter like some sinister trail of blood and flame. Higher still, the green gave way to a dull murky purple, slashed across and across with inky clouds. In one of the rifts so formed a star shuddered fearfully.

And now occurred a very strange phenomenon. A high layer of cloud was swiftly sliding up from the south-west above the Bietschhorn when, of a sudden, a wind current caught it, and with a violent clockwise rotary motion like that of a tornado, cut a hole clean through it. So amazed and interested was I at this singular spectacle, something I had never previously witnessed, that I momentarily forgot my camera, then, hurriedly recollecting it, was just in time to photograph the hole, round which it was possible to see the mists rushing before it filled in again.

Only an extremely unstable air condition could have caused such an aerial tornado. It was an earnest, if anything more were needed, of the bad weather to come.

Quickly now the mists gathered about the mountain tops. Mont Blanc vanished, engulfed beneath one arm of the grey tide creeping out of the north-west, and beneath, from the Lötschenthal, the mist sea began sullenly to flood upwards. The wind was still blowing fitfully, but now and then it fled away, conjuring its wreaths and spirals of snow along the crest of the col. Then would occur a few moments of calm, and this calm was somehow more ominous than anything else. In it a cowed earth and sky seemed to be held in suspension, as though awaiting a monstrous catastrophe. Then back would come the wind snarling and worrying, and because it was possible to attribute something human and malevolent to its spiteful assaults, the feeling of tension would pass, and we would become human beings again, not gods brooding over a universal dissolution.

Dinner consisted of soup and that kind of hotch-potch which every mountaineer knows, a miscellaneous lucky dip from the provision bag with a base of macaroni, the whole swilled down, and we were both excessively thirsty, by a gallon or so of tea. It has long been my self-appointed and somewhat thankless task to try to teach the Swiss to make tea. If we waste fuel they most certainly waste tea, and the normal method of both guide and hut guardian is to fill an egg-shaped tea-strainer with tea, and to dip this wretched contraption into some warm water which has been previously poured into a cold china or metal cup. The chilly, faintly browned liquid resulting from this operation is then served as tea.

Another point which is overlooked, and not only by the Swiss, is that water boils at temperatures below boiling-point above sea-level. Thus, at 10,000 feet it is necessary to cook the tea in boiling water for a minute or longer to produce the required result. As for such refinements as warming the teapot and measuring out the tea in proportion to the number of persons present, of these things the Swiss know nothing. For the above reasons few Swiss have ever tasted good tea, and their affection for the lukewarm, faintly browned liquid, which they so assiduously manufacture in huts, hotels and restaurants, is such that any suggestion that the leaves might be better utilised by placing them loose in boiling water is regarded as so revolutionary as to be little less reprehensible than an attack on the constitution. Thus, my efforts to teach Lehner to make tea *à l'Anglais* were from the beginning doomed to failure. Out of deference to his employer he was prepared to sacrifice his convictions to my peculiar whim, but I knew full well that once my back was turned he would revert to the methods of his ancestors.

Tea over, we spent a few minutes in conversation, during which he told me about his ambitions. Life in the Lötschenthal, he averred, was too narrow for a young man. At school he had learned something about other countries, and the opportunities in them of becoming a small farmer, shop-keeper or inn-keeper, with perhaps some spare-time guiding. There were lands beyond the seas, the United States, Canada. He would like to go to them and carve out his own line. There were opportunities, great opportunities, but in the Lötschenthal there was only a bare living to be made, and life was constricted, narrow. One grew up, one lived, one married, one had children and one died. "But it's a peaceful life," I reminded him. "Yes," he replied thoughtfully, "that is so. I do not think I could live far away from the mountains. Perhaps, though, I could get a job as ski instructor in America."

Here spoke the young Swiss of to-day, one who has been educated sufficiently to want to do more, and do better perhaps, than his peasant ancestors. This is what education will do for Switzerland on an increasing scale. The Swiss, after seven years of "captivity" in their own country, were bursting to get out of it. The tourists of all nations were bursting to get into it. Such is human nature—never to be satisfied with what you have got—and such is the result of education to-day; such, indeed, is progress—laudable enough by present-day standards of achievement, but leading to what? Never to be satisfied, always to be striving—after what? When much of Western civilisation is atomised and extinct, the Buddhist lama will still sit cross-legged and watch in

serene contentment the pale cheeks of Himachal blush
in the first caress of the sun. And who knows but that
the peasants of the Lötschenthal will be still tending
their cows?

I was tired when I rolled myself into some not-too-dry
blankets. An ascent of 6,500 feet on ski with a heavy
rucksack is no mean distance for a first day in the high
mountains. Some climb on physique and some on
nerves. The ideal is to climb on both, but that day I
had climbed mostly on nerves, and as a result was tired—
so tired indeed that I slept fitfully and in snatches,
bothered now and then by cramps in my legs and thighs.

It is not possible, either, when you are very tired to
digest a heavy meal, and for this indiscretion I paid
heavily. I mention these facts merely to warn others. If
I had profited from the experience gained when training
troops during the war, I should have realised that to
drive the body by will-power alone is something to be
kept against an emergency, not squandered away on a
mere whim. There is a danger in such cases of straining
oneself, of elongating both mind and muscle beyond the
elastic limit as it were, and I have seen this occur to
troops, seen their enthusiasm snuffed out by a permanent
fatigue gained from over-doing it in the first place. It is
better, especially in the forties, to start easily and
methodically on a ski-ing or mountaineering holiday,
and to work up strength and stamina gradually. Then,
and then only, will enjoyment follow, naturally and
delightfully.

As I lay awake I heard the wind rise. To begin with it
resembled some thief stealing round the hut and tentatively pulling at the shutters to see if any were loose.
Then, being assured there was no one within, it became
bolder and began to shake and pull with ever-increasing
determination. And awhile it whistled through its teeth
a shrill, mirthless little note. Now and again it would

fall silent, as though meditating a new evil, and all was quiet in the hut save for the deep breathing of my sleeping companion; then up it would rise again with a renewed impatience and a shriller and angrier whistle.

So it went on, from impatience to anger and from anger to rage and from rage to an insensate fury. From something stealthy and sly it became a demon, and from a demon a full-blooded giant who did not whistle or howl but roared, a solid, tremendous sound like great ocean rollers beating a rocky coast. And penetrating this roar, like rifle fire in the midst of artillery, came the sputter of snow and ice particles against the shuttered windows.

Many a time have I lain in my blankets in an Alpine hut and listened to the raging of the elements. There is something stimulating and satisfying in this. To be far from civilisation, and yet in safety and comfort amidst the unbridled forces of Nature, appeals to the elemental in our natures, so that we forget that in normal circumstances we tread city streets surrounded by all those lawful appurtenances which hedge us about, reducing our existence, in part at least, to a matter of forms and formulæ. But up in an Alpine hut away from it all there is something in the wild lawlessness of the storm which strikes deep into the wild lawlessness of our own natures. We are back in the cave with naught but a fire and a rude barricade separating us from a dangerous primeval world, and yet we can exult in that world and in ourselves. We have cheated it, conquered it; let it howl and roar. For once it can do us no harm, yet in all else it is the master of us; it awes us with its vastness, its mystery, its grandeur and its power. We are a part of it; out of it we were evolved; to it we must return.

Such, however, is our mental dependence on our physical condition that to me that night the storm was more malevolent than stimulating. Not only was I cold, cramped and uncomfortable, but I knew already that in the morning, unless the weather improved, we should have to go down. It was evident that, however well-provisioned we were, this was no time or place in which to spend two or three days in the hopes of being able to carry out an expedition, for not only was the firewood in short supply, but the prospect of living for days and nights in a temperature below freezing-point was not to be contemplated for a moment. In mountaineering when the prize is great, as in the case of a Hima-layan peak, the mountaineer is prepared to endure much hardship and discomfort, but to endure similar discomforts in order to make a ski run in the High Alps is to place himself on a par with Burmese religious fanatics who suspend themselves on meat hooks for their principles. Mountaineers are reputed to be mad, but I notice that most of them have a profound respect for the creature comforts of life, and the amenities of a civilisation which they pretend to despise.

The dreary hours passed on leaden feet. At high altitudes it is possible to lie awake and be scarcely conscious of the passage of time, but at lower elevations in the Alps this is far from being the case. Time in terms of human consciousness is certainly a variable measure. To the climber, engrossed with a great mountain ascent, the hours pass like magic, but to him who spends a sleepless night in hut or bivouac their march is funereal.

A wan light strained at long last through the single ice-encrusted window, and as soon as I could decently do so I woke Lehner and we breakfasted. If the hut had been chilly the night before it was now so cold that water left over the stove had frozen solid, while boots placed near the latter were still snow clogged.

Outside it was blowing a blizzard. Little new snow appeared to be falling, although the sky was heavily over-cast, and the peaks were buried in mist; but the wind, blowing now a gale from the west, was catching up the surface of the glacier in loose clouds and hurling it in a furious tourbillon across the col. If any further evidence as to the weather's intentions were needed, the barometer had fallen 1·25 centimetres during the night, the equivalent of over half an inch, and its needle now rested on " Stürm," an exceptionally low reading in any circumstances.

Discussion was needless, and after breakfast we packed our rucksacks and prepared to descend. Apart from what we had eaten, and some bread which we left in the hut, we carried down all that we had brought up, and this, with our ski-ing and mountaineering equipment, made up a very heavy load. Lehner must have carried fully sixty pounds, while my share cannot have amounted to much less than forty.

It needed a moral as well as a physical effort to emerge from the hut; however uncomfortable it may have been, it was preferable to the greater discomfort and fury without. As all mountaineers know, a high wind is a disagreeable and dangerous form of weather, and a high wind which blows at a low temperature strong enough to carry along with it loose snow is the worst form of wind.

It was not only the force of the wind that caught us; it seemed to sear our faces like a red-hot iron. The last time I had experienced such a wind was on the Snow Dome, a peak above the Columbia Icefield in the Canadian Rockies. This was in the winter of 1943–44 when training mountain troops. The temperature was round about minus 20 degrees Fahr. and the wind force cannot have been less than 70 miles per hour. To those who have experienced such a wind it is unnecessary to say more, while to those who have not, no description can convey the degree of physical and mental torture.

Before we could descend on to the col we had first to surmount a snow-bank a few feet high. This was so hardened by the wind that my ski, which were without steel edges, refused to bite, and it was only after two or three attempts that I managed to struggle over it in the teeth of the gale, which now seemed to be coming from all points of the compass.

Once over the bank it was necessary to make a further traverse on steep wind-hardened snow to the gentler slopes of the col. Here again I found myself at a disadvantage without steel edges, and the effort of endeavouring both to edge my ski and maintain my balance in the wind resulted in a sudden and painful attack of cramp in both thighs simultaneously. The wind chose that moment to make its most violent assault, and a sudden snow-laden squall whirling across the slope smote me to such effect that in another instant I had been blown out of balance and was sliding down the icy snow.

Lehner was some twenty feet below and to one side, and disliking the sight of his " Herr " descending in so unorthodox a manner, he promptly proceeded to intervene. He was a trifle too late. His clutch at me missed. Instead, my sliding ski struck his. The impact was sufficient to project my body outwards and downwards, so that instead of sliding I began to descend the slope head over heels. This manœuvre is ludicrous at any time, but when made in conjunction with a pair of ski, ski sticks, a heavy rucksack bedizened with a pair of crampons and an ice axe, it provides a spectacle comparable with the equestrianism of the White Knight. I fear that at the time I was unable to appreciate this, for my mouth, nose and neck were full of snow. My surroundings also were rendered quite invisible by the blizzard, and the only means by which I could tell that I was revolving was the fact that my face hit the snow at regular intervals. On such occasions it is customary for one's past life to appear before one in a cinematic panorama; truth, however, compels me to admit that I spent the descent in thinking out some extremely bad language, none of which I was able to ejaculate beyond a Blast! Blast! Blast! every time my head came round, and that with difficulty, since my mouth was full of snow.

I should perhaps now explain, however much it comes as an unwanted anticlimax to the compassionate reader, that during this descent I was happily aware that there were no rocks below, and that sooner or later I was certain to stop. And so I did. I plunged into deep soft snow and ceased suddenly to revolve. There I lay considerably winded, since the process of somersaulting down a mountainside at a height of over 10,000 feet is not one calculated to refresh the inspiration. I was still gasping like a flounder when Lehner appeared. There was anxiety in his face, but when he was assured that his " Herr " was uninjured, it was replaced by more than the suspicion of a grin.

I rose with what dignity I could muster, and a ball of snow which had wedged itself between collar and neck slid icily down my spine. Then we continued on our way.

We were well below the col and the wind was markedly less. We pointed our ski down the slopes of the Lötschen glacier and were out of the storm in a matter of minutes. The exercise was wonderfully warming, and for the first time since arriving at the hut I began to enjoy myself. Half-way down the glacier we stopped for some food. There was a flat calm at this level, and it seemed incredible that 2,000 feet higher a hurricane was raging.

The descent of the Lötschen glacier is among the classic ski runs of the Alps, but the conditions were poor, and leaden clouds doused light and shadow, merging all into a deceptive monotone, so that it was impossible to tell what lay ahead. Had it not been for Lehner's intimate knowledge of the glacier we should have run

more slowly than we did; as it was we descended at a fair
pace, I following in his tracks.

Soon we were off the glacier and down on the valley
flats. And here I greeted, with the pleasure I always
experience on returning from the snows, the first of the
pines. The Polar wastes have their austere and remote
appeal, but I know that I should weary of them in the
end by thinking too often of grass and trees. Is not the
greatest moment of the Everester's life the moment when,
after weeks on the glaring snows, he sees the first blooms
peeping out from the yellow moraines of the Rongbuk
glacier?

The first alp huts; there is a pleasure here, especially
in winter. We removed our ski, and entering one threw
ourselves on the hay for a rest and to eat another and
more comfortable meal.

As we ate we saw through the door that snow was
beginning to fall. Its flakes floated down out of a leaden
canopy of mist that was slowly sinking lower and lower
on the hillsides. All the high ridges had vanished, and a
great weight of formless snow-cloud now overhung the
world. Evidently there was to be another snow-storm.
But little cared we. We were down and it could do its
worst. I was already speculating as to our dinner that
night, not to mention a generous portion of " glühwein,"
on our arrival at Kippel. And as though to expedite the
fulfilment of these pleasant fancies, our old enemy the
wind came charging down the valley, whirling the snow-
flakes before it and whistling maliciously through the
cracks of our temporary hermitage.

On we went, and never was the sensation of " being
down " more satisfactory. Not even my aching limbs
could militate against our rapid advance on the " flesh
pots." Outside Kippel the populace of the valley was
assembled watching the third of the races in the local ski
meeting, the " langlauf " or cross-country, and we paused

to cheer some of the competitors past the post. Among them was our porter, who, despite his exertions of yesterday, was as energetic as ever, his lanky, plus-foured figure speeding over the snow in notable style.

And so at last to Kippel, and the cosy *gastzimmer* in the Pension Bietschhorn, there, over the promised " glühwein," mulled, piping hot and generously spiced and sugared by Frau Belwald, to reflect on the fortunes of yesterday and to-day, the " ifs " and the " might have beens," the pleasures and penalties of ski mountaineering, reflections happily invested in a roseate glow under the benign influence of the grape.

CHAPTER V

VERBIERS

THE weather did not belie its promise, and after our return to Kippel a great snow-storm set in. I decided that I might as well remain at Kippel as anywhere else until the weather improved. I did not then know that this snow-storm was to last for a week, and with short intermissions for nearly a fortnight, and that main-line communications were to be cut as a result. It also occurred to me that I might profitably spend some time having ski-ing lessons from Willy Lehner in an attempt to improve my ski-ing.

Ski-ing is not, as might be supposed, a matter of balance and instinct, but a specialised technique on which experts discourse learnedly on ballastics, parallelo-grams of forces, centre of gravity and other matters which I forgot on leaving school. Instinctive movements are usually wrong, and unless corrected in the beginner will result in an unsound technique leading to a permanent mediocrity. This is what happened to me. I regarded ski-ing as simply a means of crossing country and climb-ing mountains and did not bother to take any lessons. It is, however, obvious that any form of ski-ing is more efficient and better enjoyed if the ski-er is a well-trained and skilful performer.

It is tacitly assumed by many persons that the technique of ski-ing has been improved out of all know-ledge during the past twenty-five years. I am not so sure of this. Improved it certainly has been, and the general standard is considerably higher, yet I can remember just as good performers on the mountainsides in the old Huit-feldt or Bilgeri bindings as there are to-day in the Kandahar and other "high-speed" bindings. It is only on the beaten tracks that ski-ing has quickened.

Safety in ski-ing has been sacrificed to speed. The latest technique of " nose in the snow " depends on strapping the feet practically immovably to the ski. " What happens," I asked one expert, " in the event of a bad forward fall—when the ski dig in or strike some obstruction? " He shrugged his shoulders. " It's a case of either the ski or the legs, usually the legs." Something of to-day's cynical disregard for life and limb has been passed on to the sport of ski-ing.

My one and only ski lesson took place in a snow-storm. It lasted only an hour, but it was sufficient to prove the value of good tuition.

Snow had now fallen without intermission for thirty-six hours and had piled up to a depth of nearly two feet. The storm looked like continuing indefinitely, and as there was no possibility of any further high Alpine ski-ing, I decided to make for Verbiers in the western Valais.

My luggage could go down to Goppenstein on the post sledge, and I would follow; but when I arrived at the post office, a room in a neighbouring chalet, I was told by the postmaster that there was no post sledge to Goppenstein, as the track was snow-bound and the danger of avalanches already considerable.

Both Herr and Frau Belwald seemed to me to greet this information cheerfully. This cheerfulness, if grati-fying in one sense, merely hardened my determination to carry out my plans, and I decided to ski down to Goppenstein, carrying my luggage. The latter, which consisted of a suitcase and a frame rucksack, was too heavy and too clumsy to manage as a single load, and would have to be taken down in two journeys. All day, the second after returning from the Lötschenlücke, a blizzard raged, and at times the wind was so fierce that little was visible save whirling clouds of snow. It was a blizzard of Arctic severity in which it would have been

Whirlwind in the sky

Verbiers

possible to be lost close to the village, and scarcely a soul
had ventured out save to pass from one house to another.
I spent the day reading, but at intervals stood at the
window of the *gastzimmer* watching the storm, the rush
of the charging snow-clouds, and the *tourbillons* that set
the snow whirling in furious vortices until the tortured
atmosphere twisted and writhed like the cold smoke of
some Tibetan hell.

Such fury cannot be kept up for long, even with
mountain weather, and towards evening the wind
dropped, save for occasional squalls, although snow continued to fall heavily.

My suitcase was already packed and I attached it to
my frame rucksack. It was a clumsy, bulky load weighing
about 50 pounds and not easy to manage on ski in soft,
deep, new snow. Then I set off for Goppenstein.

The valley track had vanished. In many places it was
now flush with the hillside; in others deep drifts had
been formed; but there was nothing to stop a ski-er,
although it was a trifle annoying having to negotiate the
drifts with a heavy suitcase which insisted on sliding from
side to side in the rucksack straps. This, I told myself,
was quite my oddest journey to a railway station, and
since contrasts and oddities are the spice of life, I enjoyed it.

Ferden was passed, and the hamlet close to the coal-
mine. Some miners had returned there from a shift, and
they shouted at me some humorous and I suspect rude
remarks.

It is between the coal-mine and Goppenstein where the
valley narrows that avalanches may be expected. The
danger in the present instance was limited to one section
only of the track, and it was highly unlikely that further
avalanches would occur in the neighbourhood of Goppenstein or the coal-mine, where the immense
" grundlawinen " had already fallen. The new snow

A.S.—7

would have to pile up to a much greater depth before it became dangerous. In the dangerous section no avalanche had yet occurred. This was where steep slopes, overhung several hundred feet above by crags and gullies, rose from the road close to a concrete dam in the stream and a chalet, evidently the residence of the dam keeper. At this point for about 250 yards the road cut deeply into the slope, and as no drifts had formed on the former the latter was unsupported, and the slope ended above the road in a layer of snow some five feet in thickness. This layer consisted of some three feet of old, well-consolidated snow with an uppermost layer of two feet of freshly fallen snow. The underlying old snow was safe enough, but the previous thaw and rain, followed by freezing conditions, had turned its surface into a smooth icy sheet on which subsequent snow-falls would be more than likely to avalanche. Lastly, the slope was steep and long enough to originate a formidable avalanche, while the fall of even a small quantity of snow from the much steeper crags and gullies above would suffice to start a slide. Any such avalanche would not only pile up on the flat road, but would overflow down a steep slope below into the narrow and rocky stream-bed, carrying with it and quietly burying anyone who chanced to be passing along the road.

I mention these facts because all ski-ers should study avalanche craft. Avalanches are not incalculable phenomena as many seem to suppose, but are the result of the action and interaction of well-defined physical laws. Only through knowledge, observation and experience of these laws can the ski-runner ski safely in the mountains.

There was one important point. By traversing the road I would not cut across or disturb the slope above. Thus, any avalanche that occurred would fall spontaneously. There is a world of difference between

risking an avalanche of this nature and taking a chance
of treading loose a slide by deliberately traversing an
unstable slope. The one is a justifiable risk which every
mountaineer has incurred at one time or another—the
other is an unjustifiable risk which no one should incur
at any time.

The temperature at which new snow falls has an
important bearing on the type of avalanche. Then there
is the wind which may drift the snow into dangerous
slabs. In the present instance the fresh snow had fallen
and was still falling at a temperature very slightly below
freezing-point; it was neither wet nor dry, but something
in between. The wind was certainly forming wind-slabs
in many places. At this point, however, there was little
or no wind; no drifts had formed on the road, and the
appearance of the slope did not suggest wind-slab.

The mountaineer who understands his mountains and
his snow-craft weighs and sums up the varying factors
practically simultaneously. Instinct with him is often
only another word for experience. In the same way the
experienced mariner with a single comprehensive glance
takes in the weather, the sea and his ship. The essence of
good seamanship and good mountain craft lies in instant
decision and in the " feel " for a situation.

The foregoing may seem an absurd fuss to make over
the crossing of a minor snow-slope. The point I have
tried to make is that safe travel on ski in the Alps
demands much more than the ability to ski, and that only
through continual observation and knowledge can sound
decisions be made in all conditions of snow and weather.

The passage of the slope took only a minute or two.
All remained quiet, but I had an uncomfortable feeling
as of malevolent forces held in leash and waiting to be
released at any moment. I was alone, and to the solitary
traveller imagination is a powerful magnifier of risk.

When I reached the chalet, which stood on a ridge well

protected by forest, I saw that a man had emerged to watch me. We exchanged " Grüss Gott," and I went on my way to Goppenstein. The road tunnel had been completed beneath the avalanches that had fallen previously near the railway station. It was about 150 yards in length—the longest avalanche tunnel I have yet seen.

Relieved of my load and fortified by a cup of coffee, I returned quickly to Kippel. Darkness was falling, but the same man at the chalet, seeing me pass, came forth to watch me over the dangerous bit. I felt grateful towards him as I hastened on my way. In a gloom thick with falling snow, the slopes above seemed more ominous and oppressive than ever. Darkness was falling as I entered Herr Belwald's hospitable door.

That night I had a vivid dream that I was crossing the doubtful slope when an avalanche falling from above swept me down into the stream-bed. I woke with a yell which made the welkin ring, struggling desperately to free my head from the fatal embrace of the snow, kicking out with both feet and thrusting with my hands. Then suddenly my head was free and there was a soft plop on the floor of—the duvet!

According to the newspapers, people who have dreams of this nature take heed of them and by doing so escape shipwrecks, railway accidents, motor-car collisions, air crashes and other disasters. I can only say that if some of my dreams had come true I would have lost my life by now a thousand times over in a wide range of disasters.

Suffice to say that I rose at six, and after an excellent breakfast set off to Goppenstein, carrying in my rucksack the remainder of my kit.

Both the Belwalds insisted on coming out into the still heavy snow-storm to see me off, and the kindly proprietor, clad only in a voluminous night-shirt and an overcoat, insisted on accompanying me down the steps on to the track and adjusting my ski bindings. He was genuinely concerned for my safety, as a full metre of new snow had by now fallen, and entreated me to beware of avalanches.

It was still dark when I left, and in the thickly falling snow, which had obliterated my previous traces, I had to pick my way carefully along what was now an imaginary rather than an actual track across the mountainside.

The first light was filtering into a sombre world, which seemed almost to be sinking beneath the weight of falling snow, when I reached the doubtful slopes. Very dour they appeared, sweeping up into a haze of snow-flakes.

This time I did not stop to weigh the pros and cons, but hastened across as fast as I could. As I did so I must confess that my dream, despite its innocent inter-pretation, dominated my thoughts, and it was with distinct relief that I found myself in safety. Were I a popular novelist I should no doubt contrive that the moment I reached terra firma a monstrous avalanche fell on the very spot I would have been had not Herr Belwald stopped to adjust my ski bindings. But alas for local colour, nothing of the sort happened; indeed, the snow-bound mountains were strangely silent that morning as I ski-ed down the last quarter-mile to Goppenstein.

A few minutes after my arrival at the station I was summoned to the telephone. It was a call from Herr Belwald, who wanted to assure himself that I had arrived safely. It was the last of many kindly actions.

In Switzerland, as in other continental countries, luggage other than hand luggage is registered through to its destination. The traveller pays for the luggage by weight and distance, and is issued with a receipt by the railway company. It is a simple and efficient system which saves the traveller much bother, and one can only marvel that it is not adopted in Britain.

The Swiss, being a methodically minded people, are adepts at working a system, and it is very seldom that

anything goes wrong. It is, therefore, a thousand or
more to one that the registered luggage will travel on the
same train as its owner, and will arrive with him at his
destination. On this occasion, however, the system
broke down. As is usual in such cases, it was the human
factor. When I handed in my ski for registration, I was
instantly suspicious of the yawning, bleary-eyed porter
who laggingly labelled them and scrawled a receipt, so
that when the train arrived I kept a sharp look-out to see
whether they were being placed on it. They were
not. A solitary parcel on a truck was loaded into the
luggage van, but not my ski. The stationmaster,
gorgeous in gold braid, and with visible evidence of a
devoted wife in his beautifully pressed blue trousers, had
appeared, for this was a " schnell-zug " (fast train);
whether or not he deigned to appear for a " personen-
zug " (slow train) was another matter. In his hand he
carried a small green disc attached to a wooden handle.
In another moment he would slowly raise the disc with a
dignity that befitted his position, and the " schnell-zug "
would proceed on its way. Before he could do so, I
opened the door, stood on the steps of the coach and
shouted :

" Where are my ski? "

" Einsteigen ! " said the guard, a burly, apple-cheeked
man with a Hindenburg moustache. " Einsteigen."

" My ski! " I roared. " They have been registered. I
must have them."

" Einsteigen ! " said the guard again, severely this
time. " Sofort einsteigen ! " It was impossible that a
train could start with an open door and a passenger half-
way down the steps. " Tür zu ! " he shouted, evidently
taking a new line of thought. " Tür zu ! "

" My ski," I reiterated. " I must have my ski."

Up to then the stationmaster had stood immobile, a
look of shocked surprise on his face. All through his

career as a stationmaster nothing had come between him and starting a train, and now the incredible had happened, and caused by an obvious foreigner—an Engländer.

He turned. Slowly and imperiously he beckoned to his minion, the man who had accepted my ski for registration.

" Bring the ski."

He spoke in the manner of an Oriental potentate ordering in the dancers.

But already the minion was scurrying across the lines towards the station buildings. He caught his foot in something and sprawled full length. He got up and hobbled on. He entered the station and presently emerged carrying my ski. He hobbled back to the train. The ski were put into the luggage van. Once again the guard said " einsteigen," but I had already climbed in and shut the door. The stationmaster gazed about him impassively, magnificently. All was well. Slowly, like a benediction, he raised the green disc. The train moved off, speeded on its way by a bell in the station precincts which slowly clanged eight times. I had delayed the Brig " schnell-zug " a good five minutes, but my ski were on it and I was well content.

A few minutes later the train was humming in and out of the many tunnels and avalanche sheds through which the Lötschberg line passes on its long diagonal descent from the Lötschenthal to Brig in the Rhone Valley.

During the first mile or two snow fell thickly, but suddenly there was a gleam of light, and a few moments later we emerged from the mist. Snow was still falling thinly, but as we lost height the storm was left entirely behind, and a splendid prospect of the Rhone Valley opened up. The worst of the weather was evidently confined to the Oberland, and the peaks of Valais lifted serenely over the clouds.

I had not seen them since before the war. There they were—the same, their well-remembered shapes, their shining snows. The weary years vanished, were forgotten in an instant. Again I knew youth, again I knew the jump of the heart and the catch of the throat which come with the first sight and the first love of high mountains. There were the clustered peaks of the Mischabel, and beneath, the Vispthal, with the little town of Visp at its junction with the Rhone Valley. Are the Zermatt peaks visible from the Lötschberg railway, the Matterhorn and the Weisshorn? I don't think they are, but they were there for me that day beyond the great hills rising out of the level fields and straight poplar-fringed roads of the Rhone.

A single elderly porter in a blue smock awaited the train at Brig, and to him I entrusted my luggage. It was no surprise, after my previous acquaintanceships with Swiss porters, to hear him speak a university English. He was far more interested in me than my luggage. From whence had I come and where was I going? What was the weather like in England, foggy as usual? Had London been much damaged?

After he had dumped my luggage on the train to Martigny, he regarded me long and earnestly.

" I have seen you before," he said at length. " You were here about eight years ago on your way to Zermatt."

It was true. I had passed through Brig in December 1938 *en route* to Zermatt. There had been something vaguely familiar about him, and now I remembered. That a porter in a railway station the size of Brig should remember a traveller after nearly eight years was little short of miraculous. What a man for the F.B.I. or New Scotland Yard! And he appeared to be the only factotum at Brig. For how many travellers had he carried luggage in seven years?

Opposite to me in my compartment was a Dutchman,

and we entered into conversation, he speaking perfect English. He had been recently to Britain and was frankly critical.

"England has been through a very hard time. Her people are tired and disillusioned. So are we all. In Holland we have been through a hard time also, but we are determined first of all to regain as much as possible of what we have lost. We believe that a high standard of living with good food and comfort is the first step to a peaceful Europe. And we believe in individual initiative and freedom, not in everything being regulated and rules of iron. In England, which I knew so well before the war, I was shocked and amazed. Your standard of living has never fallen so low; and your young people do not know what it means to live well and, how shall I put it?—elegantly. The cooking in your hotels and restaurants is—well——" He made a *moue* of disgust.

"I was told," he continued, "that this was because there was little to cook. But in Holland we have also very little, but we think that is all the more reason to cook what we have well. Your manners also they are not what they were. In London I saw few people in evening clothes. That is a small thing, but it is the small things that matter in a nation's morale—cleanliness, tidiness, well-dressed people, new paint. Without these things a man becomes slovenly and in the end second-rate; if all citizens become thus, then the nation becomes second-rate. What is the good of trade and business and money to a people who become second-rate in themselves and their mode of living? But you will recover, you *must* recover. Any nation that withstood what you did has it within itself to recover. And when you have recovered, you will lead the world back to sanity."

At any other time I might have resented some of his criticisms, but I had asked him for his impressions, and he had given them with perfect frankness. There was

admittedly truth in what he said.   The secrets of contentment in a nation are unquestionably the material and
spiritual ideals set out in the Atlantic Charter.   But
spiritual values tend to dwindle on an empty stomach.
However much some preach on the financial virtues of
austerity, freedom from want and a high standard of living would bring peace and security more quickly to the
world than any other material factors.

There was no more than a sprinkling of snow in the
Rhone Valley, enough to give a patched, rather worn-
out appearance to its fields and farmsteads.   One day I
am hoping to spend part at least of a holiday in the
country to the north of the main Pennine watershed
between the Vispthal and the Val d'Hérens.   Most persons neglect this area in favour of the greater mountains
at the head of the valleys, yet there are numerous fine
ridges and subsidiary ranges, and the *Kurz Ski Guide*
marks out some alluring ski routes in the neighbourhood
of Gruben and St. Luc, not to mention the beautiful ski-
lands in the environs of the Val d'Hérens and the Val des
Bagnes.

The Dutchman alighted at Leuk.   Then came Sierre
and Sion.   The last-named place, historically and archi-
tecturally the most interesting town in the Rhone Valley,
had been at the epicentre of the severest earthquake
shock that this part of Switzerland had experienced for
many years.   However, except for some cracked walls,
little damage was visible.   The flat and somewhat monotonous valley floor is broken at this point by two rocky
knolls on which are perched castles dating back to the
thirteenth century and in one instance to Roman times.
Here dwelt the Bishops of Sion, who reigned as counts
over the Valais, and maintained contact with Rome via
the Simplon pass.   Sion became a bishop's see in 590,
and it was not until 1798 that the secular power of the
bishops over the canton was finally terminated.

There is some interesting flora in this region, and Ball's *Guide to the Western Alps* mentions a number of Mediterranean species that flourish in the torrid summer heat of the Rhone Valley. Some of these may have been introduced artificially or accidentally by travellers crossing the Simplon, and some possibly by birds and air currents—the *föhn* wind might well account for the introduction of some species—but plants grow here that are not to be found elsewhere in Switzerland.

At Martigny, where I had to change to the narrowgauge line to Orsières, I had to wait some two and a half hours. As there was no bank at Verbiers, I decided to cash some of my letter of credit. There had been no difficulty at Zürich, and I anticipated none at Martigny. In this I was mistaken. The first bank I went to airily dismissed the whole idea of changing a British letter of credit as out of the question and quite impracticable. The second bank treated me with thinly veiled suspicion. At the third bank I demanded to see the manager, and eventually after some delay that dignitary appeared. He examined my letter of credit.

" I can do nothing with this," said he. " I have no instructions."

" But you cannot allow an Englishman to starve in Switzerland," I declaimed dramatically.

This shook him, but he continued to shake his head.

" I have no instructions," he repeated. " You are the first Englishman in Martigny, except of course for ' Monty.' "

" Monty? " I repeated a trifle vaguely.

" He passed through Martigny the other day." He spoke as one who speaks of the Deity.

Knowledge came to me, and inspiration also in a sudden flood.

" I know him intimately," I said grandly.

The bank manager's face lit up.

" You know him ! "

" I was on his staff." [1]

" You were on his staff? "

" Certainly I was."

The bank manager seemed to lapse into a reverie.

" About that letter of credit," he said at last.   " There
will be no difficulty, of course.   I will telephone Zürich,
but it will be merely as a matter of form, you understand, just a matter of form, and to find out the rate of
exchange."

Five minutes later I marched out of the bank with a
thousand Swiss francs in my pocket.

I lunched at the hotel by the station.   So also did a
party of American officers who had arrived by train.
One of them carried a short-wave radio set, and this was
immediately plugged into the local mains.   Five minutes
later, after the usual cacophony of groans, howls and
hisses which short-wave sets normally emit, a crooner
somewhere in the United States was contacted, and
crooning and jazz followed at such volume that conversation by those lunching could only be carried out by
shouting.

Hastily gulping down my coffee, I made my way outside, and strolled up and down the station, noting with
satisfaction that the mountains were still there and had
not as yet been replaced by skyscrapers.

My journey in the little train that plies several times
a day from Martigny to Orsières was a typically Swiss
affair.   That is to say it was crowded with peasants, and
the windows being all closed, the atmosphere was com-
pounded of strong tobacco smoke, fustian, cheese and
garlic.

[1] I trust that F.M. Lord Montgomery will forgive me for this
opportune presumption.   I was not on his staff, but was attached for
a period to F.M. Lord Alexander's staff.   The juxtaposition was
perhaps justifiable in the circumstances.

Passing at first through the flat orchards of the Rhone Valley, we climbed up the rocky, twisting valley to Sembrancher. Here were innumerable vineyards large and small. Every available space had been utilised, and on the smallest patches of earth and stones were neat little rows of hard-pruned vines. The scene was southern, and presently, when we emerged from the narrower portion of the valley, the picturesque little villages of mellow brown-grey stone were typical more of Italy than of Switzerland. It was evident that this district had experienced the full weight of the recent bad weather, and at little more than 2,000 feet snow was lying three feet deep.

At Sembrancher I changed into the post motor-coach that climbs daily to Verbiers. Somehow or other our vehicle edged its way through the narrow streets of the little town past buildings old and picturesque enough to emit, so I am told by an authority on the district, powerful smells during the hot summer weather. Sound sanitation and the picturesque are seldom compatible. Sembrancher has, however, a claim to fame in that it was the birthplace in 1742 of M. Murith, a famous botanist who made the first ascent of Mont Vélan in 1779.

On the road up the Val des Bagnes the road had been ploughed out, and we passed between banks of snow several feet deep. Anything less like ski-ing country than the forests and crags of this lower portion of the Val des Bagnes would be hard to imagine.

We halted some time at the village of Châble, 2,740 feet, to refresh our vehicle and those in it, then set off on the last stage, a long ascent of the northern side of the valley up a zigzag, well-graded road.

And now, as we began to climb, still through vineyards which extend upwards to no less than 4,000 feet, there was evidence that once the ski-er is above the tree line there are several fine expeditions on the little-visited range extending north-north-west from the Combin massif between the Val d'Entremont and the Val des Bagnes.

Steadily, as we hummed upwards, an extensive panorama was unfolded. To the south-east and north-west the Val des Bagnes was revealed, then in the south-west the peaks at the north-eastern end of the range of Mont Blanc. But the King of the western Pennines is the Combin, and presently its vast mass, crowned with its several summits, showed above the nearer hills.

Such in bald language is the view as the traveller climbs the road to Verbiers. But there is something more intriguing than mountain scenery about this country at the western end of the Pennines. It is unspoiled, primitive and remote; there is about it the spirit of immemorial things. It is difficult or impossible to recapture this spirit in some of the popular Swiss resorts. Beautiful and majestic the surroundings may be, yet the thoughtful traveller, to whom the charm of travel consists not merely in seeing people and places but in identifying himself with a country, its inhabitants, traditions and history, finds something artificial and unsatisfying in the carrying of his normal life into different surroundings. In this respect I must confess to an incurable romanticism. I recollect on one occasion staying in a very swagger hotel, where to all intents and purposes one lived in the heart of Mayfair. Everything was nicely done, but a bottle of beer cost 2 or 3 francs and the same beer could be purchased down the road at an inn frequented by concièrges for 40 centimes. I used to go down the road, not so much to economise, as to drink with my back to a green-glazed, knobbly stove in an atmosphere of strong tobacco and Swiss talk.

To see Switzerland, the Switzerland of the Swiss, it is essential to deviate from the grooves gouged out by the tourist agencies. Happily these grooves are both deep and few and the sheep many, otherwise there would be little enough of the real Switzerland left for those who love it.

We climbed through the vineyards, then up through terraced strips of cultivated land laboriously wrested from the steep and stony mountainside. Several times we crossed and re-crossed a stream, and presently came abreast of a mill, its wheel frozen and immobile. Mills are rare in Switzerland where electricity is the national servant, and I promised myself a photograph. Beyond the mill was a village of ancient wooden chalets, and higher still, where the slope rolled back at an easier angle, another and larger village clustered about a small stone church, Verbiers.

Among those waiting to greet the passengers was a stocky, red-cheeked little man, dark moustached and with twinkling eyes. On seeing me he came forward with a broad smile and clasped my hand.

"You are Monsieur Smit?" (This is the nearest the average foreigner can get to my name.) "I am Maurice Bisson, of the Sport-Hotel. Your letter was received; there is a room reserved for you. My hotel is a few minutes' walk up the hill. A sledge will bring your luggage."

Together we walked up the hill, through the narrow street of the little village, passing a shrine containing a well-carved effigy of the Virgin Mary and Child, M. Bisson chattering vivaciously the while.

"You are the first Englishman I have had in my hotel since a Mr. Spencer stayed here, and that was before the war. You will like Verbiers, everyone does; it is beautiful; the ski slopes; the ski-ing—it is everywhere; and the sun, ah, the sun! If there is only one place in the Valais where the sun is shining, then it is Verbiers—see, is it not beautiful?"

As he spoke we were mounting a path trodden out in

the snow.   Now the angle of the slope eased away into a great field of pure powdery snow.   This field extended before us and to right and left at the gentlest of angles, then climbed more steeply towards a broken rim of mountains.   On the floor of this snowy amphitheatre were a few scattered chalets and small hotels, whilst beyond, on the sides, clusters of alp huts marked the summer pasturages.   Into the amphitheatre, which faces slightly west of south and is some 6 to 7 miles in circumference along the skyline ridges, the sun streams for the greater part of the day even in mid-winter with such warmth and continuity as to justify M. Bisson's claim for Verbiers as the sunniest place in the Valais.

Evening was drawing on as we walked, my enthusiastic companion puffing and blowing from the joint effort of the exercise and of the verbal torrent that flowed in praise of Verbiers.   It was all that he described and more.   Light diaphanous clouds were poised without movement.   Between them, in the mellowing rays of the declining sun, the rounded hillsides gleamed in all the virginal purity of freshly fallen snow.   And above, far above, the edges and ridges of the amphitheatre shone out across the blue gulfs of congregating shadow.   All about us stretched vast fields of snow, rolling and undulating, the billows alight in the level rays of the sun, the shadowy undulations a deepening blue.   It was difficult to determine where the snow ended and the heavens began, for the former seemed to melt into the latter, so that the eye was conscious of no solid substance, but of something unsubstantial and ethereal in the nature of a vision.

It was beautiful, and I said so to Monsieur Bisson.

" Ah, yes," he replied, " it is beautiful, and the ski-ing too.   Next year there will be a ski lift."

As yet there are no offensive buildings in Verbiers. The Sport-Hotel proved simple and unpretentious.   If there were no bathrooms, there was at least running

Ski slopes at Verbiers

The range of Mont Blanc from above Verbiers

water in the bedrooms. It was scrupulously clean. There *may* be dirty and disagreeable hotels in Switzerland, but I have not yet met with one.

On the ground-floor there was an oblong-shaped salle à manger and an adjoining room—it could hardly be termed " lounge "—where visitors sat at small tables and drinks were served. There was, of course, central heating throughout, double windows and shutters, but no comfortable chairs, lounges, etc. In this respect the continental is still Victorian. His view is that the only period in every twenty-four hours when a man should be really luxurious is the period spent in bed, and he certainly carries out this theory to perfection, for nothing is more comfortable than the well-sprung beds of even the simplest Swiss hotel.

On arrival at the hotel my friendly host promptly introduced me to some Swiss ski-ers who were staying there, and proceeded to cement the introduction with a bottle of Fendant, the white wine of the Valais, in which was drunk the health of that rare bird, an Englishman in Verbiers.

I dined well that evening, my dinner being accompanied by an excellent Dôle, which at 4 francs a bottle will make the reader sigh. After dinner my Swiss friends insisted on my accompanying them to a restaurant-bar a few yards from the hotel. This formed the first floor of a large chalet, the ground being occupied by a small sports shop, and was reached by a flight of outside steps. It was run by a cheerful young married couple who set themselves out to make the company equally cheerful and at home. A radio-gramophone did duty as band, and blared out a never-ending and motley mixture of Swiss, French, British and American dance tunes. The company, who were mostly French-Swiss from the Geneva and Lausanne districts, were dressed in ski-ing clothes. They were on holiday and meant to enjoy themselves.

They did, and long before midnight the fun became fast
and furious.   There was an atmosphere of carefree gaiety
such as I had not experienced for many years.   To all
intents and purposes the Swiss had been untouched by
war.   They had been rationed, for a period strictly and
even severely, and they had had a few accidental bombs;
there were few Swiss that I met who could resist telling
me this with a kind of mordant pride, which made me
smile secretly; and their man-power had been mobilised
against possible invasion.   But war had passed them by.
They had never known its weariness and strain, its suf-
fering and its horror.   Peoples of other countries could
also dance, but they danced as an antidote, danced to
forget the intolerable years.   The Swiss had little to forget, and during those intolerable years they had gone to
their beds in peace, knowing that they would not be
roused by the roar of high explosive, the glare of fires and
the cries of their injured fellow-citizens.

I have heard the envious describe them as smug, but
this is untrue, they are merely lucky and happily ignor-
ant.   Perhaps their ignorance as to the true nature of
modern war was best expressed in one remark I heard a
Swiss make.   " It is a pity," he said, " that we were not
in the war; it would have done us good."

The following morning I was up betimes.   Mist hung
low over Verbiers, but as the sun lifted it began to dis-
solve.   Light poured through in a sudden and brilliant
flood.   Quickly now the mists broke up; they were
sucked up by the sun and melted away in a cloudless
blue.

I hastened to fetch my camera.   There was a bush
close to the front entrance of the hotel, and the low sun
cast the shadows of its twigs in a delicate trellis-work
across the snow.   A simple-enough subject, but it is such
subjects, not the magnificent panoramas, that make the
best photographs.

A detachment of Swiss mountain troops had arrived at Verbiers for the week-end to compete in a cross-country ski race. For this light equipment was worn and rifle and ammunition carried. They were a fine-looking body of men and appeared trained to a hair. Some almost incredible feats have been performed by Swiss mountain and ski troops, the results of prolonged training. For instance, one ski patrol with full war equipment travelled from Zermatt to Verbiers in a single day, a distance of some 55 kilometres on the map, but much longer for a ski-er, and involving some 4,300 metres of ascent.

I spent the morning taking photographs in and around the village of Verbiers. The weather was brilliant. Light diaphanous clouds swam, melted and re-formed in an amethystine blue, and sunlight and shadow wove ever-changing patterns on peak and snow-field. Every twig was loaded with sparkling feathery snow, and the pollarded poplars, which are a feature of the western Pennines, were especially striking with the snow piled on them in domes and cushions. There was a prodigality of beauty, and, with a foreground of chalets and poplars and a background of valley depths, distant peaks and silvery clouds, compositions presented themselves at every step. Soon I had made some three dozen exposures, and it was time for lunch.

After lunch I mounted to the Croix de Cœur, a wooden cross situated on the rim of the bowl some 2,300 feet above Verbiers. The descent to Verbiers is a standard ski run in the area and already the slopes were extensively tracked. Being one of those peculiar persons who dislike descending in the tracks of my predecessors, I turned eastwards along the edge of the rim with the idea of finding another line of descent, and of ascending one or other of the small bumps on the ridge for the sake of the view.

A spiteful wind was blowing along the ridge.   It came
in gusts and squalls which raised the snow in sheets, but
in between its vicious attacks the sun shone generously
and warmly.   I had to change a film, and timed this
chilly operation immediately after a particularly vicious
squall on the assumption that a calm period would follow, but another squall arrived hard on the heels of the
first.   I remember consigning the makers of camera and
films to perdition for not making film changing easier,
and afterwards putting stick-like fingers into my mouth
while the circulation slowly and painfully returned. Such
are the trials of the photographer in the winter Alps.

But the photographs were worth it: they usually are.
It was late in the afternoon as I made my way along the
ridge and the sun was declining in unusual splendour.
South-eastwards were the peaks of Mont Blanc, the
Chardonnet, Argentière and the Tour Noir, and around
them a host of smaller summits.   To the left lay the Val
Ferret and at its head Mont Dolent, a peak which for
grace and symmetry has few rivals in the Alps.   Seen
across the nearer fields and slopes of snow, there was
something more polar than alpine in the scene. Between
those distant peaks and myself there were valleys and villages, and in summer the scene would have at once fallen
into its normal perspective; there would have been green
and brown hills and distant snow-fields and glaciers: in
winter, however, there is a universality in the mountain
scene which inspires a sense of remoteness and detachment such as is never experienced in summer even amidst
the high glaciers and snow-fields.

To my left snowy slopes, delicately turned and
moulded, swept down like the sides of a bowl.   Far
beneath, like small coffee grounds, were the chalets and
alp huts of Verbiers.   Lower still, where one sector of
the bowl was missing, a ragged fringe of forest fell away
into the depths of the Val des Bagnes, and beyond, the

earth lifted in a gigantic muddle of forests, alps, ridges
and buttresses to support the icy summits of the Combin.

The wind was fast dropping as I reached a minor summit and the sunny afternoon was quietly lapsing into a
calm evening.   Some grey mists formed and rose slowly
like a witch's brew from the depths of the bowl.   Caught
by the level rays of the setting sun, they were suddenly
transmuted to brilliant silver, then quickly shredded out
and vanished.

There was a touch of gold now in the silver-lit ridges,
and the shadows stole upwards in a stealthy slow-
broadening flood.

It was time to be gone.   From my feet a broad ridge
curved down into the bowl.   I removed my frozen seal-
skins, tied them about my waist, then turned my ski down
the ridge.   In an instant leisurely contemplation was
replaced by rapid movement and the necessity for instant
decision.   When descending on foot it is possible to
enjoy a prospect, but this is impossible during a downhill run on ski.   Halt if you will; you may remember
the scene afterwards, but you will not appreciate it at the
time; for ski-ing downhill has for its principal constituent
the subtle drug of speed, and speed, whatever its charms,
is incompatible with an appreciation of natural scenery.
In this, paradoxically perhaps, lies the charm of ski-ing.
The slow trudge up, the summit vista, and the swift
descent provide the same mental and physical contrasts
that difficult mountaineering possesses.

The snow was light and powdery; the ski flew through
it with a dry swish.   The slopes unreeled behind me.
Even a moderate ski-er like myself cannot do much wrong
in such snow, but I should have realised that, with a hot
sun on the slopes for the greater part of the day, I was
bound sooner or later to run into crust.   I was going
fast at the time, and had edged round on to the southernmost portion of the ridge where it sank into the hillside.

Anyone but a blissful fool drunk with a descent over perfect powder snow would have suspected the presence of
crust. I ran into it quite suddenly. My ski slowed up
abruptly and pitched me forward in a spectacular forward fall. It is a remarkable thing how violently it is
possible to fall on ski without hurt, and this was merely
another case in point. But as I distentangled myself
and rose to my feet full of snow and reproachful words, I
reminded myself that the solitary ski-er cannot afford to
have spectacular forward falls. Thenceforward, for the
remainder of my stay in Switzerland, I invariably ski-ed
with the utmost caution, and had no serious falls when
alone on unfrequented routes. It is obvious that even
a minor injury, no worse than a sprained ankle or twisted
knee, late in the afternoon with night drawing on can be
a dangerous and even disastrous affair to a solitary ski-er.

Down to Verbiers. Down the alps and past the alp
huts. Through the still air, through shadow and sunlight, hissing, drifting, skimming, flying over the bend-
ing snow-fields. Yes, already I had come to love Verbiers. There will always be a place in my heart, a
sentiment, a memory for its old-world village, its chalets
and hay huts strewn about the slopes of the bowl, the
prodigality of its sunlight, its regal panorama of distant
mountains. There is peace at Verbiers. Especially was
there peace that evening. I halted by some alp huts.
Instantly the physical rush and stress of the descent was
ended, absorbed into this peace. The bowl was filled
now with shadow, but beyond, the Combin, like some
enormous edifice aglow with internal fire, was poised on
the deepening twilight.

It was certainly a contrast to step out of the still frosty
evening into the noisy little hotel with its reek of tobacco
smoke and clatter of tongues. However "deux deci"
of Fendant, with the cheerful M. Bisson, soon had the
effect of rendering the contrast reasonably tolerable.

The fine break in the weather was doomed to an early extinction. The sky was leaden next morning, and as the morning advanced a grey ceiling of falling snow crept slowly down the mountains. The air was warm, too warm, and for part of the forenoon I sat on the seat by the wooden cross which stands by the path below the village. Weather in all its vagaries has ever fascinated me, and I was content to spend two hours or more watching the oncoming storm. A thunderstorm amidst the high mountains is the most impressive of all weather phenomena, but next comes a snow-storm. Unlike a thunder-storm, which normally gathers and breaks quickly, a snow-storm takes some hours to marshal its forces. Thus, the ski-er who is overtaken by one in winter is either careless or unobservant. The signs also are unmistakable: the densening cirrus, typical of an oncoming depression, and the gradual obscuring of the higher summits give ample warning. The atmosphere is often profoundly still, and this, in conjunction with the increasing pall of snow-clouds and the gradual draining of light, leaves a pallid, shadowless world.

During the next eight days snow fell intermittently and sometimes heavily. Within a week it had added another 18 inches to the metre and more that had already fallen. During one moderately fine day I was able to ascend to the Cabane de Mont Fort, a hut from which several fine expeditions can be made, but the weather was far too uncertain and the avalanche danger too great for any but short tours.

Sir Leslie Stephen once wrote that the next best thing to really good weather in the Alps is really bad weather. This, I think, is true, since there is something stimulating as well as impressive in a great storm; but it is certainly not true of long spells of dull and doubtful weather, and especially of *föhn* conditions, when mist may shut down for days on end with the tenacity of an

English fog.   At such times the traveller begins to take more stock than is his wont of the amenities of hotel life, and the severity of his criticisms may be said to be directly proportional to the length of the bad spell.   It is, of course, almost always possible on these occasions to spend the day on the practice slopes, but these become terribly tedious after a while, and in the end the ski-mountaineer is left to his own devices in his hotel, a poor substitute for home, where he must occupy his time as best he can in eating, drinking, talking, reading, writing, sitting (on hard seats), standing and sleeping, not to mention such an incidental as tapping the barometer.   All these occupations are pleasant enough in normal life, but not in the mountains, when the precious hours and days of a vacation are slipping away.

The mountains should teach a philosophy of serenity and detachment to those who love them.   Yet, there are some people, hearty people who eat and eat and laugh and laugh regardless of the new profundities into which the barometer is sinking, disgusting people to be classed with those who stroll breezily about the deck of a bucking steamer puffing at their cigars with a loathsome relish.   I can spend off days between climbs in meditative contentment, but not day after day of foul weather.   I chafe and fret and fidget.   I stand at the window and gaze fiercely and resentfully at the gloom outside; then I go and hit the barometer a vicious crack, after which I sit down and write a few words of a letter, getting up to scan the week-old gloom of some Sunday newspaper.   I look at the clock and calculate the time to the next meal, or battle with a weak conscience on the question of another drink, after which last I return to the barometer and give it an even greater crack than before, hoping against hope to see some response on its dour countenance—but there seldom is.

Mathematicians declare that if a coin is spun nine

times and comes up heads every time, the odds as to
whether it will turn up heads or tails are still equal for
the tenth spin.   This may be so, but it certainly does not
apply to mountain weather, and my experience has
always been that weather that has been bad for one week
is likely to continue bad for two weeks, and weather that
has been bad for two weeks will continue so for a whole
month or more.   At the same time there must come a
point at which the law of averages becomes operative,
though here again I never go to the mountains but I
become associated with some unpleasant weather record.
Such meteorological phenomena as the heaviest snow-fall
in living memory, the earliest monsoon in meteorological
records, the most prolonged *föhn* ever known, the
heaviest precipitation in three generations of man are
natural experiences of mine. The reader will excuse me.
therefore, if I take a jaundiced view of mountain weather.

On March 3rd the weather seemed to have reached a
climax, for snow fell very heavily all day. No wind
accompanied the fall, and it was evident that, given a
break and some sun, the photographic conditions would
be exceptionally beautiful.

Next morning dawned with a sullen sky through which
the sun struggled feebly and with apparently diminishing
power.   However, I determined to make a small tour,
and ordered a *déjeuner à la rucksack*. Photography
seemed out of the question, but more by habit than anything else I took with me my camera and some films.

So far I had not visited the rim of the bowl in the
neighbourhood of the peak known as the Pierre à Voir.
The Kurz guide marks a ski route to the south of the
summit, and I determined to follow this, as the con-
figuration of the ground promised some fine views over
the Val Ferret towards the range of Mont Blanc.

The sky darkened perceptibly as I climbed the hillside north-west of Verbiers. Presently snow began to

fall. At eleven o'clock the melancholy state of the weather prompted an immediate lunch, so I halted at a half-buried hay hut. As I ate, snow fell more and more thickly. There seemed little point in continuing farther. Already the light was bad, and a descent of shadowless slopes is always disagreeable. I was about to remove my seal-skins when I noticed a sudden lightening. A hint of blue showed through the murk, and as I watched it slowly expanded. I decided to wait. A quarter of an hour later there was scarcely a cloud in the sky, and the sun for the first time for many days was shining with a new-found brilliance.

Sudden changes of weather are common in high mountains, but I have seldom seen a change more dramatic. Never was scenery shifted and stage set with greater celerity. Between the swirling mists, as they were sucked up and dissolved by the greedy sun, the peaks shone out radiant in their robes of freshly fallen snow. In a matter of minutes the view had expanded to embrace the whole of the western Pennines, from Mont Blanc to the Combin, and the peaks of Arolla. Every snow-laden pine was transmuted to a pillar of silver, and the snow around glittered and sparkled as though strewn with diamonds.

Making my way upwards and across the fringe of the pine forest. I passed two huts, the roofs of which were alone visible above the snow, and began to traverse some steepish open slopes beyond. At any other time after a heavy snow-fall I should have hesitated to traverse such slopes, but on this occasion the snow-fall had been entirely unaccompanied by wind. Thus no wind-slab was to be expected; on the other hand, the slopes were not steep enough for a dry-snow avalanche, while the snow was too dry and powdery for a wet-snow avalanche.

Ahead was the rim of the bowl, formed at this point by the south ridges of the Pierre à Voir, which falls steeply towards the Val des Bagnes, and arrayed along it in a broken struggling line were a number of gnarled old conifers, outposts of the great sheet of forest beneath.

Here, if anywhere, photographic compositions of superlative quality were to be found, added to which was a lighting of a limpid brilliance only to be seen immediately after stormy weather.

A surprise awaited me on the ridge. I had been prepared by the map for a steep fall on the other side into the Combe de Pierre à Voir, but what I had casually visualised was a ghost of the reality. I found myself on the edge of an abyss 3,000 feet deep, an abyss of shaly slopes and cliffs set at a tremendous angle. Over this the eye passed at a bound to alight on gentler slopes beyond, where nestled a small village, then in another bound of 13 miles along the Rhone Valley to the familiar serrated edge of the Dents du Midi.

South-eastwards the view was equally magnificent. The vision plunged 5,000 feet in a matter of 2 miles to the Val des Bagnes, then across and up to the easternmost bastions of the Mont Blanc range.

Bald topographical facts are seldom exciting. The dramatic quality of the view, apart from the sudden great drop at my feet, lay in the weather, the lighting and the snow. The weather was perfect. Such is the magic of the Alps, the sullen skies of the past days were already forgotten. The atmosphere was of crystal clarity, and the sun blazed with a fierce incandescent heat from a sky of pure fathomless blue.

But it was the snow that made that day for ever memorable. Never have I seen such snow. Even at this altitude, and in this exposed place, it had fallen vertically and without wind; undeflected by the merest breath, it had drifted quietly down to earth. And because of this it had settled deeply on every branch and limb; twigs no wider than match-sticks were laden with it. The old trees along the forest's edge bent, weatherbeaten and con-

torted by a century's storms, had been transmuted into
objects of fragile ethereal beauty, and the sun shining
through them invested them with its brilliance, so that
they appeared to be constructed of glass—glass which in
delicacy and complexity it would have taxed the wit of
any craftsman to devise.

I remember that I stood there confounded by the sheer
beauty of the scene. And still nothing moved; there was
no stirring in the air, and there was a profound and
absolute silence, the silence of beauty just created in the
presence of its Creator.

Then suddenly, and it made me jump and set my
heart pounding, there was a sudden shush! A load of
snow had tipped off a twig and fallen in a little cloud of
scintillating particles. The spell was broken. I was on
a snowy mountainside once again. Then, as though
pulling myself out of some dream, I extracted my camera
from my pocket and began to take photographs.

I took many photographs, exposing all the films I had
with me except for two or three exposures reserved
against later possibilities. One of these photographs is
reproduced here. How bankrupt is a man, his materials
and his art in such circumstances!

Later, I descended to the edge of the forest proper and
there ate my lunch, and as I ate the power of the sun
became manifest on the walls of the combe. Avalanches
began to fall. At first small slides, wispy streams of snow
that poured down with no more sound than a brook,
then larger volumes that descended with a harsher rasp-
ing note, and at length two or three great falls with
prolonged roars that set thunderous echoes reverberating
round the cirque.

I would have stayed till evening, but for the possibility
of the slopes I had crossed becoming dangerous, and time
in hand is necessary in solitary ski-ing. It would have
been an anticlimax also to have lingered too long.

I strapped on my ski in the shadows of the pines and took a last glance around me. Was the weather again spoiling? Some bars of silvery cloud lay far and high above the mountain tops, and beneath in the valleys a sea of mist had formed. As I watched, it quickly expanded up the Val des Bagnes, concealing the toy-like villages and cutting me off from all sight of habitation, so that only the mountains were visible and I became to my fancy the sole inhabitant of some upper and forgotten world.

The slopes were safe enough and soon I was running down the alps towards Verbiers. The mist that now filled the Val des Bagnes had extended an arm northwards over Verbiers, and the bowl into which I was descending brewed a witchy vapour. I paused by some alp huts to watch and photograph the spectacle. The sun was still shining into the bowl, and beyond the level surface of the mist-sea rose the glowing Combin.

Long I sat on the threshold of the hut, my back against the sun-warmed timbers, and watched the passing of the day, sat while the mist first spread a canopy over the bowl, then, in the frosty evening shadow, began to shred out into wispy tendrils and filaments which twined about the forest and hillsides like the locks of some ghostly Aphrodite.

The sun withdrew, and was instantly replaced by a bitter cold. It was time to be gone. The snow was abominable, a vicious breakable crust, but little minded I. That day I had done something more than run up and down a mountainside on ski. Now I was in the mist, and now bumping on the lower slopes over a maze of frozen ski tracks. It was dull and grey in the bowl, but between the still-lingering mists the high snows were yellowing like corn in the remote fields of heaven.

CHAPTER VI

THE ROSA BLANCHE

At Verbiers I was joined by Mr. James Belaieff and his Swiss friend Dr. Broccard. Our original intention had been to go to Zermatt as soon as Belaieff had found his ski legs at Verbiers, and return to Verbiers by the Haute Route over the high passes and glaciers. This, however, was not possible in the prevailing weather conditions; furthermore, Zermatt had been cut off from Visp for some time by avalanches that had fallen across the railway as a result of the recent heavy snow-falls. We determined, therefore, to make the Cabane de Mont Fort our headquarters for two or three days, and from there ascend the Rosa Blanche, 10,985 feet, and Mont Fort, 10,926 feet.

The Rosa Blanche stands to the north apart from the main Pennine chain, and is a noted view-point. The first winter ascent was made in 1894, but it was not until the first ski ascent in 1920 by M. Marcel Kurz and the guide Maurice Crettez that its ski-ing possibilities were recognised. It now ranks as a ski mountain with few rivals; indeed, the district in general of which it is the highest point, including the glacier which goes by the intriguing name of Le Grand Désert, provides a number of excellent high Alpine tours.

Although we carried only three days' food, our rucksacks seemed unconscionably heavy as we trudged up the path above Verbiers. It was March 5th, the day after the photographic expedition already described, and the morning was brilliantly fine. During the month I had spent in Switzerland a fine day had been a rarity and two consecutive fine days phenomenal. The snow conditions also were better than expected, as the hot sun of the previous day had been followed by a severe overnight's frost. Altogether, the optimism engendered by these unusual circumstances was such that I for one was busy making plans for the future on the entirely unjustifiable assumption that, after so long a spell of bad weather, a fine period was logically to be expected. Alas for plans: where an Alpine holiday is concerned they are seldom based on anything but sand. As for mountain weather, the word "logic" has no more meaning than has the Christmas spirit with a Hitler.

The first hour or so of the ascent through the forest was delightful, but such was the power of the sun it was not long before we were fairly oozing beneath our weighty rucksacks. The route to the hut follows the Combe de Medran and crosses the col of the same name. From the col a minor ridge must be traversed before commencing a more or less horizontal traverse to the hut. To save the traverse along the crest of the ridge we sought to reach the latter not via the col but to the north of it. It was a short cut, and like many short cuts on mountains it did not pay. We had to toil up a stiff slope, on the upper portion of which soft snow artfully overlaid an icy crust. Kick turns were tedious, indeed almost impossible, and with our loads we were thankful to reach the ridge. I regret to state that I was responsible for this "variation" of the normal, as I was ahead at the time. My companions, however, were most tactful about it, and if I could sense some sizzling in the rear I did not actually hear it.

The hut was now in view, perched on a ridge well protected from avalanches falling from Mont Gélé, a fair sight for three thirsty ski-ers, and to reach it we had merely to follow the tracks of a previous party across the slopes of Mont Gélé. It was built in 1925 and enlarged in 1938, and is a well-built stone structure with a comfortable little winter room for ski-ers.

In any party of mountaineers certain domestic problems sometimes arise. These soon sort themselves out, but they involve in the first place a certain degree of delicacy and forbearance. Who, for example, is going to cook, who will do the bottle washing, and who should be the hewer of wood and drawer of water? When I was very young I used to fancy myself as a cook; on one occasion I concocted a soup which contained seventeen ingredients. Nowadays I am only too willing to leave cooking to someone more skilful and ingenious than myself. In the present instance, Belaieff exhibited these desirable characteristics in full measure, and Broccard and I were only too happy to minister to his needs in the matter of the subsidiary duties already mentioned.

Starting a fire is often a problem, especially in a hut that has been untenanted for some time. Looking back over a vista of many years' experience of Alpine huts, I am ashamed to recollect the harsh language this has provoked on occasion. The expert method, as applied by guides and intelligent amateurs, is to dispense with paper by burring up a piece of firewood with a sharp knife and of setting the ragged edge alight in the hope, not always fulfilled, that it will ignite adjacent pieces of wood.

Belaieff, however, has a far simpler and more effective method. He carries with him a packet of " meta " fuel and secretly inserts a stick of this beneath the firewood, which, being unable to withstand the prolonged and concentrated flame, cannot help igniting. Later, during a traverse of the Oberland, I adopted the same method, to the scorn and disgust of sundry experts. All improved methods, though they may be ostracised for a time by the conservative, must triumph in the end, and my particular triumph occurred when a guide, after several ineffectual attempts to ignite damp wood, approached me for a stick of my " meta."

It has often been said that hot tea is the best of all

The Dents du Midi

thirst quenchers. It certainly is provided enough is drunk. I suppose we had three or four pints each. After it we all breathed deeply, said Ha! and looked at one another without speaking.

The hut commands a view across the Val des Bagnes, extending from the Combin to the range of Mont Blanc, and that evening we watched a wild and colourful sunset. If the day had been perfect the weather was still far from settled, and the hut barometer had little comfort to offer us. The old adage " Red sky at night . . ." applies within limits to an Alpine sunset, but it certainly did not apply to the fiery clouds that evening. Hard and gaunt also were the peaks of Mont Blanc cut out like purple cardboard against a violent back-stage lighting. Dramatic and beautiful it was, especially when low stealing mists investing the nearer snow-fields spilled the sunlight in vivid pools about the mountainsides, but too colourful and uneasy for the liking of the mountaineer.

The day had been hot to the point of sultriness, but now a keen wind was blowing out of the west. It was possible that it might restrain the onset of bad weather for the time being, but that further snow-storms were in the offing was patently obvious, though as a matter of principle we waxed enthusiastic on the beauty of the scene while conveniently omitting all mention of what it might portend.

That evening we dined well, indeed sumptuously, thanks to the excellent cooking of Jimmy Belaieff and the good viands supplied by Verbiers. Of mountaineers and Swiss food it was once written:

> " They will dine on mule and marmot,
> And on mutton made of goats;
> They will face the various horrors
> Of Helvetian table d'hôtes."

A.S.—9

But this I hasten to add is no longer true, and after austerity England I must confess that even food carried up in a rucksack to a hut, and subsequently prepared over a smoky stove, came as a gastronomical ecstasy.

There is nothing like a good dinner to promote good talk, and we sat up late over another brew of tea. In Nature the things that matter are food, sleep and the bodily functions, and the problems to be contended with are not connected with business or social affairs other than immediate relationships with companions, but with the weather, the condition of the snow, the route to be followed and so forth. Thus, for the time being civilised man reverts to primitive man, whose essential problem could be summed up in two words, keeping alive. To the unadventurous whose sole idea of a holiday is merely a change of scene, and not a change in any mode of living, this voluntary flight to the primitive seems inexplicable. Why endure discomfort, he asks? What is the point in risking life and limb? He should not ask such questions until he has tried it for himself. There is a great deal of the primitive in most of us (how many times has war proved this?) and to revert awhile to the essentials of existence is not only a relaxation of the mind but a toning up of the body. That is one reason why mountaineering is the great sport it is. There is no sport which provides a greater contrast to ordinary life; and contrast is experience, and experience, living.

The weather was not in happy mood during the night. A restive wind moaned and stirred, now and again rising in a sudden fit of anger and slinging particles of snow against the windows. It was still blowing when we rose at dawn next morning, and the outlook, with only a few stars struggling weakly through a flying scud, was none too bright.

We were loath to start for the Rosa Blanche in such conditions, and waited until eight before setting forth

It was then a little brighter than it had been two hours earlier, but this was due more to the risen sun than any relenting of the weather. It was cold and altogether depressing for the first half-hour. A vicious wind flying from all points of the compass bombarded us with stinging snow, and between scowling mists the peaks showed a dirty featureless white.

We had first to cross the Col de la Chaux, which lies between Mont Fort and the Bec des Rosses. The route ascends the gentle and uncrevassed Glacier de la Chaux, and we obtained some shelter on its uppermost slopes. The wind, however, like some unrequited demon, met us with renewed force on the col, and we were glad to escape down the slopes on the far side over some excellent ski-ing snow into a hollow where a small lake is marked on the map.

At any other time we might have waxed enthusiastic over the view as we came over the Col de la Chaux, for the Rosa Blanche was full in view, and it was evident that the whole district had been specially designed for ski-ers. Extensive snow-fields with minor ridges, which may be crossed in many places from one snow-field to another, a number of ski peaks of between 10,000 and 11,000 feet, all commanding splendid views of the Pennine Alps, are there to delight the eye of the most critical ski mountaineer. As it was, the sky was glowering. A few weak drifts of sunlight fled wearily across the slopes, whilst a misty, formless greyness in snow and sky contributed to a sombre scene entirely lacking that vivacious and stimulating quality which the mountaineer legitimately expects of the mountain. Our attitude as we breasted the col towards the Rosa Blanche was simply: " Well, there it is, I suppose we shall have to climb the darned thing."

Neither was second breakfast a happy affair. I have already alluded to the spiritual and gastronomical importance of this function, which in normal circumstances is nicely designed to bridge that crucial period between the dozy trudge through the early morning and the exhilarating ascent yet to come. It is essentially a function to dawdle over in the sun.

There was no dawdling that day. We sat down with a kind of fierce determination to eat come what may, and hoping against hope that a snow-ridge above us would shield us against the wind. Vain hope! We had scarcely unpacked the grub when it arrived with a positive roar of joy in the midst of a predatory cloud of powdery snow that invaded our necks, pockets and rucksacks in less time than it takes to write this. Then off it went, and for a few moments we could feel the faint warmth of a misty sun. But not for long. Back it came, a nasty, hectoring, bullying brute of a thing, that nagged us to our feet and harried us up the hill still masticating with dry mouths.

Half an hour later we had reached the Col de Momin, and the last stage of the ascent. Before us stretched the Grand Désert, an expanse of snow-covered *névé*. This glacier is 1½ miles across at its widest point, but in winter, when the surrounding slopes and moraines are also snow-covered, it extends its domain and becomes a snow-field of impressive dimensions. Outside obvious limits the size of mountains has little to do with their beauty and even grandeur, and had I not previously studied a map I could have sworn that it was several times larger than it actually is. This, of course, is due to the miniature elevation of the surrounding mountains. The whole district is arranged on such a cunningly deceptive scale that the ski-er might well make the mistake of the Alpine guide who considered that two days were necessary for the ascent of Snowdon.

The Grand Désert cannot be compared with the vast expanse of *névé* on the Wildstrubel known as the Glacier de la Plaine Morte, nor can it rival the glacier systems of the high Alpine ranges; it has nevertheless its own especial character, and added to this is the sudden and unexpected revelation of its serene surface, undulating in folds of pure snow, for the ski-er who pops his head over the crest of the Col de Momin or the Col de Cleuson.

It is separated from the neighbouring Glacier de Prafleuri by a minor ridge, which appears to have been interposed on the landscape as an afterthought, and is of no particular significance or value in the scheme of things. Instead of supporting the north side of the Rosa Blanche, the ridge simply ends, leaving the two glaciers to unite and tilt jointly up to the summit of the mountain. There is, therefore, no difficulty in the ascent of the Rosa Blanche, and ski may be taken, within a few feet of the summit.

It need scarcely be mentioned that the wind faithfully accompanied us, while the heavens, jealous of any possibility of our enjoying a view, quickly augmented their already considerable battalions of mist. We reached the summit, stood for a few unappreciative moments in the company of our tenacious companion, gazing despondently at grey masses of mist that seethed about the high mountains, and over the dim valley of the Rhone to a sour-looking cloud-bank that concealed the Oberland, said Humph! or some such stronger expression, and without a further word retired by the way we had come.

We regained our ski, folded up frozen seal-skins with equally frozen hands, fumbled on bindings and set off down. And now came the best part of a disappointing day. Although the wind had ruffled the snow into little waves and ridges, it had not yet spoilt it, and the descent for a considerable distance was as perfect as could be desired except for the vague light. The enthusiastic Belaieff found it so good that with characteristic boldness and skill he turned his descent into a straight " schuss," and became so drugged with speed that, instead of descending to the west of the ridge that divides the Grand Desert from the Glacier de Prafleuri, he presently found himself on the east side descending the latter glacier. When, however, this little matter had been put right, and we had gathered together on the Grand Désert, the contumacy of the wind and sky was momentarily forgotten, and in a moment of entirely unjustified enthusiasm we even agreed that we were enjoying ourselves.

The descent from the Col de Momin was enjoyable also, for the snow was in excellent order. Even our old enemy, the wind, was left behind, and we took advantage of the fact by halting to eat the first comfortable meal that day. Food and optimism are boon companions on a mountain, and when we had eaten we agreed that the weakly illuminated mass of the Grand Combin provided quite an artistic spectacle; whereas an hour earlier, when we had toiled empty bellied in a cold wind, it had provoked not one iota of approval.

Then came the slog up to the Col de la Chaux and the descent to the hut over snow which, like the parson's egg, can only be described as good in parts, an unpleasant mixture of soft powder, windboard and breakable crust, none of them easy to detect in the weak light. And so to the hut and a great brew of tea over which we soon became quite unjustifiably sentimental on the merits of the day, forgetful now of the cold wind and the dull skies. The whims of mountains, like those of friends, are easily forgotten so that we remember only the smile and not the scowl; who would have it otherwise?

The cloud roof rolled back before evening, and once again we witnessed a wild sunset beyond the range of Mont Blanc, one of those " streaky bacon " effects which bode little future good. However, any qualms we might have entertained as to the intentions of the weather were

soon forgotten over a dinner of chops, cooked by Belaieff
to a tenderness that no *maitre d'hôtel* could have
excelled.   The sky was cloudless and glinting with stars
when we turned out for that last ritual of a mountaineer's
day—a look at the weather.

After such a Lucullian dinner we ought to have slept
well, but we had already discovered that the hut was
entertaining other guests besides ourselves, not perhaps
what the reader might infer, but mice.   Except for one
other party, these mice had had the hut to themselves for
some months past, and this had contributed both to their
hunger and agility.   It was evident that they regarded the
long bunk on which we lay as nothing short of an Epsom
Downs which we had now all unwittingly converted into
an Aintree.   The fun was fast and furious until one
beast, misjudging its hurdle, landed full on Belaieff's
face, after which a blitz was declared and all jockeys
warned off the course.

The clear sky after nightfall was succeeded by another
doleful morning.   Soon after sunrise snow began to fall,
and it appeared that we had no option but to descend to
Verbiers.   I, however, had one of my rare fits of
optimism, and declared to my sceptical companions that
the weather was going to clear up, a statement which was
greeted with the contempt it deserved under the too-
evident circumstances.   I was able to appreciate their
view, since if there is one thing worse than the confirmed
pessimist it is the fatuous optimist.   Personally, I believe
in a restrained pessimism where mountain weather is
concerned.   If you are proved wrong everyone is
delighted and prepared to forgive you, and if you are
proved right you can at least preen yourself on your
perspicacity.   The optimist, on the other hand, becomes
such a loathsome object when he is wrong that the times
when he is right do not begin to compensate for the
hatred already inspired.

Having thus burned my boats, I kept a careful eye on the weather, frequently going outside, while my companions gloomed within, and at ten o'clock, when things seemed pretty hopeless, and it was becoming too late in any event to climb Mont Fort as we had planned, my vigil was rewarded. There was a sudden thinning of the snow-clouds and a bright light smote through. Gauzy fragments of blue sky appeared; they deepened and widened; the mists broke up, and the sun leapt hotly out to devour their shattered remnants.

I called to my companions that the weather had improved. They did not believe me at first, but in the end emerged grumbling from the hut. "You see," I said complacently, with an expansive movement of the arm like some general marshalling an army. No further words were needed. In such circumstances, "I told you so" would have merited murder.

Belaieff and I were off at ten-thirty. Dr. Broccard did not accompany us, as he was not yet fit after a strenuous life in general medical practice. While Mont Fort, 10,926 feet, is only 59 feet lower than the Rosa Blanche, it can be ascended direct from the hut without the necessity for the long cross-country traverse involved in the latter expedition. The route follows the Rosa Blanche route for about three-fifths of the way to the Col de la Chaux, then bears left up moderately steep slopes to the Glacier du Mont Fort. The summit ridge is attained over steep slopes of *névé* at a point a short distance to the south of the peak.

Another party of ski-ers had some time previously made the ascent, and despite the wind and recent snow-falls their tracks were still visible on the slopes we had to mount to the glacier. And very good tracks they were, indicative of bold and skilful ski-ing.

"Those fellows know how to ski," remarked Belaieff. It was evident from the glitter in his eye that he had an

intention of descending likewise. As for me, while agreeing in the first place, I kept my own counsel as to the
manner of my descent. It seemed to me that the slopes
provided ideal scope for the kick turn, and that long
gentle traverses would give ample opportunity for enjoying the scenery.

At the point where we gained the edge of the glacier
there was a large rock with a snowy hollow well sheltered
from the wind which, I need hardly add, was still with us.
Here we ate a meal on the assumption that we were
unlikely to find any adequate shelter higher on the
mountain. It was but a brief halt, since the wind soon
discovered us and hustled us out.

The guide book reported a bergschrund between the
glacier and the upper slopes of the mountain, but in this
season of exceptional snow-fall most bergschrunds and
crevasses had disappeared, and we were some way up the
slopes before remembering that it was supposed to be
there. Personally, I experienced a sense of frustration
and disappointment, since without a bergschrund to cross
an expedition in the High Alps is a very tame affair.
How could mountaineering literature have survived for
posterity had it not been for the bergschrund, and the
agile, skilful, intrepid and dangerous manœuvres its
crossing involved? And what a zest it adds to the
traverse of an ice-slope to know that it is below gaping
like a crocodile to welcome in the little climbers?

Perhaps it was as well there was no bergschrund, as
we had neither rope nor ice axes. All the same, we felt
cheated by its absence, and continued resentfully on up
the slopes above, keeping a wary eye open for possible
wind-slab.

The slope was continuously steep, and the last portion
to the ridge wind-blown and hard. Once up to the ridge
we removed our ski and proceeded on foot to the summit,
which was only a few minutes distant. Here that old

Jack-in-office, the wind, had things all its own way and hurried us over some easy snow and rocks to the summit.

The view? I have little recollection of it. The sky was grey again. The weather had degenerated into a mere apology for a day. I have seen better views from the environs of Pudsey. Sky and earth were not even angry: they were merely colourless and sullen, and the mountains loomed out of a leaden snow-congested haze. We spent half a minute on the top, time enough for a cursory glance round and no more, then we turned and hastened back to our ski.

It should be possible now to insert some yeast into this doughy, not to say depressing account. Yesterday our descent had done something to compensate for the weather; on this occasion we had not even that consolation. To write that the snow was bad is an understatement lacking a variety of adjectives. Belaieff said it was the worst over which he had ever ski-ed. The catalogue of villainy consisted of snow which varied from breakable pie-crust into which the ski dived and jammed, to icy shields over which they skidded violently to fetch up in deep pockets of sticky, flour-like snow. Then there was the miserable light which, by eliminating all visible contrast in the surface of the snow, made it next to impossible to foretell what was coming. The slope, as already mentioned, is very steep, and quite 1,000 feet in height. Belaieff bravely essayed a turn or two in the uppermost portion, but after he had taken an imperial purler wisely inclined towards discretion, and did not hesitate to make kick turns. Thus, I was able to keep up with him, and we bumped and jolted across the slope in a manner reminiscent of the " swan-like " convolutions of Mr. Nathaniel Winkle on the pond at Dingley Dell.

Even steep slopes of execrable snow come to an end, and aching and battered—I know I was—we slid over the place where the bergschrund was reputed to be, and levelled out on the glacier beneath. Thenceforwards, the snow, if never good, was never really bad, except on the Glacier de la Chaux, where it was again unpleasantly wind-swept, and Belaieff was able to make as pretty a downhill pattern as his predecessors.

Back in the hut the worthy Dr. Broccard, perceiving us afar off, had prepared a meal, and right royally it went down. In any other circumstances we might have regaled him, albeit maliciously, with descriptions of the view, the warmth of the sun and many other concomitants of an enjoyable day's mountaineering, but what could we do in the circumstances but tell him the truth; that it had been a poor day and a worse descent. At the same time, it was a peak we were glad to have climbed. He is a poor climber, and unworthy of his faith, who climbs only in fair weather.

We cleaned the hut, then ski-ed down to Verbiers. The grey sky had melted away, and the sun shone warmly and without wind as we slid down the Combe de Médran; out of sheer cussedness, we supposed, or was it lofty contempt? With thoughts centred on the " flesh pots " who among us cared? We had done what we had set out to do, and if the mountaineer can do that, he at least gains a well-being and a satisfaction which he could never have gained in those " flesh pots " to which he now returns with a renewed *joie de vivre*.

While staying at the hotel the indefatigable M. Bisson saw to it that I was well supplied with companions at my table, and a very mixed assortment these were. One young fellow, a German-Swiss with a bullet head, bristly close-cropped hair and a roll of flesh at the back of his neck, proclaimed himself a trifle defiantly to be a socialist and proud of it, to which I replied that I was a democrat and proud of it too, after which we became excellent friends. When he left he was replaced by a Notary from French-speaking Switzerland, a well-read and interesting man with whom it was possible to discuss the affairs of the day political, social and religious.

My third table companion was so much like an Englishman in dress and appearance and so nearly did he resemble a soldier friend of mine, that it was on the point of my tongue to say, " Hullo, John, what on earth are you doing here? " However much may be argued about the equality of man and the beneficent effects of a homogeneous social set up, it cannot be denied that blood and breeding will out, and I realised instinctively, even before he spoke, that here was one of those rare personages, the Swiss aristocrat, and by aristocrat I do not mean gentlemen of whom there are many such in Switzerland born and made, but someone evolved out of centuries of sound breeding and fine culture. What is it that raises such a man above his fellows, that stamps him with that indefinable " something " distinguishing him from all and sundry? It is looks, clear-cut and refined, a profile instantly distinguishable from the herd; it is a physical something evolved through the centuries, finely drawn and beautifully shaped, tapering fingers and hands perfectly kept; it is something in which there is nothing *outré*, or that advertises itself, that is never blatant but always dignified, never excited, but always calm, yet not lacking in enthusiasm. But most of all it is courtesy and manner, not learned, but entirely natural, instinctive and sincere, the product not of a few generations but many. To such, the art of living, good taste, perfect manners and a fine discrimination come easily, and do not have to be laboriously acquired. Such qualities in a man are beyond price and beyond a material inheritance.

It was no surprise to me when he introduced himself; his name was one of the oldest in Switzerland. I asked him how far back he could trace his family and he replied with a smile, " Not very far with my branch, I'm afraid, only to the fifteenth century."

He was flaxen-haired and blue-eyed—not that this conveys very much in Central Europe—and his face, burned
ruddy by the Alpine sun, was cleanly cut, the nose being
slightly Roman.   There were many young Germans like
this in physical appearance to be seen in Switzerland
before the war, but with them one felt always that there
was so little behind, that they were young gods without
a purpose, or rather whose purpose and fate had already
been decreed.   Consequently they lacked all individuality, and were merely a Teutonic pattern of temporary
importance to their environment and none to contemporary culture or to posterity.   His voice was rich, deep
and melodious.   Even though it was never raised, it was
clearly distinguishable from the chatter of a roomful of
people as a nightingale is from a flight of crows.   There
was in his conversation a keenness and depth of vision
such as I had not previously encountered in Switzerland.
At the same time he had no hares to chase or axes to
grind, and was ready to discuss any subject strictly on its
merits and without irrational prejudice.   He was young,
certainly under thirty, and in business, but I do not think
the business meant much to him; his ambition, he told
me, was to travel and study the world.   It is impossible
to imagine a man better fitted for the task, or one who
would gain greater benefit from it.   Men such as he are
needed by civilisation to-day, else it will perish from the
earth.

CHAPTER VII
ZERMATT

OUR principal aim and ambition was to traverse from Saas Fee or Zermatt to Verbiers by the Haute Route, the now famous ski-way along the glaciers and across the high passes of the Pennine Alps. We decided, therefore, to make Zermatt our headquarters until settled weather arrived, if it ever did, and in the meantime make such ascents as were possible in the prevailing uncertain conditions. Zermatt, as already stated, had been cut off from Visp and the Rhone Valley by avalanches, the result of heavy snow-falls, but the line had been cleared during the recent snowless period, and trains were again running.

March 9th, the day after our return from the Cabane de Mont Fort, was fine and warm, so warm that the melted snow was streaming off the roofs. I said good-bye to M. Bisson and squelched down through the slush to the bus terminus.

Spring had already come to the lower Alps, and presently, as the bus zigzagged down to Châble, we passed from snow to bare macadamised road. After the glare of the high snows it was pleasant to see slopes of turf already shot with the bright green of a new spring growth. Then came the flowers. Highest in bloom was a clump of violets. Lower, the slopes were starred with anemones, and the first crocuses were showing, small, crumpled and a trifle bedraggled.

At Châble we halted for half an hour. The air was warm and caressing on cheeks dried and burned on the high snows, and the river was tumbling down the valley with a new-found strength and boisterousness. In such contrasts lies the charm of Alpine mountaineering. The traveller who spends one day high in the " Urns of silent

134

snow," and the next amidst woodland and pasture, with flowers at his feet and bird-song in his ear, tastes to the full the beauty of mountain travel.

On arrival at Sembrancher I found that in not having purchased a ticket I had committed a crime. On some bus routes the ticket may be purchased in the bus, but on this particular route it must be purchased beforehand at the post office. It would have been simple for the driver, who combined his duty with that of conductor, to have collected my fare, or to have directed me to the station ticket office where it was possible to purchase a ticket. The latter he did indeed do, but rudely after some quite unwarranted abuse, unwarranted because it was obvious to him that I was a visitor and unacquainted with the local customs. It was the only piece of rudeness offered to me during my two months in Switzerland.

At Martigny after lunch we set off in Dr. Broccard's car for Visp. The majority of tourists visit the Rhone Valley in summer. At that season the valley below Brig is often unpleasantly stuffy and subject to a sirocco-like wind. There are also mosquitoes, for which pest Martigny has an evil reputation, and a species of horse-fly known as the Rhone Valley fly, as poisonous an insect as its relative the Scotch cleg. In the spring, even as early as March, the story is another one. The warm, balmy air comes as a welcome change after the dry frigidity of the upper atmosphere, and the pastures and orchards, already thriving with life, are a sight for sore eyes after the perpetual glare of the high snows.

The main valley road runs in long, straight sections lined with poplars. The surface was poor, but Dr. Broccard explained this by telling us that the expense, labour and materials necessary to maintain mountain roads, such as that to Verbiers, were so considerable that the main valley roads suffered neglect as a result.

One day I am going to " explore " the minor valleys

that lead from the Rhone Valley into the Pennine Alps, not frequented valleys such as the Val d'Hérens and the Val d'Anniviers, but the little valleys in between. Some of them debouch into the Rhone Valley as formidable gorges, and their streams dash out of mere rocky slits to join the Rhone. Secret little valleys, with paths seldom trodden other than by the local herdsmen and cheese-makers, lead up to alps tucked away among the outpost peaks of the Pennines. What views there must be from these peaks of the greater peaks to the south and of the Oberland across the Rhone to the north. There is some fine ski-ing country here also, but it is not easy country to visit in winter and spring when the hamlets are abandoned and the valley road choked with snow and avalanches. The spring is the season *par excellence* for ski-ing in this area, as it is indeed for all Alpine areas above the 8,000-feet level, provided that the ski-er is content to doss down in the hay, or to be entertained in some humble dwelling.

We passed through Sion, a busy little town, and noted evidence of the recent earthquake in cracked walls and tumbled chimney-pots. Then came Sierre and Leuk. Although in altitude but a few metres above Martigny, which was entirely green, snow was lying here, and it increased in depth as we continued up the valley until near Visp it was over a foot deep. There was evidence even of avalanches which must be rare phenomena hereabouts.

At Visp the car was garaged and we adjourned to the station restaurant for refreshment. Although the hour was three in the afternoon, a time at which most ordinary mortals are occupied in earning their living, the tables were crowded with men playing cards. I have not as yet been able to fathom the intricacies of what is evidently a national game, except that it is a kind of whist. One thing, however, is certain; he who throws down his card

The Grand Combin

The drinking place

with the greatest vigour is he who takes the trick. It often happens that the first player projects his card in a modified manner, the second player covers it more forcefully, the third harder still, while the last thumps his down with such a crash as to cause the glasses of Fendant, with which every player is provided, to jump into the air. It is this last player who takes the trick. It can easily be imagined, therefore, that when a number of tables of players are engaged in this game, the resulting noise resembles a blacksmith's shop in which several smiths are working at the same time.

The evening train to Zermatt was crowded: it usually is, but no one minds this. The crowd was a happy one: ski-ers, guides, peasants returning from a day in Visp or Brig. Everyone was in good spirits, some in more senses than one, and there was an atmosphere of bonhomie and camaraderie. And they were going to Zermatt. Zermatt—did any name ever slip more easily off the tongue? Did any name ever promise such high and strenuous adventure? Grindelwald, Chamonix, Kandersteg, Pontresina are enshrined in the nomenclature of mountains and mountaineering. But Zermatt! It is more than a name: it is a heart-throb, an age, a past and a tradition. To Zermatt you go and to Zermatt you return. Why? Not solely because of the Matterhorn, or of Whymper, not solely to climb mountains, to play bad tennis on worse courts, to visit the Gornergrat and come down again, or to see the museum with its gruesome relics for the morbid. No, you go to Zermatt simply because it is Zermatt, because it is a part of the mountain theme, because it epitomises so much of what you have heard and thought and read and dreamed about mountains.

But we are still at Visp, squashed in among a crowd of sturdy peasants in an atmosphere charged with cheese and rank tobacco. Now we are off, and a heavily weighted rucksack, my rucksack, falls off the rack on to the head of my immediate neighbour, who is fortunately far too advanced in wine and merriment to be more than momentarily inconvenienced by such a trifle. Off we hum, ski-ers, peasants, cheeses, smoky atmosphere and babble of talk, first along the level floor of the Vispthal then, after slowing down to engage pinion with rack, up the steep grades to Stalden.

It was soon apparent that there had been an exceptionally heavy snow-fall followed by a rapid rise of temperature. Avalanches great and small had slid from every slope and down every gully. The line had been cut in innumerable places, and it speaks well for the efficiency of the railway company that it had been cleared and re-opened as quickly as it had been. Even so, Zermatt had been isolated for some time, and many were the heart-rending tales of persons who had been cut off from civilisation and their families for as long as a whole week.

The last occasion on which I travelled up the Vispthal was on a summer evening in a remote age of peace and quietude. The scent of hay drifted in at the open windows, a few small clouds lay becalmed in a sky of gauzy blue and the cold breath of the glacier river was perceptible in the warm, still air. Now, the valley seemed to reflect the subsequent catastrophe that had overtaken mankind. Splintered trees lay athwart the jumbled masses of avalanche snow, and huge rocks, dislodged by the sliding masses, lay piled in wild confusion. In one place a great slice of mountainside, possibly undermined by the melting snow or loosened perhaps by the recent earthquake shocks, had fallen, and thousands of tons of rock and earth were piled in ugly heaps close to the line. It was as though some blitz had come to the valley, but it was a blitz that scarred mountainsides, not hearts. In a few weeks and months the snow would have melted, then Nature would spread her healing green over the scars.

Long ago I promised myself a walk from Visp to Zermatt, but it is a promise that through laziness remains unfulfilled. The pioneers thought nothing of it, and Whymper in his "sixties" used frequently to make the journey. It would be an experience to do so, for the valley has changed little; there are the same villages, and when you have been many times to Zermatt their names sound like a song: Stalden, St. Niklaus, Herbriggen, Randa and Täsch. They occur and recur in the literature of Alpine travel and mountaineering, and so also do the names of the guiding families that dwell in the valley, the Imbodens, the Pollingers, the Knubels, and the Lochmatters, names known the world over wherever mountaineering is discussed.

The mule path along which the pioneers walked or rode is still there. It has been improved, but not, thank God, into a motor road. I am no bigot in the matter of motoring; I enjoy it as much as anyone; but there are some places to which there should never be a motor road, and Zermatt is one of them. Chamonix has been rendered hideous by cars, but at Zermatt it is possible to stroll about the single street in peace. There are horse-drawn sleighs and carriages, of course, but these fit into the scene; the horse is the immemorial friend of man, the motor car his upstart slave.

I should like also to turn the corner in the path as did the pioneers, and look for the first time on the Matterhorn. One attribute of this mountain lies in its power to draw the simile. To Ruskin it resembled a rearing horse, but to Whymper it was merely a sugar loaf with its head knocked to one side. In these few words we perceive Ruskin the poet, the painter and idealist, and Whymper, the draughtsman and unimaginative materialist. In his diary Whymper wrote: "What precious stuff Ruskin has written about this (the Matterhorn), and about many other things."

And so to Zermatt. An immense quantity of snow had

fallen in the uppermost portion of the Vispthal, especially between Täsch and Zermatt. The stream bed was a mere snowy hollow, and walls of snow 15 feet high hemmed the track. Great avalanches had fallen everywhere, some close to the station. Never have I seen so much snow in March at this altitude.

Darkness was falling as we walked from the station to our hotel, and the lights from the village shone gaily across the snow. Zermatt again. Seven years had passed since I was last there. The world was that much older, and much of it broken and shabbier, but Zermatt was the same, and the dance bands from the cafés throbbed across the still evening air through which a few snow-flakes were slowly falling. It was not the Zermatt of Whymper's day with its few chalets and single hotel. It had grown out of all knowledge in meeting the insatiable demands of "tourismo." Yet, unlike so many places that have been irretrievably changed, Zermatt retains an ancient charm. The spirit of the past is perpetuated in the old portion of the village, in the familiar façade of the Monte Rosa Hotel, and the low wall outside where generations of guides have sat awaiting employers. And when these are gone, as they will be some day, there will still be the Matterhorn. And of those who gaze on it: "However exalted may be their ideas, and however exaggerated their expectations, none will come to return disappointed."

CHAPTER VIII

BAD WEATHER AT THE BÉTEMPS HUT

MARCH 11th dawned brilliantly, and it seemed that at long last the weather was mending. The barometer, however, remained obstinately low, despite some imperious, not to say vicious, taps calculated to rouse any instrument from its lethargy. It was therefore with a tempered optimism that we piled ourselves, our rucksacks containing four days' provisions, and our ski, into the Gornergrat train.

Except for the lightest of mists the morning was unclouded, and the sun beamed brilliantly from the purest of pure-blue skies. One by one, as we climbed past the hoary old pines bowed down like a regiment of Father Times beneath their weight of snow, the great peaks swung up into view, and soon we emerged from the valley shadow on to the snows of the Riffelalp.

We alighted at Rotenboden, and having gathered together our paraphernalia, which included ice axes, crampons and rope, set off for the Bétemps hut feeling not unlike ambulatory Christmas trees, and the subject already of interested comment from the winter-sportsmen in the train, few of whom could discern anything in our appearance, movements and intentions but a species of mid-winter madness.

From Rotenboden it is necessary to descend 1,000 feet to the Gorner glacier. The summer route makes a traverse of the south face of the Gornergrat, but in winter this route is normally impracticable, and the ski-er must descend directly to the glacier. The slope is very steep, but a narrow ridge which runs for three-quarters of the way provides a route safe from avalanches except under the worst snow conditions. Down this ridge we ploughed, carrying our ski, and were soon on the glacier.

The Bétemps hut is clearly visible all the way across the Gorner glacier, but possesses the knack of seeming to remain always at the same distance, an all-too-familiar trick when the sun is hot and the climber's load heavy. Then lo! and behold! a miracle occurs, and it suddenly takes a jump forward and appears close at hand.

It is a large hut, and is visited in spring and summer by many hundreds of tourists and climbers. Adjoining the downstairs living-room is a smaller winter room with a bunk long enough for some eight persons (at a pinch), a stove, table and chairs. The stove was in wretched condition and smoked abominably, the piping having cracked and the joints loosened. Over this contraption, coughing, spluttering and weeping, we managed at length to melt snow and brew some tea.

We had hoped for a pleasant hour or two of sun bathing, but in this we were disappointed. The fine morning fizzled out like a damp squib, and as the afternoon drew on the wind rose and the sky filled with smooth, oily clouds behind which the sun slowly faded away. Snow began to fall, and by nightfall a blizzard was blowing.

Meanwhile two other parties had arrived, one of five including a guide, and the other a guideless party of three. There was also a solitary Swiss who had a rendezvous with a friend at the hut. The latter, however, had not turned up, having preferred the comforts of Zermatt to the austerities of the Bétemps hut.

I shall always associate the Bétemps hut with bad weather. On two previous occasions I had been confined there by snow-storms. These were doubtless coincidental; all the same, if when every time a particular place is visited something unpleasant happens, there is a natural tendency to dislike that place. Let me therefore say at once that I dislike the Bétemps hut. I associate it, not only with bad weather, but with long and profitless glacier ascents during which the wind usually blows with a bitter vehemence. I have done Monte Rosa and ascended to the Italian hut on the Signalkuppe, and both of these routes are pigeon-holed in memory as among the most monotonous grinds in the Alps. For all these reasons, coupled with the smoking stove, a continual damp chilliness, and of being packed that night on a bunk containing some dozen persons intended to take six or eight with comfort, with a man next to me who snored, I say again that I dislike the Bétemps hut.

To lie awake listening to a chorus of snores is an unsatisfactory way of spending a night. The rampaging of the wind about the hut, and the beating of the snow like small-shot on the shutters, was at least some sort of a solace, and it was possible to reflect that to emulate a sardine in a kind of vocal hell was preferable to a bivouac in the snow, but at the time the comparison did not have the point it now possesses in retrospect.

There is, I have noticed, a considerable repertoire in the matter of snoring. There are the shy, intermittent snorers, and the self-confident, continuous performers. Then there are those who choke or gurgle; others neigh like horses, and not a few grunt like pigs. There is the high, thin, sighing note like wind in the tree-tops, and the deep rumbling suggestive of a major natural convulsion. Many of these were represented at the Bétemps hut. It needed but one snorer to make the cacophony complete. This was a snorer I used to know. He was the snorer above all snorers, the very king of snorers. Although a small man, the volume of sound emitted was elephantine. He snored so loudly that he used to wake himself up, yet he never realised what a merciful dispensation of Providence this was, for he would nudge me violently and exclaim angrily: "Your infernal snoring has wakened me up again!"

Next morning—and I have never known such a laggard dawning—the storm was in full swing, and it continued without intermission throughout the day, depositing the best part of another foot of snow. It was a dull time. The stove took advantage of the occasion to become even more offensive than before, and to prevent ourselves being suffocated it was necessary to lie in our blankets and inhale through them as though through a respirator. How slowly the hours passed. There was little to do but occasionally to take a peep outside into a few yards of flying snow, study the hut book, which contained the names of a large number of persons all of whom appeared to have enjoyed excellent weather during the past several years, and range up and down the living-room like caged lions. From a conglomeration of forlorn and dirtied playing cards and other debris I managed to unearth an American novel. I cannot recollect what it was about, but I do remember that as I approached the denouement, or it may have been merely a happy ending, I discovered to my intense annoyance that the concluding pages had been ruthlessly torn out, possibly by someone who required them for a purpose more important than the development of his literary taste.

Sensible persons would have said: "To hell with this, let's quit," and would have descended to Zermatt, eaten a good dinner, wallowed in a hot bath, and gone to bed between sheets; but the mountaineer, although a constant prey to adverse circumstances, yet remains for some inscrutable reason an incurable and obstinate optimist. With him it is always "to-morrow," or, "perhaps it may clear." Needless to say the morrow is seldom any different, whilst the possibility of the weather clearing during a really bad spell is one on which no sensible punter would take a chance. In his heart he knows that there is no hope of the weather improving until after he has returned to the valley, and that he should continue to run contrary to such an established fact is merely another proof of his madness.

We merely postponed the inevitable, and when after a night precisely similar to the first we woke to find snow still falling, it was with a sense of profound relief that we realised that in any event we must return to Zermatt, seeing that we had not enough provisions for a longer stay.

Accordingly, after breakfast, we set off with the guided party. The tracks to the hut had vanished, and on the glacier nothing was to be seen save the white, impenetrable glare common to such occasions.

Although snow was still falling fairly thickly, the wind had dropped and the morning was pleasantly warm. It soon transpired, however, that not one of the guided party, including the guide, possessed a compass, and as the latter presently exhibited a tendency to proceed in circles, we were soon called on to direct the line of march from the rear. In any event it would be difficult to become lost between the Bétemps hut and the Gornergrat, and presently the slopes we had descended to the glacier loomed through the murk.

We climbed to the commencement of the rib up which it is necessary to trudge on foot, and there we paused irresolute. A considerable quantity of snow had fallen and, as already mentioned, this route can under certain circumstances become dangerous from avalanches. I do not believe the ascent would have been dangerous under the existing conditions, nor did Belaieff. What we jibbed at was the thought of having to labour up a thousand feet through knee-deep snow carrying our gear and our ski. In a word, we were lazy. When therefore someone suggested, and I think it was myself, why not descend the Gorner glacier, we agreed that it would be a preferable alternative.

Without waiting to hear what the guided party intended to do, we set off down the glacier; they, after a momentary hesitation, followed us.

Many years previously I had descended this glacier, but my memory of it was a trifle vague. Included in it is a considerable but not difficult ice-fall. The Kurz skiing guide mentions that this ice-fall is sometimes complicated, and that it is best turned on the right, the ski-er proceeding on foot beneath the crags of the Gaggenhaupt. There is, however, no doubt that the simplest of ice-falls can become difficult in poor visibility, specially to the ski-er.

Meanwhile, the weather had momentarily improved, and above us we could discern the rocks of the Riffel-horn. There was a fugitive glint of sun, and next instant an avalanche of new snow came rushing down. It was only a small fall, even though it made an impressive noise, but it served to convince us that we had done right to abandon the route to Rotenboden.

The improved visibility lasted as far as the commencement of the ice-fall, then mists formed, and once again snow fell heavily. Keeping to the right, we edged our way down the side of the séracs. until suddenly the slope dropped away, and we looked down a steep and ugly drop into an icy scoop. There was no further progress possible in *that* direction, and the sole alternative was to launch out into the middle of the ice-fall. It was curious that the guide seemed to have no definite ideas as to the route, which for some time past we had forced as a matter of trial and error. This was probably explained by the fact that he was a ski-ing instructor and not a mountain guide. In the bad visibility it appeared a nasty place. Dimly through the falling snow we could perceive lines of formidable séracs above us; below all was emptiness and mystery. It is fatally easy in such conditions to run over an ice cliff, as the lack of shadow renders it impossible to see what lies below, and the ski may slip over a drop before the ski-er can check himself. The guide, Belaieff and I all sought the route, and presently found what appeared the only practicable line leading diagonally downwards through the séracs.

After our dull time at the hut it was an undeniable thrill to have to find our way thus down an ice-fall in a snow-storm, better we all agreed than toiling up to Rotenboden and running down the standard route to Zermatt; it went, indeed, a small way towards redeeming three wasted days.

At length we had passed the ice-fall, and on the smoother glacier beneath were able to proceed with greater confidence. The visibility improved quickly as we descended, and when at length we paused for lunch in the gorge through which the glacier stream passes in summer, we found ourselves below the worst of the weather.

The day concluded with a leisurely run back to Zermatt. So ended three days of bad weather. If I have included this dull little account of a dull time it is because bad weather and disappointment are a part and parcel of ski-ing and mountaineering. Without it a full appreciation of the Alps in their glory of sun and snow would be impossible. In such a contrast between the agreeable and the disagreeable lies the true contentment and philosophy of the mountaineer. Little we realised, as we slid disconsolately down beneath a leaden sky, that our disappointments were over, and that great days were to come.

CHAPTER IX

A TRAVERSE OF THE BREITHORN

WHEN, after our unsuccessful attempts to make some high tours from the Bétemps hut, we returned to Zermatt, there seemed little possibility of the weather mending. With intermissions of no more than a day or so at a time, it had been bad since I had arrived in Switzerland, and it was small consolation to be told by the oldest inhabitant that he had never seen so much snow in March. Any hopes we had entertained of travelling to Verbiers along the famous high-level route, on which we had set our hearts, had well-nigh vanished, and it was becoming increasingly probable that we should have to return by train.

It was only to be expected that the weather should clear temporarily the moment we returned to Zermatt, and it was with cynical smiles and bitter comment that we rose next morning to find the sky unclouded and the sun shining with an almost insulting brilliance. This, we told ourselves, was a mere flash in the pan, an ebullition maliciously and expressly designed to lure us up to some hut, when the weather would promptly break once more.

The conditions also were as bad as they could be, and new snow lay to such a depth that high ascents would be out of the question for many days to come.

All these things we recounted, and many more, whipping ourselves into an access of pessimism and self-pity. We were through with it, we said. We would go home. What was the use of kicking our heels at Zermatt, where there is nothing better to do than funicular up and ski down *ad nauseam* and *ad infinitum*?

Half-way through the morning we were sitting outside

a café sipping coffee and scowling at one another. Around us the winter-sportsmen chattered away, and on the slopes by the village a concourse of persons was gathered to watch the international slalom race. Other people were enjoying themselves. Perhaps it was better after all to be a " downhill only " ski-er, and to spend the time between whiles in social gaieties; better the cocktail bar, the restaurant and the dance floor than the discomforts of an Alpine hut in March.

We were demoralised, no doubt of that. And yet, and yet, the sun was shining brilliantly that morning, shining down the colourful little street with its strolling, gaily-clad people, and its wealth of flags and banners; and beyond, and far above, the high snows were reposed, remote in a sky of vernal blue. Would we, could we, give the weather one more chance?

Belaieff, ever brimful of energy, spent the remainder of the day in being a " downhill only," while I wandered about with my camera. I, too, had the idea of making an ascent by the ski lift, a form of transport I had not yet employed.

For those who have yet to visit Switzerland, I should explain that a ski lift is simply a cableway on the same principle as a coal conveyor, only in this instance ski-ers are substituted for coal, and instead of being borne through the air are dragged up on their ski over the snow. Ski lifts are highly profitable undertakings. They require little maintenance, and unlike mountain railways, which must be continually ploughed, are not affected by snow-falls. Even in the event of the cable breaking, all the ski-ers concerned, who are spaced at regular intervals and supported by loops, will merely fall backwards and slide down the slope until they stop.

When I arrived at the ski-lift station I found a queue some fifty yards long and six abreast. I attached myself to this. At the end of half an hour I had been shuffled

and pressed forwards some five yards. A simple mathe-
matical calculation showed that I should have to wait a
further five hours before my uplift, and it occurred to
me that I might not then be in the mood for any uplift,
physical or otherwise; it would also be dinner-time.

A further objection, if any were wanting, was that the
route traversed by the queue lay directly beneath the
roof of the station, on which was poised a mass of snow
some six feet in depth and weighing several tons, which
was not only pouring steady streams of icy water down
the necks of those assembled beneath, but was obviously
ready to slide off at any moment.

Thus, for about two hours out of the five in the queue,
I should be exposed to an actual waterfall and a potential
avalanche. Having weighed these considerations, and
taken into account an objection to queues amounting to
claustrophobia, I decided to forgo the experience of
ascending by a ski lift. I must therefore apologise to the
reader in having presented him with so inadequate an
account of this interesting device.

The remainder of the afternoon I spent taking photographs in the Vispthal below Zermatt. There was a fine
assortment of animal and bird tracks in the snow, and I
identified foxes and hares. Then there were some minute
marks which might have been made by a mouse, and
along the banks of the stream evidence of birds great and
small.

Apart from these, there were numerous opportunities
for photography. Already, under the hot sun the snow
was becoming silver crusted, a condition which always
makes for dramatic photographs taken against the light.
Shadows of trees and shrubs also provided some charming subjects. In this work a 35-mm. camera with a
6-inch-focus telephoto lens is ideal, as the latter provides
the narrow view and depth of focus necessary for such
studies.

I had made my own track towards Täsch, keeping to the side of the valley opposite to that along which the road and railway pass. I was somewhat surprised therefore when I was presently overtaken by a tall fellow on ski. Shortly before reaching me he stopped and planted a red pennon in the snow. He passed without a word, and a few yards farther on planted another pennon. I thought at first that he was marking out a race-course, but when I examined the pennons I found written on them the single word BALLY. There is, I believe, a shoe-maker of this name, and subsequently I saw many similar pennons planted in the slopes about Zermatt. Without in any way desirous of being offensive to my Swiss friends, or making any attempt to teach them their own business, I would suggest that such a form of advertising on the mountains in winter is as offensive as it is unnecessary. It establishes a principle which, if not checked, might render every scene open to defilement by great posters and banners stuck in the snow. In a word, it is Ballyhoo of the vulgarest description.

Having crossed the stream, where it was bridged by an avalanche, I returned along the road. Few persons use this road in winter, and even in summer everyone who can afford to do so travels by railway between the villages in the Vispthal. It was along this road that the early visitors tramped to Zermatt. The Romans must have passed here after crossing the Théodule pass. Did they march in kilts, metal helmets and cuirasses? Here also passed the soldiers of Napoleon on a campaign of ravage and extortion, and later, the pioneers of the " Fifties " and " Sixties," the golden age of mountaineering, Alfred Wills, John Tyndall, Leslie Stephen, John Ball, Edward Whymper and many others. All ancient ways have their tale to tell, and as I slid along the deserted track towards Zermatt I would have given much to have bridged a matter of eighty years or so, to have turned the corner where the Matterhorn first springs into view and known the thrill of its virgin summit.

On the wooden bridge which spans the Visp half a mile from Zermatt, a stout middle-aged man in knicker-bockers was busy taking photographs with an enormous stand-camera, to focus which it was necessary to peer under the folds of a voluminous black cloth. I too have taken various photographs from this bridge, and more out of a spirit of mischief than anything else, I rigged up my tiny 35-mm. camera beside his massive apparatus. Unlike another photographer, a white-bearded old gentleman I once met who contemptuously addressed me as a " snapshotter "—and what a world of scorn he crowded into it—this one was perfectly civil; indeed, he seemed highly gratified that I was following his choice of vantage-point. His whole appearance and immense apparatus were, however, suggestive of a bygone age, and I began to wonder whether I had stepped back among the immortals, who with infinite trouble and patience lugged around their wet plates and clumsy apparatus in further-ance of their art.

For once the day ended as it had begun. It was never-theless with a qualified optimism that we set off next morning for the Bétemps hut, once more determined if possible to commence the proposed high-level route with a traverse of the Breithorn by way of the Schwarzthor and the Théodule pass. In Belaieff's case his optimism was so qualified that he announced his intention of descending to Zermatt by one of the Gornergrat runs and reascending in the afternoon to join me at Rotenboden, after which we would proceed together to the hut. This he said would avoid wasting yet another day. It was a proposition of which I thoroughly approved, as it meant that while he tested the seconds in a swift dash to Zer-matt, I lounged in the sun on the Riffelalp.

For a time I watched the ski-ers skimming down the icy

Shadows

The Matterhorn in winter (telephotograph)

track past the alp, then, sickening at the sight of so much speed and energy, I found a secluded spot, and with my back to a pine dozed peacefully until the time arrived for our rendezvous at Rotenboden. There is no question that the next best thing to intense activity is absolute idleness, and I look forward with hope rather than horror to an old age in which it will be both necessary and desirable to spend pleasant hours doing nothing in the sun, while youth devotes its time to straining up the mountainsides.

From Rotenboden we set off on the now familiar track to the Bétemps hut. Many persons had already passed that way, and we descended a regular staircase to the Gorner glacier. As we did so we were intrigued to notice a ski track on the glacier which, instead of proceeding towards the hut, zigzagged up the lowermost slopes of the Breithorn in the direction of the Young-grat. This last-named ridge is well known as a long and difficult summer climb, and was first ascended by Mr. Geoffrey Winthrop Young, after whom it was named. It had not been ascended in winter conditions, and situated as it is on the north face of the Breithorn massif, it scarcely seems a route which could be climbed at this season except under exceptionally favourable conditions. It was evident that a party was prospecting it, and colour was lent to this by a ski-er who followed us to the glacier laden with all manner of gear, including ropes and crampons, which it was obvious were to be employed on the climb.

On this occasion we carried four days' food, and we toiled up the Gorner glacier with a grim determination inspired both by the weight of our loads and the thought that this was positively the last chance we intended to give the weather and ourselves.

On arriving at the hut we found that a considerable crowd was already established there. This was for once an advantage, as the winter room was now unusable owing to the Huttenwart (hut keeper) having visited the hut and removed the faulty piping of the stove. Thus, the larger summer room had to be used, and the presence of a large number of persons, and well-nigh continual cooking operations, had the excellent effect of raising the temperature in this to the point of a veritable fug, and a fug in an Alpine hut in winter is something to be cherished. This fug had also warmed the bedrooms on the first floor of the hut, and in one of these we staked out a claim and disposed our belongings.

That night something I had eaten for dinner died horribly within me. We had planned next morning to ascend the Lyskamm by way of the Grenz glacier, the Lysjoch and the south-east ridge of the mountain. This is a long day's ski mountaineering, and we left in the first daylight. The weather still remained fair, but some ominous mists were pouring like oil over the high ridges and a bitterly cold wind spurted down the Grenz glacier.

For once I found myself unpleasantly cold, but this was scarcely surprising, seeing that I had been unable to retain my victuals, and had spent a large part of a sleepless night in rejecting them. My legs were also weak, and before long I found myself urging them along more by will power than anything else. Will power is something to be used sparingly at the best of times on a mountain, and then only in conjunction with a fit body, and after an hour or so I began to realise that not only was I incapable of attaining the summit of the Lyskamm, but I might easily collapse if I attempted to do so. It was very hard luck on Belaieff that this, our first opportunity of making a high ascent, should be ruined, and a less generous companion might well have shown his disappointment. As it was his sole concern was for me.

Not far ahead was a guideless party of two young fellows, and it was agreed that Belaieff should continue on up the glacier after them, in order to get the longest possible ascent, while I descended immediately to the hut.

All mountaineers know how interdependent are the physical and mental capacities on a mountain. It is possible for a chronic invalid to rise superior to infirmity, and to exercise and enjoy his mental capacities to the full, but this is not so easy in the case of anyone normally accustomed to be physically fit, and the full appreciation of mountain scenery and mountain climbing depends without a doubt on a peaceful and co-operative union between the physical and the mental.

I have seldom seen mountains look uglier than they did that morning. Monte Rosa, I decided, was one of the most unprepossessing and most shapeless mountains on which I had ever set eyes, and as for our original objective, the Lyskamm, it was a mere pallid lump. Snow was being shorn off its summit ridges by a strong wind, and as I watched it pouring away in writhing convoluting clouds it struck me as resembling all too faithfully the state of my stomach.

As for the Grenz glacier, it is a long, dull slog at the best of times, and that morning it appeared not only dreary but positively hostile. Fragments of sunlight were flying across it, and gusts and squalls of wind raised the loose snow from its surface in spirals that assaulted me viciously.

A number of British soldiers escaping out of Italy during the war crossed the Lysjoch and descended this glacier. Ill-nourished and ill-clad, and without previous mountaineering experience, they were taken by Italian guides as far as the pass, and there left to make their own way down into Switzerland, the guides being afraid to accompany them, as they were normally smugglers and scarcely *persona grata* with the Swiss frontier guards. Some stirring stories have been written, and others remain to be written, of their adventures and tribulations. Unused as they were to snow-craft, the descent of the glacier, dangerous and complicated at the best of times, must have seemed a nightmare, until they were met and guided down by the kindly Swiss. Small wonder if they hated the mountains, and that morning it came to me how it was possible to hate mountains as well as to love them.

The descent was over good snow, and soon I was back at the hut. There I turned into my bunk and slept for the greater part of the day. Belaieff arrived during the afternoon. He had accompanied the Swiss to the foot of the Signalkuppe rocks, whence he had enjoyed a magnificent descent of the glacier in a little over half an hour.

My recovery after this was rapid, and next morning we decided to ascend the Cima di Jazzi, 12,527 feet. This mountain, which rises from the Swiss-Italian frontier ridge between Monte Rosa and the well-known pass of the Schwarzenberg-Weissthor, is one of the easiest snow peaks in the Alps and a fine ski tour. The barometer had also staged a recovery, and for the first time since I had arrived in Switzerland it was climbing steadily. Only the wind still continued to blow hard on the high peaks and ridges, and any greater ascents, if not impracticable, would have been both difficult and unpleasant. In such circumstances the Cima di Jazzi is an ideal alternative for the ski-er at the Bétemps hut.

We were off at the Christian hour of 9 a.m., and making our way up a deep scoop between the Gorner glacier and its southernmost-side moraine, were soon on the expanse of *névé* which extends for miles between the Strahlhorn and Monte Rosa.

There was little wind, but enough to keep us moving briskly until at length we neared the peak—perhaps bump is more descriptive. A guided party of two were an hour ahead of us, and as we approached the final slope they descended from the summit. They were muffled up to the eyebrows and "pour encourager les autres" halted to tell us that the wind was very strong and cold, and that there was absolutely no pleasure whatever to be gained out of the ascent. Having said this they moved on.

They were perfectly right. From comparative calm we emerged suddenly into a strata of air moving over the frontier ridge with gale force. Against this we struggled, and presently found ourselves on the summit. In calm conditions the Cima di Jazzi is probably a fine viewpoint. I say "probably," because the wind made it impossible to appreciate the view, though this was both cloud-free and extensive, while a cornice prevented what must be a dramatic glimpse of the east face of Monte Rosa, which is second only to the south side of Mont Blanc in height and magnitude.

Half-frozen by the blast, which whipped stinging snow into our faces, we fumbled off our seal-skins, and without further ado set off down.

There is no doubt as to the superb quality of the descent from the Cima di Jazzi to the Bétemps hut. First came the upper slopes of the mountain, which were in surprisingly good condition considering the wind. These were followed by a level stretch and a long descent of the glacier. This last provided the finest down-hill run we had yet enjoyed together. The snow consisted of a powdery surface overlying a compacted sub-stratum. The light, however, was weak, and in one or two places patches of a rather heavier type of snow intervened. In one of these I took the fastest toss I had yet accomplished.

That was the sole incident of an uneventful descent, the best portion of which was the run down the long scoop between the glacier and the moraine, in which we flew tortuously from side to side, mounting each slope in turn, an evolution reminiscent of an ocean passage on a breezy day.

It was evident that the weather was mending. The barometer that evening was still rising, and the mountains no longer smoked their pipes with the same vehemence.

We had already discovered that among those at the hut was a party of Swiss guideless climbers who had designs on the Young ridge of the Breithorn. It was their porter we had seen on the way from Rotenboden, and they told us they had already prospected the lowermost portion of the route, climbing as high as it was possible on ski, and had dumped bivouac equipment and provisions on the ridge. The climb above that point would have to be made on foot, and their plan now was to make another dump of ski on the summit of the Breithorn.

The reader may well ask, why go to all this trouble over a route which is far more easily, safely and comfortably scaled during the summer months? There cannot be many routes with fewer attractions than the Young ridge of the Breithorn in winter, and especially when this sunless north side of the mountain is heavily plastered in powdery snow. The answer, of course, is the same as that given by George Mallory to the question of why climb Everest: "Because it is there." In this instance, it is not a question of making a new route, but simply of traversing under winter conditions a route made many times in summer.

Such climbing is an indication of the degree to which Alpine mountaineering has become specialised, and also a proof that the adventurous instinct in man is as strong as ever it was. It is interesting and significant that such ascents should be attempted nowadays by the Swiss school of guideless climbers, as before the war the Germans and Austrians made the majority of very difficult guideless climbs. Contrary to some notions I have heard, the peace with which Switzerland has been blessed for so long has in no wise diminished the virile adventurous spirit of her people.

The conditions were so far improved that we decided next day to traverse the Breithorn by way of the Schwarzthor, 12,274 feet, afterwards descending to Zermatt via the Théodule pass, and subsequently continuing with the high-level route to Verbiers should the good weather hold.

The wind dropped with evening, and a ruddy sun dipped peacefully behind the Matterhorn. It was the first fine-weather sunset that we had witnessed during our tour, and I stood on the terrace outside the hut conversing with one of the Swiss who hoped to climb the Young ridge. He and his companion were also going to the Schwarzthor on the morrow, and from that pass to the Breithorn, carrying the short ski which were to be left on the summit. He was a keen photographer, and waxed enthusiastic on the beauty of the view down the Gorner glacier towards the Matterhorn and the Dent Blanche, which stood out in sharp relief against the pale green of the sunset sky.

We were up betimes the following morning, but it was fully two hours before we left the hut, this being due in part to having to wait our turn at the cooking stove.

Pink sunrise was lighting the Matterhorn as we skidded and bumped over the frozen tracks down to the glacier. The atmosphere was frostily still, but on high, little tufts of wind-blown snow still clung to the ridges, small flames that quickly changed to a white heat in the risen sun.

We had reduced our loads somewhat by leaving a day's provisions at the hut, yet rucksacks always seem unduly heavy on these occasions. In summer, comparatively little is needed in the matter of clothing and equipment, but in winter, apart from ski, seal-skins, ice axes, rope, crampons and provisions, heavier and warmer clothing than is necessary in summer must be taken. Then there are various additional items such as ski wax, a spare ski tip and perhaps a spare strap for the ski binding. Individual items may be trivial, but they mount up to a formidable weight in aggregate. Few mountaineers and ski-ers make an intensive study of weight. It is astonishing what can be done with materials such as Shetland wool, silk, aluminium, nylon and plastic.

For perhaps a mile we descended the gently inclined glacier, then turned southwards up the buttress which separates the Schwärze glacier from the Zwillings glacier. The former glacier leads to the Schwarzthor. It is ragged with formidable crevasses and ice-falls, but the lower portion is conveniently avoided by following the buttress. Where this merges with the glacier an ice-fall must be negotiated. Above this an unbroken snow-slope leads to the col.

We had already examined the route from a distance, but any difficulty in route-finding over the buttress had been obviated by the Swiss party who had already ascended as far as the ice-fall with the object of examining the Young ridge which forms the west retaining wall of the Schwärze glacier.

At the foot of the buttress we halted to put on seal-skins, always a detestable business on a cold morning.

Then came the buttress on which we had merely to follow the tracks of our predecessors. It was an invigorating ascent and set the sluggish blood coursing. Wind was blowing higher up, as we could note from a certain fuzziness which invested the ridges, but in every other respect the day was perfect, the sky being cloudless and the peaks shining with a new-found brilliance. Here was the weather we had for so long hoped, and the thought set us tacking up the slopes at a rate of knots. What a difference good weather can make to an Alpine holiday. It banishes doubt and indecision, and promotes that superlative *joie de vivre* of which the mountains are such generous givers.

The buttress petered out into a gently sloping bay of the glacier. Ahead and slightly to the left the symmetrical snow-peak of Pollux rose from a tangle of ice. Was ever a pair of peaks more aptly named than the Heavenly Twins? Trim, neat and elegant, they stand between their massive neighbours the Breithorn and Lyskamm, beautiful incidentals of mountains.

A level traverse brought us on to the glacier at the foot of the ice-fall. Ice-falls have a knack of appearing much more difficult and complicated than they really are, especially when viewed from afar. This was no exception. The tracks we had been following had ascended no farther than the traverse on to the glacier, but the way through the séracs was obvious enough, first an upward traverse to the right, then a tack back to the left.

Some bulky blocks of ice, weighing, I suppose, some hundreds of tons apiece, leaned menacingly over the lower part of the route, but we were soon past them. A little higher we halted to tie on the rope. While we were engaged in this one of the two parties who had been following overtook us and went ahead. This consisted of a guided party of three; the two Swiss who had designs on the Young ridge brought up the rear.

Above the ice-fall it was plain sailing towards the pass, which now appeared deceptively close. The wind was strong here, and as we climbed grew steadily stronger.

The Schwarzthor is a pass as interesting as it is obvious. On one hand are the steep snow-slopes of Pollux and on the other the red precipices of the Breithorn. The wind blew violently across it, raising clouds of snow, which it frog-marched along the slopes in a succession of whirling spirals. It came from the north, an indication of fair weather, but it was bitterly cold, and seemed to pass playfully into us at one side and out at the other.

It was a relief when at length we reached the pass, where without further ado we turned right to seek shelter under the rocks of the Breithorn. The change which took place in a matter of seconds was magical. One moment we were struggling along buffeted by the cold devils of a Tibetan hell, the next we were in a complete calm through which the sun smote with a tropical intensity.

The guided party were seated against the rocks leisurely consuming their second breakfast. We joined them and set to work to lessen the weight of our own rucksacks. Five minutes earlier I had been wriggling my toes and fingers to prevent loss of circulation, now I was seriously considering how much clothing I might conveniently remove.

For the first time we became fully conscious of the day's perfection, perfection that is outside the province of the wind. There was literally not a cloud to be seen in the panorama now outspread before us. Steeply from our feet the glaciers plunged down into Italy, and beyond, range after range of peaks lay glowing in the morning sun.

The guided party presently continued on their way. For some time after they had departed we continued to sit basking in the sun. Meanwhile the remaining two Swiss arrived, and when at length we mustered up sufficient energy to get started we left them sunning themselves. I heard subsequently from one of them that they were unable to make an attempt on the Young ridge owing to unfavourable snow conditions.

We followed the guided party's tracks—there seemed no point in doing anything else—but presently came to the conclusion that, left to our own devices, we would have made both an easier and safer route across the southern flanks of the Breithorn. Not only did they keep unnecessarily high over steep, icy ground, on which it was fatiguing continually to edge the ski, but they traversed unpleasantly close to some unstable séracs, some of which had already fallen across the route.

Meanwhile, the sun did its best to grill us against the glaring snow-slopes. My eyes were stinging and bleary from the sweat that poured into them. Whatever my weight may have been at the commencement of the traverse it was appreciably less at the end.

Up and down we went, round many corners, and across hollows where we could feel, even if we could not hear, ourselves frizzling. And all the while Italy, its infinitude of ranges, peaks and valleys, lay at our feet.

Over the Breithorn pass on to the Breithorn plateau we ski-ed; the last is an almost level field of *névé* with that cheeky little parody the Klein Matterhorn and the massive ridge of the Breithorn rising from the northern end.

We caught up with the guided party, but kept politely in the rear. Yet another party was on the mountain, at least three members of it were; the fourth had ensconced himself in the snow at the foot of the final slopes. There seemed no particular reason why he should not accompany his companions until we passed him, when we observed that he was an Italian, and had made himself thoroughly comfortable both without and within, the last with the aid of a bottle of formidable dimensions kept conveniently at hand.

Climbing very slowly, so as to give those ahead plenty of opportunities to do the step-cutting and track-making, we mounted to the point at which it is usual to discard ski and proceed on foot. Here we dawdled awhile in the sun, while the leading party of Italians performed prodigies of valour on the slopes above, where they had to cut about a dozen steps, each one of which occasioned a considerable commotion and chattering.

This work completed, the second party with ourselves

following walked up, without bothering to rope, in the steps thus bountifully provided, and in due course reached the summit, which we were glad to have to ourselves, the Italians having promptly descended, possibly apprehensive that, unless they did, nothing would be found remaining of the refreshments left with their companion. The Swiss party had also left. Most guides have a rooted objection to remaining for any length of time on the summit of a mountain, and like to hustle their employers down with all possible expedition. We were thus enabled to enjoy a prospect unalloyed by the presence of our fellow-men. This may sound an ungenerous statement, but not where Italians are concerned, since this race is incapable of any form of restful meditation either on or off a mountain, and must needs jabber at all hours of the day and night.

The north wind was blowing across the summit, not with anything like its old force and viciousness, but with a shrewishness sufficient to prevent a prolonged halt. Furthermore, the afternoon was now well advanced, and we had a long descent before us. For these reasons we spent no more than ten minutes in contemplating the view. But what a ten minutes and what a view!

There was not a cloud, not a single shred of vapour in the firmament. Not only was a large portion of the Alps outspread before us, but a considerable slice of the map of Europe. Mont Blanc, 52 miles away, seemed close at hand, and in between were the well-remembered forms of many a friend, the Combin, the peaks of Arolla and the immediate giants, the Matterhorn, Dent Blanche and Weisshorn. The Oberland dominated the north, and to the east past Mont Rosa, which cut out a considerable segment of the view, was a glimpse towards the multitudinous ridges of the Central Alps.

But it was to the south and south-east that the eye most frequently turned where, far beyond the deep trench of the Val d'Aosta and the snowy summits of the Grivola and Grand Paradis, the noble peak of Monte Viso, 115 miles away, rose sharp and distinct with the blue line of the Ligurian Alps clearly discernible beyond and slightly to the east.

Close beneath were the sunny expanses of the Breithorn plateau, and beyond them the Théodule pass with its collection of unlovely huts and houses. From this height and direction the peaks of Monte Rosa, which appear so squat and shapeless when viewed from the Riffelalp or Gornergrat, are seen in their true proportion, soaring grandly above the torrents of ice and snow at their feet.

Reluctantly we turned away to be hustled off the top by the wind. We were soon out of the latter, and as we descended the icy little slope below the ridge I was conscious, even more than I had been on the summit, of the scope and extent of the tremendous southward panorama. Treading that snow-slope was like treading the snow-covered roof of the highest building in a city, and of seeing beneath thousands of other roofs extending as far as the eye could travel.

There was not so much a sensation of height as a sense of utter remoteness. Even the necessity for care in the icy section could not dispel a detached dreamy feeling which I have long associated with high mountains in winter. It was very quiet; the wind no longer pestered; a thousand glowing summits slept in the warm afternoon sun. In one sense they were substantial; so brilliant was the atmosphere that the details of each peak up to 100 miles distant could be picked out. But in another sense they were unsubstantial, since they were beyond comprehension, computation and memory. Over them through blue space the eye roamed and roamed, yet saw only mountains. Views such as this are not for men but gods.

We rejoined our ski, then sped down to the plateau.

Across this we loitered, poling gently. Then, where the *névé* bent over towards the Théodule pass, the descent, so famous among ski-ers, began.

The snow was in a queer state. It had been eroded by the wind into mushroom-like plates that projected several inches above the general level. At first there seemed a danger that the ski would drive in beneath these plates, which would have meant a nasty fall, but in practice the bend of the tip was sufficient to keep them on the surface. It was better not to run too slowly, or the ski tipped forward into the gap between the plates. This surface was perfectly consistent, and over it we rattled and bumped with merry abandon.

As we neared the Théodule pass we saw some Italian frontier guards. Before the war the arrogance and pomposity of these passed belief. Dolled up with gold braid, plumes and feathers, they strutted about like performers in some Gilbert and Sullivan opera. Indeed, one never knew whether they were admirals, field-marshals or marshals of the air. And if there was a safe excuse, and a safe distance, they would even fire on the unsuspecting traveller. Now, however, like pricked balloons, they were patently anxious to ingratiate themselves with any stranger who chanced along, and ready to discuss, not the omnipotence of Mussolini and the Fascist Empire, but subjects on which they were better informed, such as ice-cream, opera and performing monkeys.

We were glad to leave the Théodule pass. With its dreary buildings, ranges of barracks, filth and garbage, it is the most depressing of all Alpine passes.

The plate-like snow continued for some hundreds of feet below the pass, then, at the junction of the Unter and Ober Théodule glaciers, we came suddenly to a smooth floor of perfect powder.

The route bifurcates here, one arm descending directly to Zermatt by way of the Gandegg hut and the Schafberg, the other crossing the Furgg glacier beneath the Matterhorn and descending to the Schwarzsee, whence the first route may be rejoined, or a roundabout descent to Zermatt made via the Staffelalp. Of these alternatives the Furgg glacier–Staffelalp route is by far the best.

The afternoon was lengthening when we paused for a bite of food. Our old enemy the wind had long since given up the pursuit, and we stood in an area of complete calm. All about us the powdery snow stretched sparkling and scintillating in the brilliant sunlight. Such snow is far removed from the heavy, clammy substance of our British clime. It is light and dry. Pick up a handful, and it will pour glittering through the fingers. It is so full of light that you find yourself looking into its subtle texture, built up of an infinite number of spiculate crystals, and marvelling at its gem-like beauty.

Away from us stretched this snow in great fields, lifting and sinking in wide and spacious undulations. It was beautiful, that snow. There was about it a strange compelling quality. You wanted to dive into it, feel its cold caress, immerse yourself in its subtle beauty. And yet it can kill you. Slowly, stealthily, painlessly, it can drain away your warmth and your life. Then, ever so gently, will it cover you. It is beautiful but deadly, not maliciously deadly, but deadly because it is the absolute negation of life, the visible embodiment of space and eternity. Its fascination to the ski-er and the mountaineer lies in the joy of treading it and sliding over it, of becoming absorbed in its beauty, its purity and its silence. To descend a great snow-field on ski is to live more absolutely, more intensely, than is possible in any sport I know.

Over this snow we ski-ed beneath the Matterhorn. I remember a great shadow. One moment I was drifting over the sunlit snow, the next I was in the shadow. Through this shadow I continued drifting, scarcely conscious of volition. Then I was out of it in the sun, with a cold air against my face, and in my ear the whispering rush of ski. It was not until then that I realised I had passed through the shadow of the Matterhorn, and that the great peak was moving, its ridges, buttresses and precipices changing shape and position with a slow and measured precision.

I swung to a standstill, and the loose, dry snow rose in a scintillating cloud. The Matterhorn no longer moved; the world was stationary again and I with it. There were the slopes down which we had come, with our thin ski tracks drawn delicately across them in clean sweeping strokes. And beyond was the Breithorn remote in the afternoon blue. There was no sound, and the immense frozen pile of the Matterhorn emphasised the profound silence.

From the tongue of the Furgg glacier we passed under the Hörnli, then ran down a broad, steep gully to the Schwarzsee. The snow was not so good here as it had been on the glacier, but I daresay in any other circumstances we should have considered it first-rate; we had tasted perfection on that glorious descent across the Furgg glacier in the shadow of the Matterhorn.

Next came the descent over the open alp to the Staffelwald and the Staffelalp. The hot sun was beginning to affect the powdery nature of the snow, which was in the transition stage between winter and spring. Nevertheless, it was a fine run, and by avoiding the sunnier slopes we enjoyed some magnificent ski-ing.

Down we went through the scattered trees to the clustered hay huts of Staffelalp. The sunlight was fast mellowing now, and in its light the beautiful little alp, with its half-buried huts, set beneath the enormous crags of the Matterhorn, seemed to embody the very spirit of Switzerland.

I took some photographs, but whatever else a camera

Schwarzthor

Monte Rosa from
the summit
of the Breithorn

can do, it cannot capture such a scene, the subtleties of light and shadow, the glowing loads of luminescent snow on the weathered huts and the delicacies of its surface and texture.

Above the pines the Matterhorn lifted duskily blue through the delicate breadths of sun-drenched atmosphere. All was light. That day we had lived in light, skimmed over light, almost it seemed breathed light, and now that light was ebbing, and the shadows were gathering amongst the tall trees.

With our backs to the warm timbers of a hut we ate the remainder of our food, then clipping on our ski set off on the last stage of the descent.

Many others had descended by this route to Zermatt, and we had merely to follow a deep groove in the snow. This is the kind of ski-ing I normally avoid, but that evening I enjoyed the run to Zermatt. It was more like tobogganing than ski-ing; one let oneself shoot down the groove, and at speed; the rest was Kismet.

It required a degree of concentration, that run. In places the track switch-backed violently, in others it passed along the edges of ugly little drops; at some of the corners it was easy to leave the track altogether and, helped by centrifugal force, plunge down the slope into the trees. There was no time to look at the scenery, but I stopped once to photograph the little village of Zmutt on its snowy shoulder across the valley, with the glowing peaks of the Mischabel in the background.

For the rest it was down, down, down, the fast-freezing snow harsh now beneath the skidding ski. Down to Zermatt.

On the map this trip is not very impressive, an ascent of 5,000 feet in 5 miles and a descent of 8,000 feet in 12 miles. Double the miles and this gives a truer value. Few ski-ers can grumble at 20 miles of downhill ski-ing, and I doubt whether there is a finer descent in the Alps than that from the Breithorn via Staffelalp to Zermatt. There may be longer descents, such as that from the Jungfraujoch or the Ebnefluh to the Rhone Valley, but most involve a good deal of poling. On the Breithorn run there is practically no poling, while for scenic beauty the route is unsurpassed. In summer the ascent of this mountain is a long and tedious slog; in winter and spring it is one of the world's great ski-ing expeditions.

Zermatt. Once again we were bathed and respectable, well fed and relaxed. The good Rhone wine coursed warmly in our veins, but not so warmly as the memories of a wonderful day on the mountains.

CHAPTER X

L'HAUTE ROUTE

THE day after our traverse of the Breithorn was brilliantly fine, and it was evident that both weather and snow conditions were now ideal for the high-level route from Zermatt to Verbiers, on which we had for so long set our hearts. Unhappily Jimmy Belaieff had been attacked by snow blindness after descending from the Breithorn without dark glasses, and it appeared that the expedition might have to be postponed, or even cancelled altogether, as he had but four days remaining of his holidays. Snow blindness, as I know from personal experience, is exceedingly painful, but he was bravely determined to overcome his disability, and the start was accordingly fixed for the following day.

Meanwhile, it was arranged that an hotel in Arolla, which is normally reached on the second day, should be opened to receive us, and also to supply us with a further two days' provisions. Arolla is closed in winter, and the ski-er, unless he carries sufficient food for the whole traverse, must descend to Haudères, which entails the loss of a day. In our case, we were both of us determined to travel as light as possible, and not carry more kit than was absolutely necessary under the broiling March sun.

The following morning, March 20th, my companion's eyes were still very painful, but his determination to leave Zermatt was unshaken, and shortly after lunch we shouldered our rucksacks and set off for the Schönbühl hut, the first stage of our journey.

The weather was as fine as ever, but we were scarcely in a position to appreciate it. So bad were Belaieff's eyes that he could not open them fully to see ahead, and on the path up the Zmutt valley he had to follow close behind me in order to avoid stepping off the edge. The sun, moreover, burned down with a fierceness which, while materially reducing our weight, seemed substantially to increase that of our rucksacks.

We passed through the deserted village of Zmutt, then, crossing to the other side of the valley, joined the track by which we had descended two days previously from the Staffelalp.

Ascending this track was analogous to ascending a narrow ice gully raked with falling stones, for every now and then ski-ers came flying down it, and we had to leap aside out of their way. Our expedition nearly came to a premature end at one point. I had hastily given way to a ski-er, but as he passed the basket of one of his sticks caught on the point of my right ski. Instantly my ski with my foot and leg was dragged violently round, and I was flung on to my back facing away from the direction of the pull. There seemed a strong chance of my leg breaking, as the owner of the ski stick was unable to leave go of it as it was attached to his wrist by the usual leather thong. Luckily, however, he was not only an expert runner but going comparatively slowly, and was able to stop just when it seemed that nothing could save my leg.

Owing to our late start, evening was drawing on as we passed Staffelalp, and it was evident that we would be lucky if we reached the hut before nightfall. From the alp we climbed a little, then traversed horizontally on to the Zmutt glacier. The summer path to the hut follows the side moraines to the north of the glacier, but in winter it is best to keep along the south side. The glacier in summer is a dreary affair of moraines and rubbly ice, but in winter it becomes a white expanse in abrupt contrast to the enormous crags of the Matterhorn. Everyone knows the appearance of this peak from Zermatt and the Riffel, from which directions it is seen at its sharpest and most elegant, but fewer travellers see it from other angles. From Breuil in Italy it is Roman in massiveness and rises in a succession of precipices and buttresses. From the west its sharply pointed summit, firmly buttressed by the Pic Tyndall, has about it the airy touch of the Gothic. From the north, however, it is not so easily described. When travelling amongst far ranges the mountaineer frequently discovers mountains whose shapes and profiles are suggestive of those he knows so well in the Alps, but I have never seen a profile even faintly reminiscent of the Matterhorn as viewed from the Zmutt glacier. Perhaps the aptest comparison is that of a great ocean wave with its crest curling over in the act of breaking. The lowermost slope of the roller is formed by the long and slowly steepening sweep of the Zermatt ridge, and the curling crest by the precipice that falls from the summit of the mountain to the east. To the north-west the mountain bends over in a beautiful volute to form the fearsome overhanging precipice known as the Nose of Zmutt, which is buttressed in its turn by the sickle-like fall of the Zmutt ridge.

Elegance, massiveness, beauty, none of the ordinary descriptive terms is individually applicable to this view of the mountain. One does not study either profile or angle as one does with normal mountains, and this is because the Matterhorn viewed thus is so abnormal as to dam the normal channels whereby analytical thought seeks to interpret the physical images presented to it. In much the same way an outstanding personality is remembered for his personality and not for his physical form and profile. The Matterhorn when seen from the lower-most portion of the Zmutt glacier can only be described as a monstrous brooding presence.

Fear of mountains no longer exists in Alpine valleys. The dragons have vanished, the ghosts have been laid and the spirits of the damned departed long since. Yet even to-day, when the mountain has for a generation been " an easy day for a lady," he who stands on the Zmutt glacier and gazes up at that fantastic form menacing the heavens will be both unimaginative and strong-willed if he cannot sense the awe with which his forefathers gazed on its extraordinary profile. He knows that it has been mapped and measured, that every side, even the terrible northern precipice immediately above him, has been trodden. He is aware of the geological processes that went to the making of it, and of the forces of destruction that are slowly but inevitably reducing it to ruins. He will know these things, and yet " . . . ages hence generations unborn will gaze upon its awful precipices and wonder at its unique form."

Night fell as we mounted the glacier. Very slowly objects on either hand changed position. We could see the hut perched above the glacier, but toil as hard and as quickly as we could, it never seemed to grow from that first original dot.

On the glacier were the tracks of a former party, and these we assiduously followed until at length, and erroneously as it proved, we suspected that they did not go to the hut at all, but directly to the Col de Valpelline, our morrow's objective. So after apostrophising them, in order to strengthen our own case, we left them and cut diagonally across the glacier towards the promontory on which stands the hut.

It was dark now. The peaks had flamed and gone out, and there remained but the faintest of pale afterglows. Up and down we climbed over a series of humps, in which all glaciers abound at night, and at long last came to the foot of the slopes westward of the hut. And there. of course, we rejoined the track we had previously followed; it had traversed leisurely round under the Stockjé, thus avoiding the humps we had so laboriously traversed.

A steep slope of crusted snow, a grope over the level, and the dark shape of the hut loomed before us.

Mountaineers will remember the old Schönbühl hut with affection as a starting-point for several fine expeditions, including the Dent Blanche and the Zmutt ridge of the Matterhorn, but it was never a comfortable hut and often grossly overcrowded. The new hut seems to get over these disadvantages to some extent, but I doubt whether it and many other Alpine huts will be able to cope with the rapidly increasing number of mountaineers. The trouble with the Swiss Alpine Club hut is that it is a compromise between the amenities of an hotel and the inconveniences of bivouacking and camping. The mountain hotel system of the German and Austrian Alpine Club in the Eastern Alps is far to be preferred. The mountaineer has hotel facilities on a simple scale, including meals, or he can live inexpensively in a common room and maintain himself off his own food. In summer, hut keepers occupy most of the Swiss Alpine Club huts. They assist in cooking the climbers' food, and in general look after the huts. This again is merely a compromise. The present system has served its purpose, and the time is fast approaching when a drastic revision will be necessary. The mountain hotel, with the present huts retained as overflow annexes, is the undoubted solution to the problem in the more populous areas.

It was nearly midnight by the time we had finished our supper. Before turning in to our blankets we went outside for a look at the weather. The moon was rising in a clear sky. Its rays were stealing along the level reaches of the Zmutt glacier. Opposite, the enormous Matterhorn reached darkly into the stars. Sound there was none, except that now and then the glacier at our feet creaked uneasily, and once there was a sudden sharp snap as a crevasse opened. The air was still and keen.

To-morrow the snow would be hard-frozen, and we should mount rapidly to the Col de Valpelline.

We slept comfortably for a few hours, then rose and breakfasted in the dark. I must confess that I am never at my best on these occasions, but Belaieff, despite his eyes which, although better, were still painful, insisted as usual on cooking an excellent breakfast, and what a difference this makes to morale in the small hours! Yet such is my detestation of an early start, that when we set off in the first wan light, I found myself looking at the Matterhorn with no more interest than I would have found in a milk-cart at this hour.

The snow had frozen hard in the overnight frost, and we carried our ski down the slopes to the glacier. Such is human nature that it is always a cause for satisfaction to improve on the other man's route on a mountain. When therefore we contoured round the moraines close under the Stockjé, instead of following the tracks of the former party, and found that by so doing we saved an appreciable amount of climbing, we felt in better humour with ourselves. It was evident, however, that the weather had little intention of reciprocating these feelings. Already grey clouds, with here and there lengths of smooth, zeppelin-shaped mist, were gathering, and when at length the sun rose behind the Zmutt ridge of the Matterhorn, the scene, if not ominous, was scarcely one over which to cheer and rejoice. Thus, it was with a very qualified optimism that we began the ascent to the Col de Valpelline.

To begin with, the route led us into the impressive glacier cirque which is bounded by the Stockjé, the Tête de Valpelline, the Dent d'Hérens and the Matterhorn. One arm of this cirque leads up to the Tiefenmattenjoch, and the other is filled by the Tiefenmatten glacier, which lies directly under the west face of the Matterhorn and the Col du Lion. There may be higher and wider

Alpine cirques, but none that boast of a more formidable combination of precipice, ice-slope, couloir and hanging glacier than the horseshoe enclosing the head of the Tiefenmatten glacier, which begins with the Zmutt ridge of the Matterhorn, and ends with the great ice-face of the Dent d'Hérens. It is a gloomy place, where the thunder of falling ice from the Dent d'Hérens is answered by the crash of stones from the Matterhorn, a duet loud enough to appal the stoutest hearted traveller.

To reach the Stock glacier we had to climb some steep snow-slopes between the Stockjé and the Tête de Valpelline. The snow was hard-frozen and edging the ski fatiguing, but otherwise there was no difficulty, and once on the Stock glacier it was nothing but a straightforward trudge to the Col de Valpelline.

Someone once separated passes into two categories, good passes and bad passes. A good pass is one with a well-defined crest which withholds the view of the far side until the last moment. The bad pass has an ill-defined and indeterminate crest, and the view is so slowly unfolded that there is little satisfaction in crossing it.

The Col de Valpelline belongs to the latter category. It is one of those aggravating passes with a number of false crests. Each fresh rise in the glacier is hailed as the pass, but on attaining it another and higher rise is seen beyond. Any original optimism therefore undergoes a steady deterioration, so that when the actual pass is reached any fine feeling of derring-do or mountain adventure has long since been extinguished and replaced by a mordant cynicism. Thus, the view, if any, awakes no response other than a faint dislike, and is instantly dismissed as being of far less importance than an immediate ministering to the needs of the inner man, who has in all probability been grossly neglected on the interminable snow-slopes.

It is probable that I do the Col de Valpelline an injustice, for on examining my photographs I find that not only is there a view from the pass but rather a good one. The Dent Blanche is pleasing and the Weisshorn is quite its graceful and spectacular self. Unhappily, both the lighting of the scene and the development of the film leave much to be desired, and the ensemble as a result suggests a scene in the Manchester area rather than one in the high Alps.

There is no question that a dull sky, and a cold wind which had dogged our footsteps with the bulldog tenacity of an Inspector Lestrade, had much to do with a certain mutual disgruntlement. To begin with, we endeavoured to escape from the wind on the lee slope of the col. Here I was incautious enough to remove my ski and make myself comfortable in preparation for lunch. But the wind was still on our tracks, and without further ado poured its cold vials on us, seizing the loose snow and malevolently thrusting it down our necks. Belaieff said (it came to the same thing): " I commit this obstreperous element to the uttermost depths of the flaming and nethermost underworld. I am going down."

And down he went, leaving me to shovel hastily in such food as I could with numbed fingers, pack up, and presently join him on that glacier, 1,000 feet beneath, which goes by the curious name of Haut Glacier de Tza de Tzan.

So far we had seen little of the sun, which had been struggling weakly with a grey vapour overspreading the sky. Neither of us had liked the weather; it was in sullen mood, and a sullen mood where mountains are concerned is all too liable to end in an explosion. This occasion was an exception, and as we swung down and out on to the uppermost bay of the glacier under the tottering séracs of the Col de Bouquetins, the scowl peeled off the sky as though by magic, and the sun poured its radiance over the snow.

What a queer yet beautiful little glacier is the Tza de Tzan. Its uppermost limit under the rocks of the Dents des Bouquetins forms one of the smoothest and most secluded little snow-fields imaginable, yet a few yards away it falls in a savage torrent of shattered ice. Beyond is the range culminating in the Jumeaux and the blue distances of Italy.

At its southernmost extremity the snow-field rises gently to the Col du Mont Brulé, which is next door to the Col de Tza de Tzan. Both passes link Italy with Switzerland, and the portion of the traverse between the Col de Valpelline and the Col du Mont Brulé lies over Italian territory. It was pleasant to be able to ski here without being molested or shot at by Italian Fascists.

Before setting off on the run down to Arolla we paused on the Col du Mont Brulé for another meal. This, I need hardly mention, was the signal for an immediate disappearance of the sun behind a high bank of fast-moving cloud, and a renewed onset of the wind, which must have trailed us the whole way from the Col de Valpelline.

I had hoped for some photographs, especially as the Arolla country was unfamiliar, but this was out of the question, since Mont Collon and l'Évèque, the principal objects in view from the col, resembled nothing more interesting than rather dirty and ragged bits of cardboard silhouetted against an even dirtier sky. There was no incentive to wait, and having gobbled our food we clipped on our ski and slid off on the last stage of the day's journey.

The distance on the map from the Col du Mont Brulé to the end of the Arolla glacier is a little over 5 miles and the descent about 4,600 feet. It took us thirty-five minutes to cover this distance. This is not fast going; on the contrary, it is slow and well below the speed an average ski runner should be able to accomplish. For one thing, the steep slopes from the col to the glacier were in poor condition, the snow being disagreeably crusted, and the time taken to descend them was disproportionate to the whole. For another, the light was so poor on the glacier that we had to run with care. The snow also cannot be described as perfect all the way. Yet these figures do give some idea of what I firmly believe to be one of the finest straight ski runs in the Swiss Alps.

The slopes below the Col du Mont Brulé are very steep, and the snow, as already mentioned, was in poor shape. Belaieff, ever a bold and skilful runner, essayed successfully several spectacular downhill turns. As for me, on crusted snow at a high angle I am well content to make kick turns at the ends of each traverse, the traverses being as long as I can make them. Thus he was on the glacier 1,500 feet below the col several minutes before I was.

Thus far, there was nothing especially enjoyable in the ski-ing. Once on the Arolla glacier, however, we found well-nigh perfect snow. Neither of us had previously descended this glacier and the poor light made caution imperative. Presently, however, we came upon some old tracks, and these we were able to follow in one continuous swoop to the end of the glacier.

For long, long stretches it was difficult to estimate speed. As with the run down the Furgg glacier, movement was measured, not so much by the physical sensation of speed as by the time in which objects on either hand changed their position. It is a long slog from Arolla to the Col du Mont Brulé, and I can well imagine the weary time it must take to pass Mont Collon. Now, as we ran, we saw that mountain to the left steadily approaching, its cliffs and gullies growing in size every instant. Then those cliffs and gullies were passing one after another like the folds of a curtain. Soon they had all passed, and in a matter of a few minutes the peak was behind.

The trouble with high Alpine ski-ing is that it ruins the mountaineer for those long glacier trudges which are an inevitable feature of summer mountaineering in high ranges. There are many excellent rock and ice climbs to be made from Arolla where ski at any time would be of little use. This applies to most mountain ranges. But where long glacier walks are concerned, I never hope to have to do them again except on ski, for once you have tasted the magic of ski-ing on the high snows you are ruined for foot-slogging over them.

On the level, where the first stunted pines struggle out of the terminal moraine, we ran to a standstill. So also did everything about us. It was as though a film had suddenly jammed and scene and players were frozen still in a single instant. We became aware that the sun was shining and that somewhere far back we had emerged from beneath the clouds. The air which had continuously pressed against our faces or drummed in our ears did so no longer, and the snow no longer swished beneath our ski. These sounds had ceased and had been replaced by an instantaneous silence, coupled with an absolute stillness and lack of movement in every object around. Such are always my first impressions after a long, fast run on ski.

A few hundred yards away was Arolla, and we poled leisurely towards it over the snow, then through a larch forest. Everything seemed curiously flat and dead under the staring sun, and so too did Arolla when we reached it, its well-known hotel being shuttered and forlorn with streams of snow water pouring off the roof.

Two Swiss frontier guards advanced to meet us, and to them we tendered evidence as to our identity. Satisfied that we were harmless Englishmen, and not Italian smugglers, they accompanied us to the small hotel which had been opened for us.

En route to the hotel we had to pass between two chalets set close together, on the roofs of which sodden snow lay some six feet deep. A minute later the snow on one building suddenly and without warning quietly slid off in a mass that must have weighed several tons. It would have done us serious injury at the very least had it struck us. What a Gilbertian ending to a high-level glacier tour to be killed or injured by an avalanche from a house-top!

Two youths had come up from Haudères to reopen one of the smaller hotels. They were helpful and friendly. Both qualities are golden, but in this case literally so, as next morning, for some simple meals, and still simpler amenities, together with two days' provisions, we had to foot a thumping bill, the largest I have ever paid for goods and services anywhere in Switzerland.

A well-known Swiss professional photographer, his friend and a guide were present overnight. He was photographing scenes and places for a new series of picture postcards. Our talk turned to the art of mountain photography, and it soon became apparent that, like film producers, politicians and captains of ocean-going liners, he had a profound contempt for the public to which he was ministering. "People who come to Switzerland," he said, "don't want artistic pictures; they aren't interested in cloud effects, in skilful compositions or the light in the snow; they want to see things as *they* see them, just mountains, and to be able to put a cross against their hotel window." In this way was explained to me something that has always puzzled me—the artistic mediocrity of picture postcards.

Neither Belaieff nor I had been to Arolla before. Once upon a time it must have been a delightfully unsophisticated little place. Those were the days when an elderly member of the Alpine Club went up to a newly arrived guest who had incautiously descended to the salle à manger clad in a dinner jacket and remarked: "You appear unaware, sir, that dinner jackets are NOT worn in Arolla." I fear that such days no longer hold good; not that there appears any particular objection as to a guest wearing what he pleases at any hotel under the sun, and that Arolla is likely to share the same fate as most other Alpine resorts. It is, however, still delightful, and the surrounding mountains have yet to be equipped with funicular railways and ski lifts.

March 22nd saw us away in the first light bound for the Cabane du Val des Dix, which hut is reached from Arolla over the pass known as the Pas de Chèvres.

The ski route marked in our otherwise impeccable map proceeds north-west from Arolla, then bends south-west across the alp marked L'Arolla before traversing into the valley that descends from the Pas de Chèvres to the east. The obvious route, on the other hand, is to follow the valley already mentioned all the way from Arolla.

As a result of following the map route, we became involved in sundry steep climbs and traverses on an unpleasant mixture of icy crust and deep powdery snow. We blamed the map bitterly and vehemently, and for once with some justification, for when after a long and fatiguing traverse we found ourselves in the valley it was to meet with old ski tracks that had ascended directly from Arolla with no difficulty or fuss whatsoever. In this connection I should like to pay a tribute to the excellence of the 1:50,000 map of the Service Topographique Fédéral, Berne, which covers some of the most difficult and complicated country in Switzerland with great accuracy. At the same time, it is not invariably accurate in detail, and the ski mountaineer is well advised to study the remarks Monsieur Marcel Kurz has to make in his admirable guide book on ski-ing in the Valais. If anything, the map errs on the pessimistic side, and its crowded contours in some places present a false impression of the terrain.

As a result of the time lost on this needless deviation, we had to climb the long snow-slopes to the Pas de Chèvres beneath one of the most grilling suns I ever remember. In *Scrambles Amongst the Alps* Whymper describes how a Chamonix porter who had appropriated the food entrusted to him was made to lard the glacier by his emptier and lighter companions. I can only say that a very similar process attended our ascent to the Pas de Chèvres.

What a pleasant and even humorous theme such an ascent makes in retrospect, and how difficult it is to remember all those trifling details so unimportant now, yet so important then. The particular shape of a particular fragment of snow, an ordinary rock which becomes a leering profile, that tedious song or banal jargon that refuses to be silenced in the mind, the recollection of feeble, meaningless little incidents that have no bearing whatsoever on the job in hand, that momentary indecision as to whether the upward-sliding ski shall go a little more or less of an angle, and a thousand things more. To climb a long, hot and fatiguing slope on a mountain is to realise the greatness of the small and the smallness of the great.

On the pass at last we slid our heavy rucksacks off our backs, mopped the sweat from our eyes and gazed languidly across the smooth surface of the Glacier de Seilon to the Cabane du Val des Dix perched on a promontory, then to the left, and up the thin, rocky edges of the graceful Mont Blanc de Seilon. What a ski-ing country! The hut rose from the midst of beautiful and extensive snow-fields culminating in the flowing summit of La Louette.

The Dent Blanche
from the
Furgg Glacier

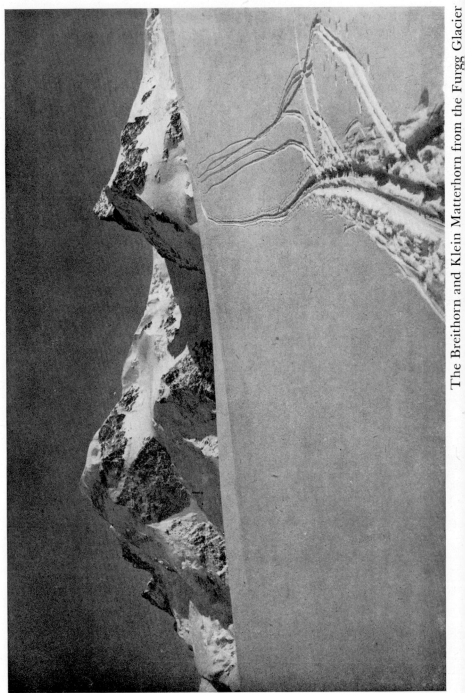

The Breithorn and Klein Matterhorn from the Furgg Glacier

[18

But we were in no mood to linger; a cold little wind was licking past the col, and I for one was soaked with sweat. The hut was but a half-hour distant, and already our thoughts were centred on tea, gallons of tea.

As might be suspected from its name, the Pas de Chèvres is not, or was not when so named, an easy snow pass. To the west a sheer little rock cliff some 100 feet high falls to the Glacier de Seilon. In its natural state this must have afforded a pretty little climb, but authorities other than the mountain gods have decreed that an iron ladder should be placed to assist the traveller.

In the past I must confess to an irrational fanaticism in many things, and purism in mountaineering was one. By purism I mean climbing without artificial aids other than nailed boots, crampons, and an ice axe and rope. Like many more, I have long looked askance at the extensive use of pitons and of making climbs by their aid. I am also at variance with those logicians who falsely argue that because one thing is justifiable then so is another. It is necessary in every field of human activity to know where to draw the line. The same strictures apply to permanent fixtures on mountains to assist the climber. Many routes in the Eastern Alps have been ruined by lines of hand grips, pitons and ladders. At the same time my purism suffered contamination at a very early stage. There was, for instance, a piton in the Dolomites at the top of one of the most exposed walls I have ever scaled, and knowing that it was necessary to descend by the same route, I own to a positive thankfulness at sight of it. Then there are the fixed ropes on the Matterhorn; it is a solid satisfaction to handle them when time is pressing and a blizzard blowing. There is no doubt also as to the safety value of pitons on the crumbling limestone of the Canadian Rockies, where sound belays are often non-existent.

A.S.—13

As for the ladder on the Pas de Chèvres, no one but a fanatic could find anything to object to in it, for it is both comforting and helpful. Without it the rock cliff would become an awkward problem, and what is the point of awkward problems of this nature on an otherwise excellent ski route? If, however, someone was to substitute a railway for the ropes on the Matterhorn I, for one, would object bitterly. It is, as already stated, a matter of knowing where to draw the line.

I descended the ladder and Belaieff let down our goods and chattels on the end of a rope. Then he joined me and we made our way across the level surface of the glacier to the hut.

The Cabane du Val des Dix is an excellent ski hut, not only as regards the expeditions possible in the immediate vicinity, but as a link between the Cabane Chanrion and the new Jenkins hut. These three huts open up a high Alpine ski-ing district comparable with that above Zermatt. It is true that the scenery is not so impressive as that in the environs of the Dent Blanche, Matterhorn and Monte Rosa, but it is wonderfully varied. It is essentially a spring ski-ing area, and to visit it in winter would be to invite a risk of being snowed up and caught in an avalanche trap.

The hut is also comparatively newly built, and is well fitted out for the ski-er. Best of all, it is remote and outside the range of the Swiss week-ender who, however personally estimable, does at times crowd certain of the huts. We were pleased to find it unoccupied, and having prepared the before-mentioned gallons of tea, we planted ourselves outside on a bench for an al fresco lunch in the sun.

What a jolly hour that was. Belaieff's eyes had greatly improved, and he was now enjoying the traverse as much as I. The sun was fierce, but we were inured to it and could expose our faces with impunity. So we lounged, half drugged by the vast quantities of tea we had consumed, our gaze wandering vacantly over the surrounding snow-fields. We could have spent the remainder of the day in complete indolence doing absolutely nothing, but there were two of us and therefore a composite voice of conscience. And this said:

"Do you really think you can spend half of a perfect day like this, you lazy louts. Why, all you have done is to cross a minor pass. Up with you, you sluggards, and climb La Louette!"

Once more the toil, once more the sweat. But we were without our rucksacks, and a keen little wind blew across the snow to temper the blistering sun.

It is an easy mountain, La Louette, a ski runner's "bümmel"; just a long snow-slope to a ridge and along the ridge for a few yards on foot.

As we climbed, an oily-looking cloud slid up the sultry blue sky and settled on Mont Blanc de Seilon, expanding rapidly as it did so. It was a signal. Other clouds appeared. They did not approach from afar, but suddenly made their appearance, gathering stealthily like a pack of timber wolves. Wind rose. We could see the loose snow snatched off the ridge between Mont Blanc de Seilon and the Ruinette like spume from the crest of a wave. This wind caught us on the upper portion of the mountain and drove the snow like needles into our sun-burned faces.

My memory of the view from the top of La Louette is a trifle vague. There certainly was a view and an extensive one. I daresay we saw Mont Blanc and the Combin, and I certainly remember the pyramid of the Dent Blanche, with some long, ominous clouds athwart it. There is also an impressive drop from the summit on the northern side of the mountain.

The fine weather seemed to be fizzling out. The atmosphere was no longer tranquil but uneasy; in places it was in a turmoil, and conflicting air currents tore and worried at the fast-growing clouds.

The light was fast deteriorating as we descended to the hut, and the day faded out into a sullen and threatful evening.

We did not, as we had hoped, have the hut to ourselves. Two young Swiss university students arrived before dark. They had come from the Chanrion hut, and carried enormous loads, including provisions of all sorts in innumerable tins. We had previously toyed with the idea of reaching the Val des Bagnes and Verbiers by way of the Chanrion hut, but had been deterred from doing so by the dangerous and difficult nature of the descent from the hut through the narrow avalanche-swept gorge in which the Val des Bagnes terminates. What we now heard from the newly arrived ski-ers confirmed the rightness of this decision. Apart from avalanche danger it would have been a wretched descent on ski by this route. Moreover, the Chanrion hut is a perfect trap in bad weather, and the ski-er is advised to give it a wide berth, beautiful though the ski-ing district is in which it is situated, in all but the most settled weather conditions, and then preferably in spring. We decided therefore to follow the route we had planned via the Val des Dix and the Rosa Blanche to Verbiers.

With a long day ahead of us involving ascents totalling some 6,000 feet in a cross-country distance on the map of some 14 miles (20 miles and more on ski), we turned in early.

Once or twice I woke in the night to hear the wind blustering past the hut and a spattering of snow on the shutters.

We rose before dawn. Driven snow on a gusty wind intensified the gloom. Our breakfast was no less gloomy. If the weather broke completely we would have no option but to descend the Val des Dix to the Rhone

Valley, and a long and weary way that would be. However, when we at length stepped out of the hut the weather showed signs of relenting, and the red gleam of the rising sun shone through the thinning mists.

In better spirits we set off down the Glacier de Seilon over rough, icy and exceedingly fast snow.

The Glacier de Seilon ends in a gorge so narrow and steep, and of such formidable appearance, that we would have hesitated to descend it had not our ski-ing map decreed otherwise. Down a twisting ribbon of icy snow enclosed by sheer rock cliffs we rasped and skidded, to emerge presently on to the broad Alp de Seilon.

From the alp the route makes a long, ascending traverse across a series of slopes under the Rochers du Bouc into the broad valley containing the Glacier des Ecoulaies. The uppermost portion of this traverse is over steep open ground, and an array of red arrows on the map rightly indicates the possibility of avalanches. On this occasion, however, the snow was safe, yet not frozen hard enough to necessitate an undue amount of edging.

The weather was now excellent, and the curdled sky of dawn had sweetened to a serene blue. Beneath us was the long lake which had been artificially formed in the Val des Dix for the generation of electrical power, but it was then almost empty. The spoliation of beautiful scenery in the interests of commerce is a matter to be fought whenever possible, but there are many localities which would be improved by an artificially formed lake. The Val des Dix is a case in point, and there are other Swiss valleys where similar development might be carried out without offence.

As we gained height we noticed a suspicious blurring about certain of the ridges, and it was no surprise when a cold wind began to assault us vigorously. As so often happens on these occasions, its onset coincided with a sudden craving on our part for second breakfast. We would halt, we said, at the first sheltered place. There were many sheltered places, or so they appeared from a distance, but when we came to them it was to find the wind fairly frolicking at that particular spot. Hungry and angry we came at length to the point where three ski-ing routes meet. One passes the Rosa Blanche to the south, the second traverses the summit of the mountain and the third passes it to the north. We decided on the northern route.

Sheltered now in some degree from the wind, we managed a fairly comfortable meal in the sun, which was now doing its best to make up for its original tardiness.

This area in the neighbourhood of the Rosa Blanche must be as remote a ski-ing area as any in the Valais. It is certainly not to be excelled in beauty, variety and interest by any other area in the 9,000–11,000-feet category. We had the mountains to ourselves that day, and I must confess to a selfish satisfaction in being able to gaze over miles of untracked snow-fields.

From our breakfast place we leisurely ascended to the crest of the north-east ridge of the Rosa Blanche and descended on the far side for a short distance on to the Glacier de Prafleuri. Our intention was to cross this glacier and the Col de Prafleuri to the great snow-field known as Le Grand Désert, and so join the route we had previously made from Verbiers up the Rosa Blanche, but for some reason, attributable partly I think to the deceptive scale of this country and partly to our laziness, we decided that the Col de Prafleuri looked a weary way off, and that instead we would ascend the Glacier de Prafleuri to the Rosa Blanche.

In point of fact, the Col de Prafleuri was little more than half a mile away, even if it looked 2 or 3 miles, and the alternative route involved a further climb of close on 1,500 feet.

I like to think that our decision was actuated solely

by a desire to be energetic rather than the reverse, but I am not so sure.

The north wind did much to temper the heat of the sun as we climbed the Glacier de Prafleuri, and the view that opened up was, we vowed, an ample compensation for the additional work. On the last occasion we had climbed the Rosa Blanche we had seen little or nothing, but now away to the north and north-west the whole range of the Bernese Alps stood up beyond a level bar of haze that marked the Rhone Valley. For once the Oberland was unclouded, and not a vestige of mist marred its array of peaks, which extended from the Wildhorn in the west to the Grimsel in the east. And it was very blue that day; the whole world about us was blue, the snow at our feet, the valleys beneath and the sky above. There was nothing impressive in the immediate vicinity, no bold ice-slope, crag or precipice to set off the tranquil background. I, for one, could have lain down on the spot and comfortably slept. Belaieff, I think, felt the same. We trod a plateau rather than a glacier or a mountain, and plateaux are somnolent places whereon to rest and dream.

We should, of course, have continued on to the summit of the Rosa Blanche, in order to see the higher peaks of the Pennine Alps, which are not visible from the Glacier de Prafleuri, but when we came to the point, which is only some 300 feet beneath the summit, where the route of our previous descent was joined, we tacitly agreed to make for Verbiers. It was a reprehensible decision and dictated by pure laziness, though the wind, which was blowing forcefully, may have had a hand in it. During the past few days we had seen many and beautiful views: was it really worth while going to the top of the Rosa Blanche just for another? So we argued in our hearts. Can one have too much even of sun, glacier and mountain?

This is the way to climb mountains, never through any mistaken sense of duty, however trivial that may be, and seldom through self-abnegation; except, of course, where the prize is great and your efforts are dependent on the efforts of others as in a Himalayan expedition.

So we turned our ski downhill, sweet downhill, over good snow, where once again the air thrummed in the ears, and the loose crystals whisked and gleamed comet-like behind us.

Almost before we had time to think we had run out to a standstill on the broad levels of the Grand Désert. Then followed the second instalment from the Col de Momin, and another glorious descent over equally perfect snow into the combe beneath.

The afternoon was veiling over when we paused for a rest at our old breakfast place before trudging up to the Col de la Chaux, and the brilliant snows of the Combin had relapsed to a duller sheen. There was not a breath of wind, and as we sat eating the silence of the afternoon seemed to settle down so heavily upon us that I for one found it almost an effort to speak. It was as though we were hypnotised by some unearthly drama which we could no more than dimly sense.

And so to Verbiers over the well-remembered route. Belaieff had flown on. I lagged, as usual, behind. An icy track which he followed did not commend itself to me, and I preferred a leisurely descent across the pastures. The snow was melting fast, and here and there were patches of brown and sodden turf. The chalet roofs were dripping in the sun, and there was a faint sound of awakened streams. Spring had come to the Alps.

CHAPTER XI

THE OBERLAND TRAVERSE

ON the morning of March 24th I said good-bye to Belaieff and Mrs. Belaieff at Verbiers. It was a sad occasion, for the weather was now perfect, and the conditions for ski mountaineering ideal. Unhappily, that grim and exacting devil Business had called a halt to Belaieff's holiday, and he had to return to Geneva and England. As for me, after so many disappointments with the weather during the first five weeks of my tour, I was anxious to make the most of my few remaining days in Switzerland. The question remained how was this to be done when I had no companion, and not enough foreign exchange remaining from my allotment from the Bank of England with which to hire a guide? In any event, it was necessary to return to Zermatt, and I decided to postpone any planning until I had done so.

When I last descended from Verbiers, the first breath of spring had wakened into life the slopes of the Val des Bagnes. Now the genial weather of the past few days had garlanded them with bloom. Galaxies of anemones now beautified the pastures, and the crumpled, newly-born crocuses, expanded to their full and gallant stature, rivalled the shining snows above with their silvery drifts. The warm air of spring pulsed with eager life, and its moist, soft breath was a balm to my sun-scorched face. To visit the Alps in mid-winter and high summer is to see much, but it is to miss much also, and I can only recommend those who can to reserve at least one of their Alpine vacations for the magic months of April and May, when Nature attains to the plenitude of her beauty.

Already by Martigny the peach orchards were spreading their bloom over the wide floor of the Rhone Valley, and the brown and sodden herbage of winter had been replaced by a carpet of brilliant green.

At Visp, having nearly three hours to wait for the train to Zermatt, I repaired as before to the station restaurant. There, to my surprise, I found the same tables of players, busy at their card thumping, and what is more, I recognised the players. Had they been there in continuous session for the past fortnight? If so, what a tournament they must be having! Did they play day and night without even a break for meals? And what happened to their businesses, wives and families? Was it possible that they had none, and that some inexorable fate decreed that they should spend their lives playing cards in the station restaurant at Visp? Were they perhaps the ghosts of card players committed to some fearful doom, much as the ghosts of mountaineers might be doomed to spending their time climbing unending scree slopes?

If so, they were fleshy and noisy apparitions, capable of lifting their elbows to no mean effect and filling the atmosphere around them with pungent tobacco smoke.

Long I puzzled over this singular phenomenon. Then suddenly, like a lightning flash, the true solution struck me. The last time I had seen them it had been a Saturday afternoon, and now it was a Sunday afternoon. It was possible, then, that their activities were limited only to week-ends, and that they did indeed live, work and function as ordinary human beings during the remaining five days of the week. But what a way of spending the week-ends of springtime in Switzerland!

This solution arrived at, I devoted the afternoon to wandering about Visp. Ebel, in his guide of 1867, mentions a tendency here to malaria during the autumn, but this has been stamped out. It was once the seat of many noble families, but suffered greatly from inundations due to the overflowing of the Visp and Rhone. Nowa-

days, these rivers run harmlessly along beds raised artificially above the floor of their valleys. It was severely
damaged during the great earthquake of 1855. The two
inns at that time were, he mentions, plagued with flies.
Nowadays, Visp is a flourishing little town with a thriving community, and I was impressed with its cleanliness and the up-to-dateness of its shops, restaurants and
hotels.

Passing the old church which overlooks the town, I
climbed a small anemone-sprinkled hill, and there sat
down on the turf with my back to a low wall to enjoy the
warm sun. It was a pleasant little belvedere, commanding a view up the Vispthal to the serried peaks of the
Mischabel and across the Rhone Valley to the great Oberland wall.

And there, as I gazed, what had previously been a
half-formed idea became a resolution. I would spend a
day at Zermatt completing some photographic studies on
the Riffelalp and then, if the weather continued fine and
settled, travel by train to Ulrichen, in the Rhone Valley,
ascend to the Corno hut and make the ascent of the
Blindenhorn. After that, if time remained, I would go
to the Grimsel Hospice and traverse the Oberland to
Goppenstein.

It was perhaps an ambitious programme for a solitary
ski-er, but it provided alternatives, and was inspired by
the fact that the glaciers were as safe as glaciers were ever
likely to be, owing to the heavy snow-falls, thaws and
frosts of late winter which had effectively bridged the
crevasses with firm snow.

Furthermore, I had a score to settle with the Blindenhorn. In the winter of 1926-7, Mr. J. de V. Hazard and
I traversed from Andermatt to the Corno hut on ski via
the Rotondo hut and the Wytenwasser and Rotondo
passes, intending to ascend the mountain, which is reputed to be one of the finest ski tours in the Alps. At

the Corno hut we were overtaken by a prolonged snow-storm, and, our provisions running short, were forced to retreat to Airolo.   The descent was distinctly unpleasant, and as we came down the steep-sided and narrow upper-most portion of the Val Bedretto in a dense mist, we heard, but could not see, the snow-slopes cracking omin-ously on either hand apparently preparing to avalanche. Repaying an old score on a mountain is a pleasant, harm-less and eminently satisfactory pursuit, and this is what I now promised myself.

Zermatt when I reached it that evening had changed greatly during the past week.   The visitors had drained away, and with the once-splendid snow ornaments dis-integrating into ruin beneath the spring sun, the slush in the street and the floods pouring off the roofs, it was but a shadow of its former proud self.

The following morning I travelled to the Riffelalp by train, intent on my photographic studies, but as usually happens to a photographer, even during a prolonged spell of fine weather, my appearance coincided with a general darkening of the sky, followed by a drizzle of snow.   Long and impatiently I waited for a lift in the curtain, until presently my impatience gave place to resignation and from resignation, as is so often the case on a mountain, to appreciation.

The morning was strangely warm and still.   Some-where the sun was struggling to penetrate the sluggish vapours, but without success.   All around me, as I sat with my back to a tree stump, the trees of the forest were silhouetted against the mist.   They were useless photographically except as vague shapes, for light and shadow were merged into one, but beautiful to con-template.

It may be invidious to particularise, but I do not believe there is a more beautiful alp in all Switzerland than the Riffelalp.   The railway, the telegraph posts, the electric pylons, the ugly barrack of the hotel, not even these can spoil its pristine beauty. Nowhere are trees to be found more appropriate to the mountain scene. Densely the forest of tall pines flows up the mountainside, then, broken by height, weather and temperature, it breaks up and tails out into an Old Guard of noble trees, gnarled, weatherbeaten and twisted into fantastic forms, the incarnated phantoms of the mountain storm. And between them, between their stark arms, their branches half stripped of foliage, or gaunt and dead, but still defiant in their time-long battle with the elements, the great peaks shine in eternal array.

Edward Whymper's description of the view from the summit of the Matterhorn has been criticised as being merely a catalogue of names. But what names for him and the readers who have followed his adventures in *Scrambles Amongst the Alps*! There is poetry in this catalogue, poetry and romance. From the Riffelalp you will see them: Monte Rosa, Castor, Pollux, the Breithorn, the Matterhorn, the Dent Blanche, the Gabelhorn and Weisshorn. How much of history, how many human associations are locked up in these names, how much of hope and frustration, triumph and disaster?

I can think of only one other comparable view, that of the Himalayas from Dr. Kellas's grave at Khampa Dzong. You should stand there, not in the bitter winds of spring, but in the monsoon season, in the same still warmth as that of the Riffelalp, when the yeasty mists congregate along the Himalayas, and the moist, warm air flowing out of the south settles on the frigid Tibetan plateau like a benediction, so that it blossoms miraculously with flowers; when there is scarcely wind enough to urge the tall clouds across the deep-blue firmament and send their showers drifting northwards to blur the far blue hills with their skirts of rain. Then you will see mountains whose names, sonorous and majestic, live for ever in

memory: Kangchenjunga, Siniolchu; Chomiomo, Kang-
chenjau; Chomolhari, Arma Dreme; Chomolonzo,
Makalu. And, lastly, Everest, Chomolungma, Goddess
Mother of the World. You will see them in the early
morning beyond the level wastes of sand, the ochre-
coloured hills, the turquoise lakes and swelling uplands,
radiantly pure, immeasurably remote. You will see them
in the afternoon shining through rents sundered in the
massive curtains of monsoon cloud by the uprush of
mighty winds, and you will see them in the evening
with battlements afire, their snows shedding a perpetual
splendour over the leagues of golden plain.

Later I made my way to the Grünsee, near the end of
the Findelen glacier, then doubled back at a lower level
following downhill tracks through the forest beneath the
Riffelalp. The warmth seemed subtropical, and even in
the dense forest I found that I was by no means safe from
small avalanches which were cascading down between
the trees almost like water. They were not all small
slides either, and lower, where the track crossed the
Gornergrat railway between Zermatt and the Riffelalp, a
fair-sized fall had occurred, blocking the line to a depth
of some 15 feet. A gang of thirty men was already busy
shovelling away the snow. The Gornergrat railway is a
paying proposition, and incidentals such as avalanches
cannot be allowed to interfere with paying propositions
in efficient little Switzerland. And how those men
worked, continuously, steadily and methodically. Anywhere else it would have been necessary first of all for
such a working party to establish itself firmly on the spot
with canvas shelters, charcoal braziers, sausages and tea,
then to sit down and contemplate the job for a couple of
days.

The snow was wet and sticky during the whole of the
descent; it was still in the transitional stage between the
loose snow of winter and the firm, wet, crystalline snow

of spring. The sun broke through before I emerged
from the forest, and the harsh roar of avalanches from the
crags of the Untergabelhorn alternated with an occasional sharp crash as huge icicles broke loose from the
cliffs immediately above Zermatt. Winter's shackles
were being knocked off, and in double-quick time, by
Blacksmith Spring.

At Zermatt that evening I came to my final decision.
The break in the fine weather could only be temporary, the little finger of some distant and passing
depression, for the barometer hand was high, half-way
indeed across that exalted quadrant of Herr Aufden-
blatten's aneroid, which begins with " Schönes Wetter "
and ends with " Sehr Trocken." I would leave Zermatt
on the morrow and carry out the scheme already pro-
pounded. So far I had not worked it out in any detail,
partly because I had been unable to obtain a map which
depicted the approach from Ulrichen in the Rhone
Valley to the Corno hut. That evening I was able to
borrow one and study it for the first time. What I saw
immediately convinced me that a change of plan was
necessary.

To reach the Corno hut from the Rhone Valley the
ski-er must follow a narrow, steep-sided valley for a considerable distance. The weather, as already mentioned,
was exceptionally warm, and avalanches were peeling off
everywhere. A narrow valley in such conditions is an
obvious trap. It might have been possible to ascend at
night, or in the early morning when the snow was frozen,
but this is a fatiguing business on hard-frozen snow
carrying a heavy load, and it meant hanging around for
many hours at Ulrichen, in the Rhone Valley. The
problem is typical of those that frequently confront the
ski-er in early spring—how to reach the relatively safe
glaciers and snow-fields through the lower avalanche-
swept valleys during a spell of hot weather.

The alternative was to traverse the Oberland glaciers from Münster, in the Rhone Valley, via the Galmihorn ski hut and the high passes of the Galmilücke,[1] Grünhornlücke and Lötschenlücke, including, if conditions permitted, an ascent of the Finsteraarhorn, the highest peak of the Bernese Alps. I had no guide-book describing the ascent to the Galmihorn hut and the Galmilücke, but it was obvious from the map that the former could be reached over a forest-clad shoulder, which should be safe enough from avalanches, while the route between the hut and the Münster glacier, which leads up to the Galmilücke, crosses a series of shoulders where the contours did not suggest any prolonged and dangerous slopes. I argued, therefore, that it should be easily possible to reach the hut in one day from Zermatt, since it is only some 2,500 feet above Münster, and by starting from it at the crack of dawn next morning be across any doubtful ground between it and the Münster glacier before the snow frozen by the night's frost should become soft and avalanchy. Once on the Münster glacier the avalanche danger is at an end, as the route lies entirely over wide glaciers and snow-fields.

If I have expounded at length on the planning of this little expedition, it is because of the necessity for making plans, and of studying the route well beforehand, when engaging on a high Alpine tour in spring. In winter, accidents due to that pernicious form of avalanche, the wind-slab, may be deplorable and often reprehensible, but in some degree they are understandable, and on rare occasion accidents in the strict sense of being unforeseen even by skilful mountaineers. In spring conditions of wet snow the ski-er has no such excuse, and it is his own fault entirely should he become involved in a wet-snow avalanche. Care in working out the route, an accurate appreciation from a large-scale map of the ground to be

[1] Lücke = pass.

Arolla and Mont Collon

Jimmy Belaieff and the writer at the Cabane du Val des Dix

covered and a precise estimate of the time necessary to cover it are essentials in ski mountaineering, apart of course from equally essential mountain craft.

As regards provisions, I estimated for a total of five days: half a day for the ascent to the Galmihorn hut, two days for the actual traverse to the Lötschenthal and a day for the ascent of the Finsteraarhorn. This allowed for an extra one and a half days against contingencies, the most likely of which was bad weather. Should a storm break when the ski-er is at the Finsteraarhorn hut, he may have no option but to stick it out, the hut being isolated and difficult to escape from in a heavy blizzard.

Next morning, March 26th, I bade farewell to my host and descended to Brig on an early train. At Brig, when I alighted, it was, almost literally, into the arms of my friend the elderly porter. He greeted me as one would a long-lost son.

"Where are you going now?" he inquired.

I told him to Münster, and that I intended to leave the bulk of my luggage in the cloakroom until I returned.

"You are going up the mountains with a guide, of course?"

I replied a trifle evasively that I was indeed going up the mountains, and that I wanted to buy some food in Brig, especially honey. At this he ruminated awhile.

"You would do better," said he at length, "to buy food at Münster, not Brig. As for honey, you will not get it in Brig, except possibly that stuff the hotels give to the tourists, which is not honey but a cheap syrup. That is no good for *you*. It is honey you want, honey from the Alpen blumen. You will not get it in Brig, but you *may*—I say *may*—get it in Münster."

In summer it is possible to travel from Brig to Chur via Gletsch, Andermatt and the Furka and Oberalp passes, but in winter the narrow-gauge train plies only as far as

Oberwald, in the upper Rhone Valley. The scenery of this portion of the valley is as diverse as it is beautiful. Between Brig and Martigny the Rhone flows along a regular and almost level trench, but beyond Brig the valley climbs rapidly, soon reaching that happy level of alp and forest, stream and village. The last are indeed little gems of places arranged at regular intervals along the valley, each clustered about its tall, whitewashed church.

Nothing could have exceeded the beauty of that morning. The weather had recovered from its lapse, and a full-blooded sun beamed from a cloudless sky. It was one of those mornings that elevates the spirit of the mountaineer beyond every mundane matter and fills him with a keen anticipation of great days to come. Even the sober Swiss peasants who formed the bulk of the passengers were infected by it, and for once the windows were opened all along the train to admit the vitalising mountain air.

No snow lay at Brig, but within a few minutes we encountered it, at first in patches, then in a continuous carpet, which rapidly increased in depth as we climbed, until it was presently apparent that the snow-fall hereabouts had exceeded that of Zermatt and the western Valais.

Innumerable avalanches had fallen, many of them across the railway, which in places ran for hundreds of yards between walls of debris 15 to 20 feet high. Due to this exceptional snow-fall, and the extensive catchment areas, particularly on the north side of the line, these avalanches were many of them of enormous dimensions; indeed, I have never seen so many monsters within so few miles.

Intent on capturing some of the beauties of the scene, I took a number of photographs through the open window, a procedure which evidently interested one of the passengers as he transferred himself to the seat opposite me and began to ply me with questions.

He was a tall young man and obviously not of the peasant class, since he was immaculately dressed—in his Sunday-best, I should have put it.   He appeared in great good spirits and was brimful of enthusiasm for every-thing he saw.   Yes, it was a beautiful valley, " wonder-schön," and the accent was on the " wonder."   There was no more beautiful valley in the Alps.   He knew it well : had he not been stationed there as a soldier during the war, when the neighbourhood of the Furka and St. Gotthard passes had been turned into a last-ditch redoubt against a possible invasion by Hitler?   And now he was revisiting old scenes, and especially Münster, where he had been quartered.

" I also am going to Münster," I told him, " for the start of a ski tour.   Can you tell me where I can buy some provisions? "

" That is easy," he replied.   " There is a *gasthaus* there, an excellent *gasthaus*.   You must lunch with me. The people there, they are excellent too—' sehr freund-lich.' "

There was a light in his eyes, a far-away light.   I began to suspect that there was a motive stronger than the scenery of the valley, even the excellence of the *gasthaus*, behind his return to Münster.

Along the sunlit valley hummed the train.   My acquaintance had relapsed into silence.   He was gazing out of the window, but I do not think at the scenery.

We alighted at Münster, into an oblong space cut out of the snow, where stood the single little building con-stituting the station.   Beyond were the roofs of the vil-lage grouped on the lowermost slopes of the hillside that passed forest-clad in its turn towards the Oberland wall. But it was little more than the roofs that we could see, except for the larger buildings and the inevitable tall church.　Never have I seen so much snow in late March. The village is 4,560 feet in altitude, 755 feet lower than Zermatt, yet there were several feet more snow than at the latter place.　There cannot have been less than 9 or 10 feet on the average.　It was necessary to descend steps or else paths from the street into the houses.　It was not a Christmas-card village, but something from a fairy story, on which some snow queen had put her spell, and the genii who controls these matters had emptied snow until he had no more to empty.

Through this snow we trudged until we came to a fair-sized building with a space cleared before it.　We entered and found ourselves in a little *gastzimmer*. There was an old man with a glass of schnapps before him in one corner, and a serving girl, rosy-cheeked and petite, clad in a chic black bodice with a colourful little apron.　Her eyes were very bright, and when she saw my companion she ran forward to greet him in a manner —well, not one she would have assumed to an ordinary guest.　I looked away, and when I looked back I caught the eye of the ancient in the corner: there was, I could swear, a twinkle in its rheumy old depths.

I stood my companion a drink and wished him all health and happiness.　I put the stress on the "Glück-ligkeit," but he had no need for it, he had discovered it already.

After this we adjourned to the salle à manger, which was in a new building across the way.　Our hostess ushered us in.

"What do you think of it?" she inquired.

My companion stood in silence for a full half-minute, then he drew a deep breath and exclaimed:

"But it is beautiful! beautiful!"

And so it was.　It was quite new, and had been con-structed in its entirety by local craftsmen out of local timber.　The walls, the ceiling, the floor, the furniture, the picture frames, even the ash trays and other oddments were made entirely of well-seasoned pine. There was nothing flimsy about anything. Heavy beams crossed the ceiling, the tables were solid, and the chairs had seats and backs inches thick. The builders had exercised an obvious talent for wood carving in the beams and walls. This carving was not, as is so often the case, a poor attempt at fulsome elaboration, nor was it simple to the verge of crudity, but something in between, and it was done with an eye to the general ensemble, to the proportions of the room, its appointments and its furniture. In two words, it was in good taste. Gay chintz curtains and coloured tablecloths and napkins leavened any suggestion of heaviness, and these too were in excellent taste.

In this charming apartment we were served with an appetising lunch, which was accompanied by some soft red wine. Afterwards my companion, who insisted on my being his guest, asked me for my requirements in food. I told him, not forgetting the honey, and he went into consultation with Rosycheeks. Yes, it could be managed quite easily, but she was not sure about the honey; it was not easy to get these days, but there was a friend and neighbour. . . . If the " Herr " would not mind waiting half an hour?

The " Herr " *did* wait outside by himself on a bench in the sun. Inside he felt a trifle *de trop*.

Seldom have I experienced such a combination of sun and snow during an Alpine spring, and not only sun, for the air was positively sultry. There was a thermometer hanging nearby in the shade, and I was amazed to note its reading of 20 degrees Centigrade (68 degrees Fahr.). Very high sun temperatures are a commonplace on mountains, but so high a shade and air temperature is surely unusual in March? High air temperatures during an Alpine winter are associated with *föhn*; the latter, on the other hand, is not as a rule associated with cloud-less skies and a complete absence of wind.

I was not, however, disposed at that moment to puzzle my head over meteorological phenomena. Suffice to say that it was the warmest and sunniest March day I can recollect. The snow-buried chalets slept in the sun, and except for the water running off the roofs, there was not a sound to be heard; Münster lived as a thrall under some subtle enchantment.

Rosycheeks returned laden and triumphant.

" I have got you some honey," she said, " nearly a kilo, and here are the other things: bread, butter, sugar, ham, dried meat, ' Maggi ' soup, macaroni, dried fruits and nuts, sardines, tea, salt, some eggs also—I have packed them carefully—and some chocolate."   I endeavoured to decline the chocolate—it could only have been accounted for out of the household coupons—but it was useless; to have insisted would have caused these good people offence.

" The honey is good," she smiled; " it comes from our flowers."

" I must return when the snow has gone," I told her. " It must be very beautiful then."

" It is always beautiful in Münster," she returned proudly.

I added the provisions to some oddments I had brought from Zermatt. The cost? It was absurdly small, in all well under one English pound. Then I swung my weighty rucksack on to my back and prepared to take my leave.

She stood pointing up the mountainside.

"There are many avalanches still to fall. Keep up through the trees on the ridge, but do not go too far to left or right, or you will be in danger. They fall every-where in this weather."

It was sound advice. In normal circumstances it is

possible to ascend almost anywhere in safety through the forest above Münster, but the exceptional heat, coupled with the enormous quantities of snow on the slopes, made all steep slopes dangerous, whether tree-clad or not.

The slopes immediately above the village were in shocking condition. It was not so much a question of the ski sinking deeply into the snow as the latter collapsing beneath the ski. For the first two or three hundred feet I went in up to the knees at every step. Added to this was the terrific sun on my back and a rucksack containing five days' food and ski-mountaineering equipment. It was not long before I began to wonder whether it would not be preferable to spend the night at Münster and ascend to the Galmihorn hut next morning when the snow should be crusted. However, the hut is normally within two easy hours of the village, so I decided to carry on, even though the ascent took twice that time.

The lower slopes proved the worst, and when, after a toilsome struggle, I reached the broad ridge above, I found better consolidated snow.

Here I paused for a breather. Already I was soaked with sweat, thanks to the broiling sun and my heavy load, by far the heaviest load I had carried during the past seven weeks.

Below lay Münster and, in spite of the realistic toil of the past half-hour, it seemed to my vagrant fancy that I had emerged from some sugar-caked hamlet in the realm of fairy-land. Surely, I told myself, Rosycheeks was none other than Snow White and my youthful companion some gallant and princely adventurer for her hand? As for the Seven Dwarfs, doubtless they were at work under the very hillside on which I stood, quarrying precious jewels for their beloved mistress.

Some old ski tracks zigzagged up the ridge, and I followed them through the gradually steepening forest, halting every twenty minutes or so on the convenient excuse of admiring the view, but in reality to rest my aching shoulder muscles. The sun was declining now, and as the shadows of the tall pines lengthened, a welcome coolness awoke in the still air.

The ridge, at first broad but clearly defined, slowly petered out into steeper slopes sparsely dotted with trees as the forest thinned out. Innocent though these slopes would have been in all ordinary circumstances, I should not have fancied them an hour ago, but already the fast-growing coolness in the air was doing its work, and the snow, if not already crusted, was becoming firmer and less like a waterlogged pudding.

Ahead there was light and blue sky, and presently the slope curved out of the forest on to an open alp.

My map, an old one, did not include the Galmihorn hut, and as the tracks I had been following had vanished, I began to look about me. At the upper end of the alp was a likely-looking building, newly constructed of stone and three-quarters buried beneath the snow. It did not look much like a club hut, but evening was now drawing on, and it seemed best to investigate.

Little more than the side containing the door was visible, and as the latter was arranged in two halves, an upper and a lower, a type common to Alpine club huts, it seemed possible that it was the hut. The door was overhung by a huge mass of snow some 12 feet in thickness, but I insinuated myself beneath, and after some difficulty managed to effect an entry. Inside it was cold and dank, and smelt faintly of cheese. It was evidently a cheesemaker's summer residence, but to make sure I struck a match, which at once confirmed this supposition, as there was nothing to be seen but some milking stools and wooden buckets.

As I crawled gingerly out under the cornice of snow, it occurred to me what an unpleasant thing it would be if it collapsed and buried me beneath a ton or so of snow.

To be found a month or so later when the snow melted trapped on the threshold of a cheese-maker's hut was scarcely an appropriate end to a mountaineer!   Fate has sometimes bizarre notions as to the manipulations of its puppets, and this thought quite illogically (since every- thing that falls has its moment for falling) expedited my exit.

Above the alp were some scattered pines.   Then came open slopes, and on them an old but clearly-defined uphill ski track.   It led over a brow, and there, a few hundred yards away, was the hut.

What is the ideal Alpine club hut?   It is scarcely pos- sible to dogmatise.   Huts are placed and built for par- ticular purposes, and these purposes are often more important than situation.   Some, such as the Solvay hut on the Matterhorn, are mere refuges for those overtaken by night or storm and unable to descend.   Some are placed high up for the ascents or traverses of particular peaks and passes, some are primarily for summer climbers and others for winter ski-ers.   In some fuel is expensive and difficult to transport.   Some have a purely utili- tarian quality and some an æsthetic quality.   Some are comfortable and some uncomfortable.   And within these wide limits there is always the matter of personal prefer- ence.   I can merely state, therefore, my personal preference.

It is for a hut at the top of the timberline which com- mands a wide and unobstructed view and which receives the sun for the greater part of the day.   Such a hut should necessarily be comfortable, since it is easily acces- sible from the nearest valley and village.   Fuel is also available in unlimited quantity.

The Galmihorn hut fulfils these conditions.   From a utilitarian standpoint it has its limitations.   Some local ski-ing is possible on the neighbouring snow-fields, but it is primarily a jumping-off point for the Galmilücke and the glaciers and peaks of the Oberland massif. It commands a panoramic vista of the Rhone Valley and its villages for many miles in both directions. In its wider scope the view extends from the Weisshorn and the peaks of Zermatt and Saas, past the peaks of the Simplon and Binn, along the range bounding the southern side of the Rhone Valley, including the Blindenhorn, over the Rotondo group and the Furka to the Galenstock group eastwards of the Grimsel pass.

The sun was still well above the horizon when I arrived, and I straightway set about making myself comfortable. The hut is large, but easily heated by an excellent stove in the main downstairs room, the kitchen being separate, and I was soon cosy. It is unnecessary to enlarge on the details of my dinner, which ended with some of the most delicious honey I have ever tasted, and a silent thanksgiving to my good friends of Münster.

My solitary meal over, I stood outside smoking in great peace and contentment. The sun had passed behind the western Oberland, and the slopes whereon the hut stood were in shadow. Already the snow was crusted by frost, yet the air still seemed strangely warm, due no doubt to the complete absence of wind. The evening was marvellously tranquil, not a breath stirred, and except for a few threads and filaments of cloud, the sky was unmarred. Deep at my feet lay the level floor of the Rhone Valley with little villages arranged at regular intervals along it. It was as though some giant had strode that way and at every stride dropped a pinch of seed from which had sprung the clustered houses.

The evening shadow was lipping slowly up the opposite hillsides, but far above the peaks still warmed themselves in the sun which, although close to the horizon, had lost none of its brilliance.

The summits which bound the upper Rhone Valley

to the south-east are arranged with a striking regularity, as though they had been marshalled there by some ser-geant-major of fabulous geological antiquity. Shoulder to shoulder they stand, as prim and proper as any Guard, and now this regularity was even better defined by the sun, which picked out the buttresses and ridges with its declining rays.

But it was not to them that the eye instinctively turned, but to the west, to the peaks of Zermatt where the Weiss-horn, Lady Godiva of the Snows, rode the ranges in unashamed purity and beauty. In the gap between it and the massive Mischabel rose the solitary spire of the Matterhorn. At a distance of 45 miles the area it occupied was an infinitesimal fraction of the whole panorama, yet again and again the eye was drawn to it as though to a magnet. A personality seemed to radiate from it, a quality of steadfastness and eternal splendour was perceivable across those miles of mountains. " Men," wrote Whymper, " who ordinarily spoke and wrote like rational beings, when they came under its power seemed to quit their senses and ranted, and rhapsodised, losing for a time all common forms of speech." And this quality which influences the near beholder still continues to influence him from afar, so that if the Matterhorn be visible from any point of the Alps, the eye will instinc-tively seek out its unique peak.

And now, as the shadow tide lifted higher and higher, the colours in earth and sky and atmosphere began slowly to change. In the west and south-west the Matterhorn and the peaks of Zermatt, previously dark and severe in tone, lightened to a powder blue as the rays of the sink-ing sun were absorbed in the breadths of intervening atmosphere, whilst the sky behind changed from saffron to a vivid sea-green. Then, suddenly, the sun sent a single ray diagonally across the Vispthal, which caught the east ridge of the Weisshorn, so that the mountain seemed to have suspended against it a scimitar-like ellipse of light.

Slowly the light continued to recede, and as slowly the night welled from the valleys. And now came the phase that every tourist knows, the Alpine glow. No phenomenon of Nature has been more vulgarised than this, no advertising agent of Swiss wares could manage without it; gaudy and lurid, it appears on trinket and chocolate box. And yet it is always beautiful, invariably wonderful. And the reason for this is that beauty in Nature and in Art is imperishable and beyond the clutch of vulgarity. That evening the mountains lit up as they have always lit up, and I stood, as I have always stood, enthralled by the beauty of the scene. There was nothing dramatic about that sunset, no fierce colourings, no glowing clouds drawn across the sky, no threat of storm. It was just the end of a fine day and the promise of a fine morrow.

I felt myself to be privileged to witness such a scene in solitude. To some it is anathema to be solitary, but to others solitude is something to be prized. I do not mean the solitude that cuts itself off from its kind and will have nothing to do with others, but that of a rare occasion—solitude in the presence of Nature and its Creator. Such solitude is not to be associated with any feeling of loneliness, which is a purely negative state of mind, but has about it a positive spiritual quality.

I do not know how long I stood there. I remember the purple stain of night spreading out of the east behind the glowing snows of the Galenstock, and the faint tolling of church bells from one of the villages, and finally, when all the lights were out, a solitary star and a world of snow left softly glowing like a vast pearl.

The following morning I was up before dawn, but cooking, breakfast and tidying up the hut took so long that it was full daylight before I was away. There was not a cloud in the sky, and already the peaks were gilded in the rising sun. As I had hoped and expected, the snow was hard-frozen, and I progressed easily and quickly uphill on my ski across the gently sloping snow-fields.

The route crossed the east ridge of the Kastlenhorn. Here the slopes were steeper, and I found it simpler to carry my ski than to edge them into the board-like snow. The sun was now well up, and I halted for " second breakfast " on the ridge.

It was the best moment of the day. Many hours of glorious ski-ing lay ahead. Everything promised well, and life seemed very good up there in the morning sun beneath a cloudless firmament in an air so still, and a silence so profound, that I could hear my blood-stream pulsing in my veins.

From the ridge I traversed to the north of the Kastlenhorn, then ascended steeply over a series of slopes so as to strike the Münster glacier to the east of the secondary summit (Point 3,091 metres) of the Firrenhorn. This last portion was heavy going, and it was with relief that I found myself on the edge of the broad ridge bounding the glacier.

So far so good. The snow had been as safe as snow could be. Within a few hours it would become unpleasant for a ski-er, later still it might well be dangerous. Thenceforwards, until I descended into the Lötschenthal, my way lay across glaciers and passes free from all avalanche danger.

Before me stretched the Münster glacier, a broad and undulating expanse. Except for an ice-fall in the lowermost portion, which I could avoid by traversing on to the glacier above it, there was not an open crevasse to be seen. The Galmilücke was out of sight, hidden behind the Hinter Galmihorn, but a single glance assured me that the ascent was as easy a ski route as can be imagined.

A diagonal downhill traverse brought me to the glacier. What would otherwise be a dull plug is often relieved by the changing scenery. This cannot, however, be said of the ascent of the Münster glacier. It is frankly a long, uninspiring ascent up a broad, gently inclined snow-field, which is enclosed by trivial peaks and rock ridges.

There is no doubt that a combination of broiling sun and a heavy load materially detracts from a mountaineer's appreciation of an ascent, but I still maintain that the Münster glacier is a glacier to descend, not ascend, on ski. It resembled a burning-glass, which seemed to concentrate every ray of a burning sun on the solitary little insect that slowly crawled up its glaring expanses.

On such an occasion it is fatal to chafe or fret, and best to relapse into a kind of apathetic resignation or coma. One expedient is to hum a tune beneath the breath, but even " Onward, Christian Soldiers " is liable to pall, while the " Volga Boat Song " becomes positively revolting after a while, especially when the shoulders are aching abominably and trickles of sweat are coursing down the ribs and spine.

I was labouring thus when I heard a sound above, and saw a party of three descending towards me. They were ski-ing well. First came a guide, then a man and a woman, following dutifully in the tracks of their leader, a process that scarcely seemed necessary on this unbroken glacier. They stopped when they reached me, and the guide, a red-faced fellow with blue eyes, eyed me questioningly and with obvious disapproval.

" Where have you come from? " he asked.

I told him from Münster.

" What is the snow like to the Galmihorn hut? "

" All right if you lose no time," I replied, " but possibly bad later."

" You are quite alone? "

" Yes. Good-day."

I moved on.   I knew what was coming.   Few guides can resist an opportunity for a homily on the follies of solitary mountaineering, and here was a heaven-sent opportunity in the presence of his " Herr."   I had no intention of presenting him with the opportunity.

I little later I glanced back.   The three were halted and talking animatedly, the guide gesticulating with his arms.   I could not hear, but could easily imagine, what he was saying.

" There goes an ' alleinganger,' a fool, a wooden-head. Look at him now.   You will never see him again, nobody will.   He will fall into a crevasse; he will perish in the first storm; he will be buried in an avalanche; he will break his leg and die in the snow; he will . . ." And so on and so forth.   And the tourists would be listening to this diatribe with goggling eyes.

I can understand the guide's point of view.   It goes against professional pride when you are paid a considerable sum of money to conduct someone across the Oberland to pass a fellow who is doing it on his own, free, gratis and for nothing.   And of course criticism of solitary mountaineering is more than justified by many lamentable accidents and disappearances.   But I have an Englishman's belief in the right of every man to risk his neck if he wants to.   In solitary mountaineering it is possible to draw the line between prudence and folly. The solitary traverse of the Oberland in spring is to my mind a far less dangerous proposition than many a standard route climbed regularly by guided parties.   Stones on the Matterhorn and falling ice beneath the Grépon are far more likely to kill you, however many guides you employ, than the Oberland glaciers in spring.   The point in all this is that anyone who climbs a mountain by himself should have the requisite skill and experience to do so.   It has been customary among mountaineers, when writing of their experiences in solitary climbing, to apologise to the reader for their misdeeds. I do not propose to do so here. I prefer to write that I thoroughly enjoyed my traverse of the Oberland, and consider such an experience as being well worth the small risks entailed, risks far smaller than scores of previous expeditions made with companions.

At long last the Galmilücke came into view. It is simply a low notch in the ridge connecting the Oberaar Rothhorn with the Hinter Galmihorn and cannot be described as either an obvious or a beautiful pass. To the south-east of the pass a hanging glacier clings to the face of the Hinter Galmihorn. It is quite unnecessary to pass beneath it, but I noticed with sardonic amusement that the guide had led his party well within range of possible bombardment, a small risk but an unnecessary one.

A rocky edge formed the crest of the pass, and there I disposed myself for what I had come to regard as a well-earned lunch. I quenched a formidable thirst in a very simple manner. There were both snow and rocks on the pass, and by plastering the former against the sun-warmed latter, trickles of water were induced, which filled my cup again and again.

It is usual for a pass to command a view in two directions. The Galmihorn is an exception, and the view eastwards was blocked by the ice and snow of the Galmifirn, which rose higher than the pass and was separated from the latter by a deep wind-carved hollow. However, that to the west was unobstructed, and the hanging glacier on the Galmihorn provided an imposing foreground to the serried array of peaks beyond the Furka and Grimsel passes.

An hour passed in the apparent space of five minutes before I could muster up sufficient energy to continue on my way.

Descending into the hollow, I climbed up on to the

The Cabane du Val des Dix
with the Weisshorn and Dent
Blanche from La Louette

The upper Rhone Valley from the Galmihorn ski hut

Galmifirn.   Instantly beyond the *névé* of the Studerfirn
the Finsteraarhorn soared up to greet me.   Viewed from
every angle, it is a shapely peak, but it is especially impressive from any point in the eastern quadrant, as from
this direction the great precipices which fall to the north-
east and east are revealed.   The Finsteraarhorn is not
only the highest peak in the Bernese Alps, but a pivotal
point of the massif.   It rises from the remote heart of the
high snows, and from it radiate three great glaciers.   No
peak in the Alps commands a wider vista of ice and snow.

My plans included an ascent of the highest point of
the Galmihorn.   No doubt this ascent would have been
made, and another peak added to the " bag," had I had
a companion with me, but alone I found myself disin-
clined to make the effort.   The sun was hot, and the still
air drained of vitality.   In a word, I was lazy.

Now, one advantage of solitary mountaineering is
being able to indulge a whim or change a plan at a
moment's notice.   This is impossible, or at least difficult,
with a companion, and the larger a party the more
" according to plan " do its actions become.   Had I been
with a companion, I might have tried to find out by
devious means whether he was lazy also.   I would have
said, " By jove, it's hot," and " Looks a pretty awful
sweat, doesn't it? "   And if he replied, " Yes, it is hot,"
and " The snow's about its worst now," I would insinuate
my propaganda still farther, and would enlarge on the
advantages of arriving early at the hut, and of a siesta
outside in the sun, until he was thoroughly demoralised
and ready, not only to agree to anything, but to suggest
it himself in the first place.   But if he greeted every suggestion tight lipped and bleakly, and while agreeing that
it was hot, and that the ascent would be a sweat, we had
planned to do it and had jolly well got to, then, of course,
it would have to be done.

The descent of the Galmifirn to its junction with the

Fiescherfirn was over snow typical of the season. The alternate hot days and night frosts of the past week or more had consolidated it well, and the ski slid fast at the gentlest of angles. At the same time it was rough in patches, and there was a tendency towards breakable crust where it had been caked by the wind. It was snow in the transition stage between winter and spring, and would continue to improve throughout April and May. Thus, the run down was not consistently smooth, and it was necessary to keep a wary eye open for patches of breakable crust. Heavy falls should be eschewed at all times when ski-ing alone, and this is especially the case on glaciers where there is always the possibility of a fall occurring on a snow-bridge over a crevasse. Throughout my solitary traverse of the Oberland, I made it a point not to fall at any time, a process achieved by a poor ski-er like myself only through slow, ultra-cautious running.

Yet I enjoyed the descent. If the ski now and again rasped and bumped over the crusted snow, there were long stretches where they lipped over a silk-like surface.

At one point, where the *névé* steepened a little, its smoothness was broken by some crevasses, but the majority of these were visible only as shallow undulations. Then came the junction of the glaciers, a level plain littered with moraine heaps and boulders.

From this point there is an ascent of less than 1,500 feet in a distance of 2 miles to the Finsteraarhorn hut. It is not much, but it came as the most fatiguing section of the route. The glare and heat reflected from the unbroken snow of the broad Fiescherfirn were terrific, then there was my heavy rucksack and, finally, the scale, and the consequent monotony due to lack of change of scene. This last is a powerful factor in the ascent of any great glacier. I toiled for a quarter of an hour, then half an hour, and lo! everything was as before, the peaks in the same position as to make no difference, the hut on its promontory of rocks the same elusive speck. Every ski-er and mountaineer knows what I mean. The distance is small and the time to cover it relatively short, yet both seem interminable. The hour spent lounging on the Galmilücke had passed like a drifting mist; the hour spent slogging up the Fiescherfirn dragged on leaden feet.

You know, of course, that it is merely a matter of time and effort, a case of so many pounds raised through so many feet by a treadmill-like movement of the legs. One day you will be seated in comfort with a map of the Oberland outspread before you and a pair of dividers in your hand. In a single stride those dividers will cover the distance you have covered over those burning snows. And then, as though to emphasise to my further disadvantage this implication of time and space, there was a sudden humming, and from over the Fiescherhörner swept a fighter aircraft. In a matter of seconds it was past and gone. I too have flown over mountains. It is an interesting experience in the first place, but in its ultimate it provokes little sense of time, space or beauty.

The new Finsteraarhorn hut stands on a rock rib some 300 feet above the Fiescherfirn. Below it is the old hut, which is still used as an overflow for visitors. The quickest approach is from the railway station on the Jungfraujoch via the Concordia Platz and the Grünhornlücke. Were it not for the Jungfrau railway it would certainly rank as the most remote hut in the Alps, since all other approaches are long and arduous. Even taking this into account, it is no place at which to be overtaken by prolonged bad weather. If in good weather and clear visibility the Oberland glaciers are nothing but a promenade, in blizzard conditions they present problems in route finding which even the expert use of map and compass may fail to solve.

There was no one at the hut, as I noted with pleasure, not because I am unsociable, but because the charm of solitary mountaineering depends on being solitary. Fire-wood, as I knew from past experience, is in short supply and also expensive, being 2 francs 50 centimes for a small bundle, an understandable sum, as it has to be carried from the Jungfraujoch. During the past winter the hut had been visited by only two or three parties, and it felt both cold and damp. I did my best to remedy this state of affairs, and having made a fire brewed tea.

It was 3 p.m., and time remained for some pleasant and idle hours in the sun. There is a small terrace, and here I ensconced myself on a stool, teacup at hand, my back to the sun-warmed wall of the hut.

If there is anything more delectable in mountaineer-ing after hours of hard slogging than to sit thus in the sun, sipping tea between mouthfuls of good rye bread generously plastered with butter and honey, I do not know it. The hard work was well behind, and the only memory of it lay in the thin line of my ski track on the glacier beneath. With what lofty superiority did I now contemplate it, and with what solid satisfaction. What a dull view is a view unearned; what splendours unfold to him who toils!

How much enjoyment is animal and how much spiritual on these occasions it is impossible to say. Taut muscles relaxed, tired limbs spread in delicious repose, thirst quenched and appetite satisfied, these are powerful contributors to an appreciation of the mountain scene. The Yogi claims to rise superior to bodily needs and ills, but he recognises the importance of a healthy and uncon-taminated body, since no fleshly disability must retard the full expansion of the spirit. Yet there are many interacting factors. The Yogi believes that physical energy can be transmuted into mental energy. This, I am sure, is untrue. Superlative physical fitness is not conducive towards mental activity. This is especially the case in mountaineering, and I have often noticed that notes and descriptions made at the time seem poorly written, banal and ill-conceived when studied later.

At the same time, the brain is registering impressions and the memory photographing them for subsequent use. When, therefore, the mountain lover experiences an attack of nostalgia, he is not only resurrecting these impressions, but probably experiencing as strong a feeling for the beauty of the mountains as he did on the spot. There are, of course, many occasions, almost visionary occasions, when impressions made at the time cannot possibly be recalled with the same vividness. Such impressions are usually associated with comfort, for beauty associated with bodily discomfort can only be appreciated in retrospect. While, therefore, it is possible and desirable to make factual notes of experience, much as an artist makes colour notes, it is certainly not possible or desirable to endeavour to record the beauty and interest of a mountaineering expedition except in retrospect, since the physical so far predominates over the mental at the time as to stultify any possibility of lyrical description. History, indeed, seems to show that the large majority of notable poets, writers and artists were men who led sedentary and physically inactive lives, their natural, inherited, physical energy having been transmuted into mental energy. This is why so little writing of literary merit has been produced by sportsmen. The " flannelled fool " is no coincidental phenomenon, but the product of definite physical and psychological factors. In the same way, the mountain poets and writers have been drawn, not so much from the ranks of those who climbed the mountains, but from those who were content merely to contemplate mountains from below.

Long I sat. The shadows broadened on the dark precipices of the Grünhorn, then began slowly to extend out-

wards on to the smooth Fiescherfirn. The ice-crowned
ribs extending from the long-convoluted edge linking the
Fieschergabelhorn, the Schönbühlhorn and the Wannehorn became more clearly defined as the sun swung westwards, and the harsh glare of noon began almost imper-
ceptibly to soften. Except for an occasional clatter of
falling ice and stones from the southernmost facets of the
Grünhorn, all was motionless, so motionless indeed, that
of a sudden my wandering gaze was arrested by something that moved, a minute something, a dot that
appeared on the snowy curve of the Grünhornlücke. The
dot moved downwards; it was followed by a second and
a third dot. I sighed resignedly. After all, I could
scarcely expect to have the hut to myself in such perfect
weather.

The party descended rapidly, and always in line.
Evidently they were ski-ing on a rope. When they had
reached the level glacier I retired into the hut to relight
the fire and prepare them some tea.

They proved to be a party of two Swiss, accompanied
by a guide from Adelboden. I recognised the guide and
he me, as at one time I had tentatively approached him
in case the weather should mend sufficiently for a traverse
of the Wildhorn and Wildstrubel.

As expected I had to endure the usual barrage of
questions. Where was I going? What was I doing?
Why was I alone? Etc., etc. I dislike those who pry
into others' personal affairs, and the Swiss showed little
restraint in this; but it is not easy to be rude when you
must share the cooking and other chores in a hut a few
feet square; in any event, a solitary ski-er in March at the
Finsteraarhorn hut is a rare bird. As a matter of fact,
we soon became excellent friends, and before we parted
I was to experience many courtesies and kindnesses at the
hands of my companions.

Very slowly and very quietly the day ebbed away. I

have known many fine days in the high mountains, but none finer. All day long there had not been a cloud in the sky, not the slenderest thread and not the faintest stirring in the air. And when at length evening came, and the sun withdrew to the high summits, crowning them with its final glory, the peace deepened into something so profound that we sat on the terrace without talking, absorbed in this portentous drama of Earth and Space.

Could such weather last? The answer seemed to lie with the stars that night. The sky was thick with them. From horizon to horizon they were assembled, not trembling through a watery atmosphere, but steady and serene over the mountains.

I slept little. One reason was that the blankets were damp; another was sunburn. I lay uneasily, my body clammy and my face burning. Most mountaineers know what it means to lie thus at night in an Alpine hut. It may be due to over-fatigue, or to excitement, or, more prosaically, to indigestion. The worst feature of such sleeplessness is the mind, which often involves itself in a recondite labyrinth of morbid worrying. At high altitudes on Mount Everest it is possible to lie awake all night in a kind of coma which takes small account of time, but at low altitudes time becomes a tyrant who passes by on leaden feet.

Wind is common at night in the High Alps, but that night there was none. Instead, there was a heavy silence broken only by the breathing of my companions. I thought of the morrow and what lay in store. During my ascent of the Finsteraarhorn in 1923 my companion had trodden through a snow-bridge and fallen up to the waist in a concealed crevasse. I endeavoured to remember where that crevasse had been but failed to do so. Once a fall of ice occurred somewhere. I must have been half asleep, for its sudden thunder made me jump up with a bumping heart under the momentary impression that I was once again in camp under that terrible west wall of Kangchenjunga.

So passed the night, and it was with profound thankfulness that I noted that the hand of my watch had crawled round to 3 a.m. We all of us rose and set about preparing breakfast. What a miserable business this is in a cold hut by the light of a guttering candle. It is on such occasions that the bootlace breaks and other minor catastrophes occur.

The Swiss party had announced their intention of ski-ing as far as possible up the Finsteraarhorn. I, however, had decided to climb entirely on foot, my assumption being that the snow would be hard-frozen the whole way.

At five, while the Swiss were packing their rucksacks, I was off. The dawn was faintly showing, but it was in virtual darkness that I picked my way up the rocks above the hut, then traversed left on to the snow-slopes that fall to the Fiescherfirn.

The snow, as anticipated, had frozen board hard under the night's frost, so hard that in places a number of kicks were necessary to form a step. The exercise quickened my sluggish circulation, and for the first time a suggestion of enjoyment entered into the proceedings.

Soon I was well out on the slope. The snow was in excellent order here, and a single kick alone was needed to fashion a step.

Some 500 feet up I bore diagonally to the left towards the ridge known as the "Frühstückplatz." At the junction of the *névé* with the ridge, there were indications of a small bergschrund, and I advanced with caution, probing with my axe at every step. This, I now remembered, was the crevasse into which my companion had fallen.

Above, on the broken rocks of the ridge, there was

plenty of evidence as to why the spot had been named
" Frühstückplatz " in the shape of numerous tins and
bottles.   I paused here, but not to eat, for I was not yet
hungry.   There was no sign of the Swiss party.   I had
seen them once; they had left the hut a few minutes after
me, and they were making heavy weather of the ascent on
ski.   It is difficult to understand why anyone should
wish to labour up slopes of hard snow on ski when it is
so much easier to climb on foot, but, of course, a run
down later is a consideration to an enthusiastic ski-er.

Northwards of the ridge on which I stood steep snow-
slopes descend from the level section in the north-west
ridge of the Finsteraarhorn known as the Hügisattel,
13,416 feet, named after Hügi, two of whose guides
reached the summit in 1829.   This slope is mainly
unbroken in its uppermost portion, but lower down it is
considerably crevassed.   To avoid the crevassed section
I found it best to continue along the ridge above the
Frühstückplatz, and then descend from the latter on to
the slope above the crevasses.

It was an easy enough scramble along the ridge over
screes and boulders, then across a steep little slope of
snow to the glacier.   The latter was a mere uphill walk,
except that there were stretches of breakable crust, into
which I plunged half-way to the knee.

The sun had long since risen.   I had seen the peaks, at
first cold and pallid, flush a calm rose, and the rose
replaced by a swift rush of radiant light.   I had seen
the shadows shrink on the snows, and the revelation
of mountain beauty in all its wondrous and infinite
complexity as the sun flooded over peak, glacier and
snow-field.   I had climbed rapidly, upborne by the
beauty, the exhilaration, the adventure of the morning,
my legs like steel levers, my heart pumping deeply and
rhythmically, my lungs filled, not only with oxygen, but,
as it seemed to me, the latent power of the Universe.

And now, as though transported thither by some subtle agency, as though I were no longer a fallible structure of flesh and blood, a hulk that has spent a miserable night of tossing and turning, an earthbound creature clad in a singularly shabby and unsavoury suit of clothes, I found myself levitated suddenly and mysteriously to the Hügisattel!

The sun rose to meet me over the ridge; an immense gulf fell away at my feet, and below were mountains, hundreds and thousands of mountains. It stretched away, this splendid world, and the eye passed over it in a single step as over the faces of an assembled multitude of persons, paused without movement and waiting in absolute silence.

Southwards this congregation of mountains shredded out into single entities and isolated groups, and this was because a vast sea of mist, level and calm like a Venetian lagoon covered the valleys, the plains and the hills to an altitude of some 8,000 feet.

I seated myself on a rock and rummaged in my ruck-sack for food. I did not want to eat, but it was necessary to eat. There is little doubt that climbing high mountains alone is a matter more of nervous than physical energy. To a large extent this applies to mountaineering as a whole, and I do not believe that the strongest and most skilful mountaineer in the world is capable of climbing Mount Everest unless he has a large reserve of nervous energy on which to draw. Man being by nature gregarious, solitary mountaineering is much more exacting on this store of nervous energy than climbing with companions. It is a luxury to be indulged in sparingly. Like a drug it is wearing to both body and mind if taken in excess.

Had I been with a companion, we should doubtless have made ourselves thoroughly comfortable on the Hügisattel, and spent an hour or more in consuming a substantial meal and in studying the view. In the present instance a long halt was not advisable, as it was essential to return to the hut before the sun softened the snow, bridging any crevasses that might lie concealed across the route. Even so, half an hour had passed before I continued on my way. My ice axe and rucksack I left on the sattel, and all I carried was some food in one pocket and a camera in the other.

When free of snow the north-west ridge of the Finsteraarhorn is an easy rock climb. Although no one had climbed it as yet in 1946, it was evidently in excellent condition, the fine weather of the past week having cleared most of the winter snow from the rocks. Like so many Alpine ridges, it appears a formidable edge when viewed end on. And there is no denying its sharpness. To the west, broken rocks fall at a steep angle, but the precipices to the east are abysmal. It is indeed one of those delightful and inspiring ridges which is thoroughly sensational without being difficult, a ridge on which, if the climber were to make a false step or was not equipped with one of those " perfectly steady heads " so eloquently recommended by Herr Baedeker, he would undoubtedly descend an unusually long way in a remarkably short space of time.

Doubtless the pioneers had to contend with loose rock, but this has been largely removed, and the ridge was scored and polished by the boot-nails of countless climbers. The route does not yet resemble certain British climbs, which are steadily becoming more difficult as the holds become increasingly worn and polished, but to miss it would be impossible.

Along this pleasant and stimulating edge I made my way, stepping up steadily and without pause. Here and there it was necessary to traverse a small tower, and sometimes in between these towers were snow edges with cornices overhanging the depths to the east. Now and

again, also, the route divided, some climbers having preferred one way and some another.

It was a luxury to feel the good red schistose beneath
the nailed boot. Ski-ing has its pleasures, but, truth to
tell, the grit of a nailed boot on rock is as much music in
my ears as ever the whisper of ski on a slope of powder
snow.

Now and then there were puffs of cold wind, but these
were of small account, and suggestive merely that the
shadowed gulf to the east was sighing to wakefulness in
the warm caress of the sun.

Not far from the summit I came to the only two
obstacles that gave rise to even a momentary halt. This
was where snow had accumulated to a considerable depth
on the ridge. The latter is at its narrowest at this point,
and the addition of the narrow snow edge piled up along
it made it narrower still. This snow edge was corniced
to the east, and to follow its crest was out of the question.
It had to be circumvented along its westernmost flank.
The traverse was not more than 20 yards long, but it lay
across very steep snow. Up to that point I had had no
cause to regret having left my ice axe on the Hügisattel,
but here I would have been happier with it. The snow,
however, was in reasonably good order. The surface of
the slope was loose and floury to a depth of several inches,
but beneath was hard, well-consolidated snow, into
which, after several kicks, it was possible to fashion a
step. The angle, however, was such that without hand-
holds balance was too critical to be comfortable, while
there was always the remote possibility of the step
breaking away, in which case an ice axe would have been
a useful reserve.

It is one thing, as the reader may readily imagine, to
kick footholds with a nailed boot and another to employ
the hand in the same manner. The snow at handhold
level, once the loose surface had been swept away, was if

anything harder than at foot level, and it was only after repeated blows with my gloved hand that I was able to make a nick deep enough to grip with some confidence. It was not possible to make the nick with the fist: the fingers had to be held stiffly and driven tips first against the hard snow. In such a manner, step by step and handhold by handhold, I spread-eagled myself across the slope.

There was another but shorter and easier section of a similar type which I tackled in the same way. It was the last difficulty, and three hours after leaving the hut the Finsteraarhorn was mine.

Many persons imagine that to reach the summit of a mountain is the sole motive in climbing that mountain. This is far from being the case from the mountaineer's standpoint. The summit is a part, and a very necessary part, of a day's climbing, but still only a part. It is the climb that matters, and sometimes the summit comes as a positive anticlimax. How many times does it happen that one is chased off by a chilly wind, and what an unpleasant place it can seem in mist and snow! It may even be associated with the prosaic or the disagreeable. One mountaineer records how he spent precious minutes in having a patch sewn on to the seat of his breeches.

There are, however, occasions when the summit comes as the true crown of endeavour, and this was one of them. During the ascent there had been a small cold wind, but the summit was absolutely windless. On it, I lit a cigarette with an unshielded match. Calm days are common in the mountains, but there is a difference between a day of fair weather and the absolute stillness reigning that morning on the Finsteraarhorn. I have known other still days in the High Alps, but I have never sat in a greater stillness at an elevation of 14,000 feet in March. And out of this stillness, this absolute silence that united Earth and Heaven, the sun blazed with a fierce incandescence.

And now the view. Purely panoramic views are notoriously unsatisfactory from an artistic standpoint. That from Mont Blanc is substantially the same as that from an aeroplane, and I have never recorded any impression other than that of an unending jumble of mountains. The views from the Pennine peaks are more satisfactory, but are of local significance, except for the splendid sweep of the eye across Piedmont to Monte Viso. The Piz Bernina is better situated, and from it one January day I gazed from Monte Viso to the Black Forest and from Monte Rosa to the Gross Glockner, which is probably the most extensive view of the Alps possible from any point. The Bernese Alps stand well apart from the main watershed of the Alps, and from the Finsteraarhorn a substantial portion of the latter is visible.

A level wash of opaque blue haze lay to the north, concealing the Jura and the lowlands of Switzerland. In the west, the northernmost peaks of Savoy stood up from it, with the Buet prominent among them. Then came Mont Blanc. It was exactly in line with the nearer summit of the Aletschhorn and, although far off, every detail was marvellously distinct. Even with the naked eye I could make out the main features of the Brenva face and the fall of the great Pétéret ridge, while a little closer the dark precipices of the Grands Jorasses were in abrupt contrast to the immaculate snows of the Monarch of Mountains. Next came the Pennine Alps, with the Grand Combin bulking above their western-most extremity. Then followed the peaks of Arolla, breaking in serried array against the stern bastions of the Dent Blanche. Closer at hand the Weisshorn raised its sweeping ridges, and beyond, at the head of the long Vispthal, the Matterhorn stood out in lean, grim contra-

distinction from the gently flowing snows of the
Théodule pass. And of all the vast array of peaks this
was the most memorable of mountains. It could have
been removed without causing any appreciable physical
or topographical change in the panorama, yet without it
the Alps would lack a force; it is a veritable Churchill
among mountains.

Monte Rosa, the Mischabel, the Fletschhorn and
Weissmies, Monte Leone and the Simplon; there was
much to remember here and much of history also.

There followed the peaks of Binn. At the Furka the
Alps split into two main arms. One stretches by way of
the Dammastock range to the Alps of Uri and Glarus, in
which I could distinguish the Tödi, King of the Little
Mountains, the first high peak I climbed, thence passing
to the Rhätikon Alps and the Vorarlberg. The other
continues along the main watershed to the Adula and
Bernina. The clarity in both directions was extraordinary, and the Adula was clearly visible beyond the
Valle Leventina.

Over every valley southwards of the watershed the mist
stretched level in a vast floor of vapour. It covered the
whole of northern Italy, but above it, on the high hills,
the sun shone and a score of ridges and ranges in the
south-east rose above it like a labyrinthine archipelago.

Ninety miles away the Piz Bernina rose in faultless
distinction. Even at that great distance it was much
more than an outline, and it was possible to distinguish
the details of its ridges, glaciers and snow-slopes. To the
south-west the ever-graceful Monte della Disgrazia
dominated the tangled peaks of the Bregaglia, and to the
south of that, and far beyond, rose the ridges of the
Bergamo Alps, extending south and east towards Bergami
and Lake Garda for a distance I should judge of quite
150 miles.

What was the longest distance at which a recognisable

range could be seen? It is hard to say. Beyond the Silvretta rose ridge upon ridge of the Austrian Alps. Is it theoretically possible to see the Gross Glockner from the Finsteraarhorn? Most likely not; but if so, it was in view that day, as the visibility in this direction was limited only by the curvature of the earth. A little to the north of the Piz Bernina and in line with the nearer Piz d'Err group a range of three bold peaks rose at a distance far greater than the Bernina. These can only have been the peaks of the Ortler group, in particular the Ortler and the Königspitze. What is more, they appear in one of the photographs I took.[1]

If I have referred at length to this view, it is because it was a remarkable view, the most extensive I have ever witnessed in the Alps, with the exception of that from the Piz Bernina. Views such as this are only possible in winter, or perhaps after a long spell of bad weather in summer. What is the greatest view from a point on the earth's surface? I presume that from the summit of Mount Everest. One of the longest views I have myself witnessed, was that from the summit of Kamet in 1931. We saw, or thought we saw, the eastern wing of the Karakoram range, some 280 miles distant along the Himalayan chain.

So much for topographical detail. Reclining there in the sun, I gazed out on many friends. This is the charm of the Alps. You may only tread a mountain once, but many a time you will see it again, so that when you have climbed mountains in the principal ranges you find yourself always among friends.

It was easy to dream up there in the sun and the silence. In that panorama rested the friendships, the experiences and the adventures of twenty-five years. In

---

[1] It may interest photographers to know that the photographs taken of this panorama include the peaks and ranges here referred to. They were made with a standard $2\frac{1}{4} \times 3\frac{1}{4}$ roll-film camera on Panatomic X film, using a ×4 orange filter.

those small shapes over which the eye passed tranquilly, on those shining summits where memory paused to refresh itself, youth was renewed. Our friends the mountains, our friendships on the mountains, can man ask for stauncher than these? Is there any sport, any pursuit in which a zest of living is blended more perfectly with a noble environment than in mountain climbing? No mechanisms are employed, no animals suffer; the issue is between mountain and man. The statesmen of the world might well exchange the stuffy conference chamber for the sun and the wind of the hilltop. Did not the Wisest of all Men seek His inspiration and decisions in the high places where the clamour of the multitude is replaced by the silences of God?

An hour passed. It was necessary to descend if I were to find firmly crusted snow. I took one long last look at that matchless panorama, then set off down the ridge. Except for the snow edges it was all easy going, and within half an hour I was approaching the Hügisattel. There, on the ridge a little above it, I encountered my Swiss friends, who were wisely taking their time, as there was no need for them to return early to the hut, and enjoying every minute of the ascent and the day.

I collected my rucksack and ice axe and bounded down the slopes. It was nothing more than a walk, and within an hour I was back at the hut brewing a welcome draught of tea.

It was not yet noon, and for a while I toyed with the idea of continuing with the traverse to the Hollandia hut on the Lötschenlücke, or at least as far as the Concordia hut over the Grünhornlücke, but truth to tell I was lazy, and the broiling sun offered a powerful inducement to remain at the Finsteraarhorn hut rather than toil through the afternoon glare. There was also a possibility of soft snow and insecure bridges over crevasses. These last arguments. slender as they were, since the route over the

Grünhornlücke is safe enough at any time in spring to the ski-er, settled the matter, and with a conscience satisfactorily compromised I spent the remainder of the day in the sun outside the hut. There was nothing to do other than this, as I had no reading matter of any kind, but sunlit hours in the mountains fly on swift wings.

The shadows were fast lengthening when the Swiss returned. With considerable labour they had carried up their ski 1,000 feet or more above the hut, and in the soft afternoon snow had enjoyed a pleasant descent. They were as grateful and enthusiastic as I for a memorable day, and I spent a cheerful evening in their company. They were insistent that I should join them on the morrow, since they were also travelling to the Lötschenlücke. It seemed churlish to refuse, but I still preferred to be on my own, if only to halt when I pleased to take photographs, always a difficult matter for a photographer who is one of a party. They insisted, and with better success, on my sharing their dinner, though truth to tell I had enough food remaining for a further three days.

An invariable feature of all my conversations with the Swiss I met was international politics. It is rare to hear a Swiss talk about his own country's administration, though he will always oblige if opinion or information is requested; but he likes above everything to discuss the chequered political board of Europe, a very natural tendency, since the fate and well-being of Switzerland are dependent on the disposition and economy of her neighbours. The Swiss have a profound faith in the integrity of Britain. Political trends in other countries are watched with concern, but whether there is a Conservative or a Labour Government in power in Britain is of small interest. This is because, like us, they have a regard for tradition and evolution, abhor extremism in all its forms, and believe in the middle way of political and social evolution. The bonds between them and the British and American democracies are stronger to-day than they have ever been. The Swiss have indeed evolved a well-nigh ideal compromise between the individual's contribution to the State and his right to freedom in his personal enterprises. Happy, lucky little country it is, a sunlit clearing in a dark jungle of hate, misery, self-seeking and suspicion.

During the early years of the war Switzerland was over-loaded with Nazi propaganda, which had the effect of inducing a small Nazi party; but against the vast majority of those who loved freedom this gained little headway. What mattered most was the radio, and over the radio in the worst days came the voice of Winston Churchill.

"We knew you had little or nothing to fight with," said one of the Swiss; " but when we heard Churchill, we knew you would fight, as we too would have fought in the mountains had Hitler invaded us. When I was stationed in the mountains I used to stand outside at night in the snow and listen to your bombers passing over on their way to Italy. That was my only contact with war, but it meant a great deal to us Swiss. We knew they fought for the same things that we were pre-pared to fight for. You are the first Englishman I have seen since the war, so we are glad if you will share our dinner."

During the afternoon we watched a party of two ascending the Wannehorn on the opposite side of the Fiescherfirn. It is a fine ski-ing mountain and ski can be taken to the summit. They descended late, and we watched them zigzagging fast and skilfully down the great snowy shoulder of the mountain. Arriving once again on the Fiescherfirn, they made their way to the hut, and presently to my surprise I was welcoming the same guide I had met on the Münster glacier. On reaching Münster he had straightway returned by rail to Grindelwald, a long and circuitous journey, and the following day, with another employer, a young Swiss, had travelled to the Jungfraujoch and retraced his previous route over the Jungfrau glacier and Grünhornlücke. To do him justice he seemed this time quite glad to see me and was positively affable, though he was quite unable to resist giving the homily on the folly of solitary mountaineering which had been denied him in the first place.

My laziness persisted overnight, and the Swiss were away an hour before me next morning. My plan was to spend the night at the Hollandia hut, the following day being devoted to an ascent of the Ebnefluh, and a descent from the Lötschenlücke to the Lötschenthal.

The weather was again perfect, and I climbed leisurely up the slopes of the Grünhornlücke. It was a cold morning, with a slight but bitter wind pouring up from the Fiescherfirn over the pass, and I was glad to wear woollen mitts and extra pullovers.

Like the Lötschenlücke, the Grünhornlücke is a snow pass, but unlike it, there is no downward glimpse to a low and populated valley. It stands in the very heart of the most extensive system of glaciers and snow-fields in the Alps. On the one hand is the broad, sweeping Fiescherfirn with beyond it the long, rocky mass of the Finsteraarhorn, and on the other the *névé*, whence the greatest of all Alpine glaciers, the Aletsch, draws its strength. Seven miles away, over the level floor of the Koncordia Platz, where four ice-fields unite to form the Aletsch glacier, and the gently sloping reaches of the Grosser Aletschfirn, the glowing parabola of the Lötschenlücke was outlined against the deep blue of the retreating night.

The snow-slopes descending from the pass to the Koncordia Platz were hard-frozen and exceedingly fast. From side to side I ran in a series of sinuous loops, yet seemed to lose but little height in so doing. As a

The Schreckhorn from the Finsteraarhorn

The Pennine Alps from the Finsteraarhorn

1. Monte Leona. 2. Simplon Pass. 3. Weimies. 4. Fletschhorn. 5. Monte Rosa. 6. Lyskamm. 7. Dom. 8. Théodule Pass.
9. Matterhorn. 10. Weisshorn. 11. Dent Blanche

" schuss " it is only 2 miles of downhill running, but I must have traversed three times as much at a speed as great as I dared before the slopes levelled out on to the Platz.

Then began the 5 miles' trudge up the Grosser Aletschfirn to the Lötschenlücke. I know of no Alpine snow-fields to which the words of the Red Queen apply better. " *Here,*" said she, " it takes all the running *you* can do to keep in the same place." It is with infinite slowness that the Dreieckhorn is passed. As for the Aletschhorn, it seems always in the same position. It is one of those ascents measurable purely in terms of time and effort. Presently I passed the Swiss, who were very sensibly going at a reasonable pace. The solitary mountaineer has always a tendency to go too fast, though what are the psychological factors underlying this vice I cannot say. What virtue is to be gained out of speed on a mountain I do not know? Personally I abhor it, yet frequently find myself going far too fast.

The kilometres passed. The great snow-field slowly, slowly unreeled. The Dreieckhorn was behind and the Aletschhorn to the left, its summit slope shining, the ribs and steeps falling to the Aletschfirn picked out by the slanting rays of the morning sun, its frozen cataracts of ice a pale fluorescent green. Up lifted the eye, and up in a single bound of 3,000 feet over the façades of ice to the shattered edges of the broad summit *névé*, where the lurching séracs were ranged like a row of sardonic gargoyles.

The mountaineer and ski-er have at least some motive behind their reputed madness, but what about an animal? I was but a short distance from the pass when I came across a chamois track in the snow. It wavered away to the left towards the Aletschhorn, then traversed the slopes of that mountain in the direction of the Lötschenlücke as though it intended to cross the pass,

not at its lowest point, but across the steep ridge rising
from it to the Sattelhorn. Never have I seen a chamois
track in such a high and remote place so early in the
year. The tracks came from the direction of the Jungfraujoch. Had they come from the Lötschenthal they
would have been to some extent understandable, as access
to the high snows is easy from that valley, but how had
the beast reached the Oberland glaciers from any different direction other than by a long and difficult climb?

The tracks were freshly made, and must have come
from some point to the north of my track from the Finsteraarhorn hut to the Lötschenlücke. Having thus
crossed the route to the latter pass, the beast had only two
alternatives—one was to climb the north side of the
Aletschhorn, and the other to turn west and cross the
Lötschenlücke. The last I am positive it did not do, as
no traces were to be seen on or near the pass, or on the
Lötschen glacier below the pass, while any possibility of
it having made a line to the south of the usual line
over the pass was eliminated when, during my descent
from the pass, I ski-ed so close to the rocks of the Distelhorn that I could not have failed to see a track. This
leaves as the sole route open to the animal an ascent of
the Sattelhorn or Aletschhorn, or a crossing of the ridge
linking these two peaks. Any route in this direction
involves a most formidable climb up slopes of ice at an
angle of about 45 degrees. Even the Hasler route, the
easiest line up the Aletschhorn from the north, which
follows a rock rib to the ridge linking the mountains with
the Dreieckhorn, is a long, steep and difficult climb, then
heavily plastered in ice and snow.

To climb like a chamois is a common aphorism, but
what precisely does it mean? On rough ground, on
broken rocks, screes and grass slopes a chamois is unsurpassed. It thinks little of steep snow-slopes, and has an
obvious instinct for route finding on slopes exposed to

avalanches; I have seen tracks which ascended slopes laden with wind-slab by the one and only safe line. But what are its capabilities as to really difficult climbing on rock and ice? A chamois can maintain a footing on steep slabs provided there are sufficient roughnesses for its sharp hooves, but its limitations on rocks where friction is insufficient, and on which the climber must employ both hands as well as feet to keep himself in position, are obvious. The same applies to steep hard ice, where the climber must cut steps, and it is difficult to see how a chamois could manage to ascend the north faces of the Sattelhorn or Aletschhorn. The affair therefore remains a mystery. It is a remarkable proof of a chamois' endurance, and capacity to do without food, that it should wander about in the heart of the most extensive glacier region in Europe. The question arises as to why it should leave the protective woods and feeding grounds in favour of a foodless waste. It may, of course, have been frightened away, or it may have been an outcast from its herd. The ways of animals in their cross-country wanderings are often quite inexplicable.

I was still puzzling over the tracks when I reached the Lötschenlücke, but it was impossible to puzzle long over any problem that morning, and removing my ski I seated myself on them to eat a long-delayed meal.

The morning was now perfect. The wind had dropped and a few filaments of cloud had withdrawn into space. It was one of those silver-blue mornings in which the snows were the purest silver in the brilliant sunlight, and every ripple, hollow and undulation was filled with blue shadow, as though the heaven above had distilled itself on earth. And all around the snow glittered and sparkled with prismatic colourings.

It was my last glimpse of the high snows. Now I must go down. Like the morning I felt very calm and peaceful. I was still outside the clutch of civilisation. I had read no newspaper, and heard no news, since leaving Zermatt, and my way had lain over a remote and timeless land. The world had revolved four times, and its struggling ants had revolved with it. One had escaped from the throng and in peace pursued a solitary path. He had seen and contemplated many beauties, and had been granted every favour in the manner of his going. Now he must return whence he came.

And strangely enough I felt glad. It was not that any sense of solitude was beginning to oppress me, but rather that such perfection as I had experienced during the past days could not endure longer, and that any further ascents after that of the Finsteraarhorn would be in the nature of an anticlimax. The wine bibber had bibbed enough of the gods' strong nectar.

My Swiss friends had not followed me to the pass, but had turned aside to visit the Hollandia hut. There they would doubtless lunch; I preferred to reserve that meal for the first turf of the Lötschenthal.

The Lötschen glacier on the far side of the pass was still shadowed and frozen. It was bumpy also, and the wind of past storms had carved and eroded it into innumerable ripples, cakes and soup plates. As a crown to perfection the run should have been over the same silk-like powder snow of the Furgg and Arolla glaciers, but I could scarcely grumble. Down I went from side to side of the trough in which lies the glacier. It was by no means an ideal descent, the ski skidded sideways on the icy surface, and it was necessary to control speed with frequent jerked Christianias, a fatiguing mode of descent on fast snow when carrying a heavy rucksack.

I did not stop until I was off the glacier on the level valley floor, where it was a relief to slide and ski flatly forward once again. Thenceforward, it was mostly a question of poling down the gently sloping valley.

On the last occasion the valley had been lifeless in

winter's grasp, but now spring had come.   The snow was still deep, but the trees had shaken themselves loose of the snow cumbering their branches and among the larches was a hint of green.

The now familiar huts of Guggistaffel, Gletscheralp and Fafleralp were passed, until I came to the place I sought.   This was where the track crossed the Lonza by a rude little bridge.   Here was a patch of dry turf carpeted with thyme.

I slung off my rucksack, stretched out my limbs, and lay for some time in that complete mental and physical relaxation which supersedes many hours of strenuous travelling.   Up to then there had been snow, always snow, and the world and I had been two separate entities. Now, and suddenly, we had come together again in repose and peace.   The air, no longer cold and ener- gising and charged with the dry, nipping tang of snow, rock and mist, was soft, warm and sweet with the scents of damp earth and living herbage.   It was a balm on my sun-scorched countenance, and I lay relaxed on the turf with the song of the stream in my ears.

The snow became wetter and wetter as I ski-ed down the valley.   The thaw had come.   In places the path had been bared, and I had to remove my ski, but it was not until I approached the village of Wiler that I had finally to carry them over my shoulder.

At Kippel I looked in on my former host and hostess of the Pension Bietschhorn, whose greeting was as surprised as it was cordial, and there enjoyed an excellent tea.   My host wanted to hear about my experiences, but he was engrossed with some tax collectors.   Who these tax collectors were and what taxes they collected I did not inquire.   There were no less than three of them, pasty- faced men, all conventionally dressed in dark suits and looking very much out of place against the surrounding landscape.   It struck me as a trifle incongruous to descend to a remote Alpine village and find tax collectors present in strength.

That evening I strolled down to Goppenstein. Is there anything pleasanter than the final walk down the valley in the gathering dusk after a great day on the high hills? The air was like milk, and everywhere the earth was blossoming forth.

Far away now the Lötschenlücke, full and warm in the westering sun, dipped into the deepening blue. It was the end of my tour, and I looked upwards and backwards to the high snows with gratitude. I had returned to the mountains after some wearying years of war, and in some way they had restored my faith. Quite what this faith is I cannot define, but I believe in beauty. I believe also that this world, for all its troubles and miseries, is one in which man is capable of rising to even greater heights than on those which his Maker has so wonderfully created.

APPENDIX

SWISS WINES

COMPARATIVELY little is known outside Switzerland on the subject of Swiss wines, and these notes, for which I am indebted to Herr A. Kuhn, proprietor of the Adler Hotel, Adelboden, may be of interest to all interested in wines, and particularly to visitors to Switzerland.

Few Swiss wines are exported, the reason being that production is small and little is available for outside consumption. The better-class wines may, however, be purchased in some of the European capitals, including London, The Hague, Amsterdam, Paris and Brussels. Actually Switzerland is a large importer of wines, especially from France On the average the country produces some 80 million litres of wine per annum. In 1944 the yield was 105 million litres and in 1945 only 65 million litres. The quality of the 1944 wine was slightly under average, but the 1945 wine is known as " the wine of the century," a very high-quality vintage. About four-fifths of the produce is white wine and only one-fifth red wine.

There are several districts famous for wine, out of which the first four mentioned below contribute over eighty per cent. of Switzerland's total production.

LAKE OF GENEVA

Most of this belongs to the Canton of Vaud, and about one-quarter to the Canton of Geneva. This is about ninety-five per cent. a white-wine country. The white grapes are of the same variety as those by the Lake of Neuchâtel and in the Canton Valais, yet the wine is different. In the Canton of Neuchâtel it is lively with a champagne-like quality, in the Valais fiery, and on the Lake of Geneva still and settled. Lausanne produces half the wine of the Lake of Geneva district, whilst Lavaux, east of Lausanne, is in quality more famous than that of La Côte, west of Lausanne, although La Côte has its specialities, such as Mont, Vinzel, Bougy, Féchy and Luins, but it will never reach the popularity of Dézaley, especially Clos des Abbayes, of the City of Lausanne, Yvorne, Aigle, Villeneuve (a mild and suitable wine for anyone), Corsier, Cure d'Attalens, Chardonne, Epesses and many others. The quality of these wines is becoming better and better, thanks to the skilful treatment of grapes and soil by the hard-working wine-growers, a tradition of many centuries.

VALAIS

Like the country, the red wine from the hillsides of Contan Valais is of a strong, wilful character. This canton produces more red wine than the Cantons of Vaud, Neuchâtel and Berne together, and it is known under the collective name of Dôle, of which there are, to name only a few: Dôle, Clos du Château, Dôle de Sion, Dôle Pinot noir, Dôle du Valais, Dôle Clos du Ravaney and Château Latour. It is a fruity wine like that from Burgundy, where the Dôle grapes came from some centuries ago.

The best-known white wine of the Valais is Fendant, and the name applies to any Swiss white wine apart from that produced in the Vaudois. The most famous district for white wines is known under the name of Johannisberg. There is an interesting history attached to this wine. It is said that many years ago a Swiss who spent some years at Johannesburg, in South Africa, found the wine so good there that when he returned to Switzerland he determined to bring back some vines with him. These were the days of long sea voyages by sailing-ship, but he managed to preserve the vines, and after some years produced a wine of excellent quality, although it

Chamois track near the Lötschenlücke

The
Finsteraar-
horn and
Grünhorn-
lücke from
the
Lötschen-
lücke

has been discovered that this vine can only be grown on certain slopes.

The Malvoisie, also a speciality, is one of the strongest of Swiss wines and, like the character of the Valaisan wines as a whole, is representative of the people of the Valais, strong, ardent and never failing. Unlike other districts, the year to year quality of the Valaisan wines varies little, and wine of any year may be drunk with confidence.

Another speciality is Flézry. For this the grapes are not pressed when fresh, but left on the vines, or on straw, until they are almost dry, the result being an excellent sweetish wine, not white and not red, resembling Tokay. An opposite wine to this is the glacier wine, best consumed in summer, as it is a great thirst quencher. Other specialities are Fendant Molignon, Fendant Uvrier, Johannisberg Uvrier, Fendant Fully, Chamoson, Conthey (of which Château Conthey is best known), and Lens. Amongst others is Païn, which is producing up to 4,000 feet, the limit in Central Europe. Specialities much appreciated by connoisseurs are Ermitage, Arvine, Amigne, Humagne, Montibeux, Etoile du Valais and Johannisberg Mont d'Or.

NEUCHÂTEL

These wines cool the body in hot weather and heat it in cold weather. Neuchâtel produces a certain amount of red wine, which nearly reaches the character of sparkling Burgundy if carefully stored for some years. If kept for only a short time it is usually found to be a good red wine with a fruity flavour. In a good vintage year it is excellent and comparable with the vintages of many another country. Certain districts produce a white wine which nearly reaches a champagne flavour. Well-known specialities are: Château d'Auvernier, Clos de Champreveyres for white and Cortaillod for red. The

Neuchâtel wines, especially the white ones, should not be kept for longer than three to five years according to vintage.

FRIBOURG

These wines, of which there are more white than red, are something between the Neuchâtelois and the Vaudois. Red Vully is the best known.

BERNE

The biggest and best-known district of that canton for vine growing is the Lake of Bienne, and lesser known but also good the Lake of Thun. The wine of the Bienne district is almost like Neuchâtelois, whereas the Thun wine resembles the mild white wine of the Lower Rhone Valley. Twanner and Schafiser are the collective names of the Lake of Bienne wines, and the Thun wine is known as Spiezer.

TESSIN

So far as isolation is concerned, the Canton of Tessin should produce one of the best wines in the world; if that is not so, it is due to the soil. Yet the Tessin does produce some fair wines, the white Nostrano and the red Nostrano, the latter akin to Bordeaux. The Tessin wines are usually drunk cool. It is an unwritten law that wines of certain kinds should be drunk where the vines grow, and the Tessin wines are a case in point.

ZÜRICH

This canton was at one time a large producer, where part of the town of Zürich stands to-day, but the wine industry has been swamped by the industrialisation of the canton. There are, however, a few dozen villages left with vineyards which turn out a passable wine.

SCHAFFHAUSE

This little canton at one time produced a considerable amount of wine, over ninety per cent. red, of which Hallauer is well known. The Schaffhause wines are popularly known as Blue Burgundy.

ARGOVIE

Like the Canton of Zürich, few vineyards are left in this canton. The best Argovien wine is the Gold-wändler (Gold Wall), white, a mild wine.

ST. GALL

About ninety per cent. of the wine is red, from Blue Burgundy grapes. It is not exported, as the amount produced is too small.

GRISONS

This canton, with its mountains and high valleys, produces excellent wines. Between Ragaz and Coire there are some well-known vineyards, producing such wines as " Maienfelder " (red), Malanser (ninety-five per cent. red), Schiller (red), Jenins (red), Fläsch (red), all strong and fruity. The Grisons people are great wine bibbers, yet very little of the Grisons wine is consumed higher than the valley between Coire and Ragaz. The wine consumed in the higher valleys is the Veltliner, with its specialities: Sassella, Sfirzato, Grumello, Barba Grischa (an extra-good one), Inferno, Montagna and probably a dozen more. These wines are imported from the Val-tellino valley, and cure in the Swiss climate remarkably well. Certain vintages can be stocked for sixty years or more, when they become almost like strong liqueurs. The average for a cure is about twelve years, with fifteen years for a good vintage wine, but an eight-year Sassella would suit a delicate palate.

TOURGOVIE

The same applies as to the Canton of Schaffhause. Their speciality is Karthauser.

BASLE

Even that lowland canton produces wines, mostly white, which in character approach Hock.